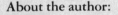

About the author:

Stephanie Dowrick has been actively interested in psychotherapy since the late 1970s. She trained in Britain and Australia in analytic psychotherapy and psychosynthesis, as well as in Gestalt therapy, and marital and individual counselling. To the creation of *Intimacy and Solitude* she also brings extensive publishing and writing experience.

She has been writing full time since 1983, combining writing books, literary journalism and teaching writing with care for her two young children. Her novel, *Running Backwards Over Sand*, has been translated into Swedish and Dutch. Stephanie currently works part time as Fiction Publisher for Allen & Unwin, while continuing to run a small therapy practice and to write on human relationship issues.

Stephanie has worked in the publishing industry since 1972 and was co-founder and Managing Director of The Women's Press, London, from 1977 to 1982. In 1991 she was appointed Chair of The Women's Press.

About the book:

Intimacy and Solitude went into five printings in Australia in its first five months of life, and was Number 1 on two New Zealand bestseller lists. Among the comments from reviewers:

'I opened it and found myself hooked. Here was an analysis of close relationships which struck home, readable but not over-simplistic, based on informed research and extensive interviews. You don't have to agree with it all to appreciate its exposition of the social pressures which go into forming our view of ourselves.' *Sun-Herald*

'In the detailed and loving, thorough explanations of how we feel, and how important it is, in her ability to make me cry and re-evaluate my life, and the way I have treated others, on many levels, this is a very good book. It may even change your life.' *Adelaide Advertiser*

'Dowrick leads the reader from restriction to freedom through self-reliance . . . It is this learning *how* to do something rather than just learning something that makes *Intimacy and Solitude* such a rewarding book.' *The Australian*

'Genuinely illuminating of the business of understanding oneself and others. It is by turns intelligent, eloquent and wise.' *Metro*

Also by Stephanie Dowrick from The Women's Press:

Why Children? with Sibyl Grundberg (1980)
The Intimacy and Solitude Self-Therapy Book (1993)

STEPHANIE DOWRICK

intimacy

&

solitude

First published in Great Britain by The Women's Press Ltd, 1992
A member of the Namara Group
34 Great Sutton Street, London EC1V 0DX

Reprinted in 1992 (twice), 1993, 1994, 1995

First published in Australia by William Heinemann Australia, 1991

British Library Cataloguing-in-Publication Data
A catalogue record for this book is available from the British Library

ISBN 0 7043 4308 8

Typeset in 10 on 12pt Garamond Roman
Printed and bound in Great Britain by Cox & Wyman Ltd, Reading, Berks

For Lisa Alther and Joanna Ryan

'To transform the world, we must begin with ourselves. However small may be the world we live in, if we can transform ourselves, bring about a radically different point of view in our daily existence, then perhaps we shall affect the world at large, the extended relationship with others.'

J. Krishnamurti

CONTENTS

During 1988 I was the recipient of a Fellowship from the Literature Board of the Australia Council. I am deeply grateful for the writing time this gave me. That vital grant notwithstanding, I hope that this book, for all its faults, will serve as some encouragement to those writers attempting large, ambitious projects without the benefits of institutional support, especially when those writers are also mothers.

Work on this book would have been impossible to sustain without the background of loving sustenance and intellectual stimulation I brought with me to Sydney from London, and without the following people.

I should like to thank, first, my therapists and teachers: Luise Eichenbaum, Diana Becchetti-Whitmore, Jenner Roth and Dr Neil Phillips. Not just thanks, but love to each of you for giving so much of yourselves so that I might discover and reclaim more of myself.

Several people gave me essential space to work during times when I could not work at home: my thanks to Drusilla Modjeska, Pam Benton and Bob Connell for their cheerful generosity.

Over the years there have been many people with whom I have had vital conversations about concepts this book develops. I must single out Niki Honoré, an intimate friend of the most inspiring kind through almost two decades and across continents. Her wisdom and compassion thread through this book and shine like gold.

My children, Gabriel and Kezia Dowrick, and their father, Ric Sissons, have been with me through the highs and lows of this project, which has been bubbling through most of the children's lives thus far. I have written this book much more slowly because of the family life I share with them and sometimes that was hard to bear, but it is incomparably richer for what I have learned and I thank them with all my heart.

I also want to thank my sister, Geraldine Killalea, as well as friends who have sustained this project: Wiebke Wüstenberg, Jetske Spanjier, Amanda Lohrey, Hanan al-Shayk, Harko Keijzer, John Baxter, Lucy Goodison, Eric Hansen, Susanne Kahn-Ackermann, Klaus Endler, Sheila Ernst, Michael King, Sally Belfrage, Sally Gillespie, Jocelyn Krygier and Michael Stephens. Thanks too to Margaret Newman and David Jansen of the Relationship Development Centre, and the course members with whom I learned during part of the writing time, especially Cheryl Assuage.

Towards the end of a dark year when I was unable to finance further work on the book, Luisa Valenzuela read what I had written and gave me the courage to go on. Her generosity of spirit literally renewed my writing life.

My gratitude also goes to those people who allowed me to interview them and who shared with me experiences, insights and feelings which have brought this book to life. I cannot name you, but I was changed by our talks and will not forget you.

I have been delighted to work again with Jackie Yowell who 'earthed' this project with graceful, persistent suggestions. My thanks to her; to Judy Brookes of William Heinemann Australia; to Louise Adler who undertook to publish it; and to Bruce Hunter of David Higham Associates who is as cool and rock-steady as a literary agent should be.

Several books were so important to me at various stages during the period of writing that I feel indebted at a deep personal level to their authors: D.W. Winnicott, Harry Guntrip, Alice Miller, Irvin D. Yalom, Carl A. Whitaker, Selma H. Fraiberg, Charlotte Wolff, Michael King, Nancy Chodorow, Carol Gilligan, Piero Ferrucci, Drusilla Modjeska.

Almost a decade ago Lisa Alther believed that I might make

writing my working life when there was little reason to do so. More than that, she made it possible. Joanna Ryan has been not only the best, the most loving of friends but also an intellectual mentor of the finest kind. My gratitude to those two women is expressed in part through my dedication of this book to them.

This is such a large book in the breadth of its concerns that during the years of writing I have often been asked why I took it on. All sorts of emotions have been implicit in that question, from envy that I should be dealing with such universal experiences to incredulity that I could be so bold or stupid as to take on two subjects as infinite in their implications as intimacy and solitude are.

A brief and somewhat partial answer is that I came to this subject matter because I felt more in touch with my own power in almost every area of my life *except* the most personal. I intensely wanted to be good at intimacy but could not trust that I was (or am). Yet what on earth does 'being good at intimacy' mean, and how is it that trust and closeness — if they are part of intimacy — are easy or easily rewarding for some people and elusive or even impossible for others? How is it that some people — I among them — love to be alone, find it stressful, in fact, when there is not enough opportunity to be alone, while for others being alone must be avoided at all costs, even at the cost of being in company that person does not really enjoy?

What are the differences between us? How did they begin? To what extent are they or can they be matters of choice?

In attempting to unravel some of those questions I learned that I had come to this work on intimacy and solitude with the

restless curiosity characteristic of writers who find in their own
psyche some disturbance — which is also all around them.
Despite an abundance of good will, despite our shared needs to
love and to be loved, when it comes to our intimate relationships
we can hurt ourselves and those closest to us with relentless,
awful accuracy.

As my work progressed, and especially once the interviews
began, I found myself continuing to look at intimacy and solitude
as different reflections of the way someone feels about him or
herself, while adding to that a need to explore issues of gender.
This is because women and men often bring different and
sometimes mutually unintelligible meanings to being alone and
being with someone else. I wanted to explore the history of those
differences and their effects, to question what could be changed
and whether change is desirable.

In trying to understand those differences I talked to many
people whose most intimate relationships are with people of
their own gender, as well as those whose 'other people' choices
for sexually intimate relationships seemed outwardly more conventional. The variety of self-expression which emerged was
inspiring and can be felt throughout these pages. It also exagger-
ates the paradox at the heart of *Intimacy and Solitude*: that there
are as many ways of expressing intimacy and of being in good
contact with your own self as there are human beings. *And the
differences between us are very slight.*

There is a good deal of theory built into the foundations of this
book. Intimacy and solitude are, in their various manifestations,
topics which have concerned writers from many disciplines,
most notably psychoanalysis, philosophy and sexual politics, as
well as writers of prose and poetry. But it is from psychoanalysis
that the most elegant and useful insights emerge which allow us
to discover why things come to be the way they are, and how
things could be different.

But this is less a book of theory than it is of shared experiences
and new insights. These come largely from the interviews I have
done which bring vividly to life useful theoretical insights. That
story-telling is not separate from the theory; they reflect each

other. In this way *Intimacy and Solitude* mirrors its own central theme: that how people experience their own sense of self reflects the way that they experience other people (as trusting, lovable, knowable, real/unreal, equal/unequal, a source of anxiety or of pleasure).

What that adds up to is understanding that we are not different people when we are alone and when we are with others. We may behave differently when we are alone and when we are with other people, but nevertheless these behaviours spring from the same source: our trust or lack of trust in our own existence; our trust or lack of trust in the validity of the existence of others.

These ideas owe much to the psychoanalytic theories of the British school of object relations, also known as Interpersonal-Relations Theory. D.W. Winnicott, Harry Guntrip and W.R.D. Fairbairn developed convincing explanations about how we become adults with greater or less capacity for self-love and with more or less freedom to relate comfortably to other people.

There are other godfathers and godmothers too who have unknowingly waved a wand over this book. In its emphasis on self-responsibility, *Intimacy and Solitude* reflects Alfred Adler's belief that we are affected less by the events which happen in our lives (which we cannot always control) than by our attitudes to those events (which we have rather more chance of 'choosing'). The book also benefits from the theories of the existential psychotherapists, especially Irvin D. Yalom, who convinced me that living life to the full comes when the ultimate concerns have been faced: death, freedom, isolation and meaninglessness. How we face or avoid those concerns has profound effects on the ways in which we experience intimacy and solitude, closeness and freedom, awareness of self and of others.

Jung has played an essential part, as has Freud, for psycho-analysis is, above all, a theory of the unconscious and it is impossible to write a book such as this without constant reminders that in experiencing intimacy and solitude, what is *not* remembered, what is *not* available to the conscious mind, is often just as present (and sometimes more powerful) than what can be consciously analysed.

The book is (or rather, I am) also influenced by Roberto

Assagioli, founding father of psychosynthesis. Assagioli left a rich legacy for making any individual's discovery of meaning more of a pleasure than a burden.

'Meaning,' Carl Jung said, 'makes a great many things endurable, perhaps everything.'

I think Jung was right. If this book is in pursuit of anything, it is to find meaning in those events which are closest and most significant in your individual life: What is it about intimacy that rewards or eludes me? Why am I alone when I want to be with someone else? Is solitude an easy escape for me from the dilemmas which intimacy poses? Why don't I know what I want?

Out of the discovery of meaning comes a changed sense of power, and of choice.

That unusually diverse theoretical base and the literally shifting personal insights I have gained from living in New Zealand, Britain and Australia and spending a good deal of time in Germany and the USA adds to the breadth of *Intimacy and Solitude*. This, in turn, is emphasised by the range of people who share their stories; and by my personal experiences: my own failures, successes and dreams of what intimacy and solitude can or might mean. Perhaps it also comes out of my diverse but interconnecting roles as I have written this book: as writer, publisher, teacher, psychotherapist and, not least, mother.

Writing *Intimacy and Solitude* has taken me to my limits. Often I felt like cursing whatever crazy compulsion had led me to take on a project encompassing some of the biggest questions human beings face. The sheer scope of this project severely tested me. Then, when I needed it most and expected it least, I began to get a strong impression of the book's reader.

Not that I imagine there is only one kind of reader for this book. On the contrary, I am confident that its very openness means that many people can and will feel 'There is a place for me here.' But without a sense of a reader, I was having an 'I' relationship without a 'you'. That is not intimate. It wasn't any fun either.

If I cannot be aware of 'you' (in this case, you the reader), my knowledge of 'I' is likewise limited: that is crucial to what this book has to say about intimacy. Working on *Intimacy and Solitude* gave me a totally practical lesson in that theory. When the reader's 'you' came into focus, my writing 'I' became bolder. Then, at last, the book came to life.

I lost the absurd anxiety that I must find and say everything that mattered on intimacy and solitude. I gained strength from the knowledge that some of the gaps would be filled in, individually, by each reader, and that others would remain — open places, moments to breathe, pauses.

I had needed reminding: the space between words also counts.

Stephanie Dowrick

Hope sleeps in our bones like a bear
waiting for spring to rise and walk.

Marge Piercy,
'Stone, Paper, Knife'

It has happened again.

You wanted a little space for yourself. You were feeling restless and somewhat irritable. You were intending to retreat into your paper or book, but suddenly an argument began. The same argument you have had a thousand times. The same ugly words; the same power to hurt. And now your partner has stormed out, vowing never to return. And you? You are left, not with any pleasure in your own company, but with feelings of anger, guilt and all-too familiar self-denigration.

Or maybe it has never got to that.

Maybe you are at home, alone, night after night. Not because you choose to be, but because you never meet anyone you believe you could love or trust. Or maybe you never meet anyone who wants to love and trust you. You know your company is good. But tonight and most other nights it does not feel good. It feels restless, lonely. You are missing something.

You are missing the life you want to be living. You do not understand why. You do not know how to change things.

Most of us want to love and to be loved. Yet in this age of instant communication many of us still know less about ourselves and about the motives of other people than almost any other subject. We may find ourselves behaving in ways which shock or distress us, or we may find ourselves feeling helpless when other people disappoint us or refuse to be the people we want them to be.

We may find it difficult to take pleasure in our own company. We may find it hard to be 'ourselves' or to find ways to behave which accurately reflect who we are.

At the heart of many of our difficulties is a lack of conscious understanding that each of us needs closeness with others, and also a knowledgeable, nurturing relationship with our own self. Each of us needs to find a delicate, shifting balance between dependence and independence, between being open to others and taking care of ourselves. Each of us has our own needs for solitude and for intimacy — yet we must also remain alert to the sometimes different, even conflicting needs of those around us.

How we experience ourselves is reflected in the way we can approach and experience other people: we cannot know other people better than we know our own selves; we cannot trust other people more than we trust our own selves. When we avoid knowing how we feel or what we think, we cannot learn to empathise with other people and take their feelings and thoughts seriously.

Balancing your own individual needs for intimacy and for solitude, while also remaining aware of the needs of those people whose happiness affects your own, is possible. It is not easy, but it is possible. And the process starts — and continues — with self-knowledge.

Many people are uncomfortable with this idea, confusing self-knowledge with self-absorption. Yet understanding and accepting your own self absolutely precedes making rewarding two-way contact with other people. In fact, self-knowledge leads away from self-absorption and towards the luxury of being able to 'forget yourself' in order to get on with your own life.

Knowing yourself and having some sense of your own emotional history; knowing what you are doing and more or less why you are doing it; trusting yourself and having reasonable confidence in your emotional future: this subtle, shifting combination would generally allow you to enjoy your own company, to feel good about your own self, and to accept and remain aware of other people even when they are not being useful, or acting in ways which please you.

Bringing intimacy and solitude together explicitly acknowledges that those needs exist in relationship to each other: that your knowledge of others grows with knowledge of your own self; that you are likely to need relationships while also wanting to express your individuality; that you need closeness and protection as well as autonomy; that you need understanding and also want to guard your secrets.

These are quite normal desires — which can only too easily become conflicts. Then what you have can feel almost like the opposite of what you want. Intimacy can come to feel like a binding trap; solitude can come to feel like unbearable loneliness. And who should you blame? Yourself? Your mother? Your partner? Life?

And when you have blamed and raged and despaired: what then?

A creative shift in perspective, and with it new meanings and a refreshed willingness to go on: that's what is available for any one of us, though sometimes this feels far out of reach. For when your needs for intimacy and solitude are scarcely known to you, or when you believe you have needs that cannot be met, your feelings of personal power become markedly reduced ('I am in a terrible/boring/frightening situation and I can't get out of it.' 'I am so lonely, no one could possibly want me.' 'I feel used/abused/misunderstood: this is the best I can expect.').

In a world which is increasingly out of control, such lack of personal power can make life seem grim or frightening. Turning in upon yourself and acting only in your own self-interest can seem like a rational response. Yet it is a response likely to increase your anxiety and to reduce your inner vitality, while also cutting you off from the warmth, humour and connection that human relationships can, despite all problems, undoubtedly provide.

Intimacy and Solitude understands those conflicts and the confusion which can follow them. It supports your life-long processes of discovering how to make rewarding, enlivening contact with other people without also losing your sense of who you are and what you want.

It is not a recipe book for human happiness. Seductive as the 'quick fix' may be, human beings are too unpredictable and complex for that kind of approach to have long-term benefits.

That should not suggest that the book avoids practical information. Most of us can be inspired by knowing how other people have faced difficulties much like our own.

But *Intimacy and Solitude* goes further than that. It allows you to develop your awareness of the choices that you have made, while also exploring new possibilities. As you move through the book, you will come to understand your own emotional history: the series of events and the web of feelings, interactions and responses which have made you who you are. From that exploration — and the insights which will follow it — will come the possibility to make lasting, rewarding change when change is needed. This experience can, as *Intimacy and Solitude* persistently shows, literally transform the way you experience your own unique inner world, as well as the larger world in which we all live.

PART ONE

Self: Is that who I am?

'Come sit down beside me,'
I said to myself,
And although it doesn't make sense,
I held my own hand
As a small sign of trust
And together I sat on the fence.

Michael Leunig,
'Sitting on the Fence'

1

Meeting your own self

Two adults sit side by side on a park bench.

The day is bright, but cold. The bench is rather oddly located as if marooned in a sea of scrappy grass. As they sit, a little apart, apparently motionless, three dogs appear from behind some trees. They race, barking, tumbling, separating, coming together again, disappearing and reappearing from behind the solid trunks of old trees.

Two children come into view. They are about seven or eight years old. Each has an arm around the other. Their heads lean together as they talk, both at once. They laugh, spring apart, then punch each other amiably before tumbling, shrieking, giggling with the dogs.

The children disappear momentarily, then return, each pushing a stroller carrying a lively infant crowing with pleasure as the strollers pick up speed. The dogs join in. Surely this game is also for them? As the infants sing out with delight, two sets of tiny feet beat a rhythm of joy in the air.

You and I were once capable of expressing our feelings of joy and connection with every atom of our body. We too were once able to know what we wanted and to demand it. We were able to abandon ourselves entirely to the moment. We were able to approach others and to be approached with relatively little prejudice and pre-judgement.

What has happened to us?

Why has the expression of joy, of spontaneity, even of affection become something that so often seems like a weighty problem which has to be worried about, discussed, with new strategies to be tried out, then those strategies observed and judged, and ourselves along with them?

It would be quite wrong to over-idealise childhood, but it is impossible not to wonder if it has to be the price of adulthood to feel vulnerable, awkward, tense, locked-in, needy or lonely. To sit, chilly and cramped on a hard park bench, perhaps alongside someone you know well, while children, infants and dogs experience their aliveness to the full.

Somewhere on that long trail between childhood and adulthood many of us, perhaps most of us, lose touch with vital skills which allow us to know what we want and how to get it; which allow us to know what we are feeling and how to express it; which allow us to reach out to others with trust and confidence, and to be reached toward in much the same way.

Part of the problem may be very simple. It may be that we set ourselves ideals of human interaction that could be met only by angels. Then disappointment is inevitable. Other parts of the problem may be much more complex and stem from our individual knot of anxieties, conflicts and defences.

What most of us want also seems pretty simple. We want to love and to be loved. We want to like ourselves, rather than despise ourselves. We want to feel that we are running our own lives, and that those lives are more or less the way we want them to be.

It doesn't seem too much to ask, and yet we know — from looking at our own lives and those of friends and neighbours — that we often cannot manage one part or even any part of this equation.

So maybe things are not as straightforward as they first appear. For it is in our most personal relationships — with our own selves in solitude and with other people in intimacy — that we frequently feel least competent, least knowledgeable and least likely to get what we think we need.

Many of us, when we feel overwhelmed by these kinds of difficulties, turn our minds hopefully outward. Perhaps there is someone else who can save us, save us from ourselves? Others harbour no such optimism and feel doomed to loneliness, or to living alongside another human being with little hope of happiness.

The odd thing is that whether we are looking outwards with hope, or with pessimism and uncertainty, we are, to some extent at least, looking in the wrong direction.

This is because in all our relationships we start with our own self. How we feel about our own self, how well or little we know our own self, whether we feel alive inside, largely determine the quality of the time we spend alone, as well as the quality of the relationships we have with other people. This is even more marked when those relationships are close enough, or are self-revealing enough, to be called intimate.

It could be that how you experience your own self might even determine whether you can, on a bright cold day, get up from the park bench and walk away from someone who has hurt you, whether you can turn to your companion and say what you feel and want, whether you can take their hand and leave the park, or whether you continue to sit, in comfortable or deathly silence.

Intimacy — closeness to yourself in times of solitude or closeness to others in moments of sharing and connecting — reflects your inner world as almost nothing else does. And intimacy begins from the inside; it begins with your own self.

This idea of self is nothing you can safely bet on. As an idea, self, or even sense of self, can barely be defended. Yet how you *experience* having a sense of self so dramatically affects how you experience 'being in touch' — whether this 'being in touch' is with others and is called intimacy, or whether this 'being in touch' is with yourself and is called solitude — that it is not possible to discuss intimacy and solitude without first finding out: *Who is it* who is feeling intimate? *Who is it* who is experiencing solitude? *Who is it* who feels like hell some days and on top of the world on others? *Who is it* who is capable of being both loving and vile?

Finding your answer to the question *who is it?* is central to this book, not least because that goal of intimacy — feeling known by someone else; feeling capable of knowing someone else — is out of reach until you have some idea of *who it is* who is reaching out, and *who it is* who is being reached toward.

Exploring *who* leads to answers like 'me' or 'my self'.

And that is only the beginning.

Not just identity

What I am describing as self might include what is called identity, but it goes beyond that. Identity is something you can tack on from the outside which changes as you move through your life.

Let's imagine, for example, that you and I bump into each other in a public place. Perhaps it's a busy airport lounge. Let's imagine that we literally bump, which breaks through our usual guard against contact with strangers. After we have laughed, apologised, recovered, we assess each other. You notice my age and my smile. I hear something in your voice which makes me feel comfortable. I love your raincoat. I had one like it years ago. We get talking.

I tell you that I am a writer, that I have lived in this city for seven years, that I have two energetic young children and that although I cannot possibly move again, I am nevertheless restless. You tell me that you used to be an interior designer and now you are studying for the priesthood. You have no children but you do have a partner of fifteen years to whom you are apparently devoted.

At the end of our time together we have shared a good deal of information. This information is more complex than the visual signals we had gathered in the moments after our collision. We know about each other's professional and marital identity. We have some clues about each other's political and social, perhaps even moral attitudes. We may have a sense of some of the emotional issues which are sensitive for each of us. But do we yet have a sense of the other's self?

Talking, even writing about self, is extremely challenging. This is in part because there is so little to say that is concrete; it is also because we have so little practice in everyday life in exploring what self might mean.

Descriptions of self do not come wrapped in a familiar vocabulary. Even forthright conversation would rarely enable someone to ask: 'Who are you beyond your identity?' But it is precisely into that territory — beyond the identifying landmarks of job, town, children, religion — that we move when we take on the challenges of intimacy and of solitude, when we are, or long to be, most 'ourselves'.

Some of the limitations of what self might mean are unravelled by the following lines:

I have a body, *but I am not my body*.

I have feelings, *but I am not my feelings*.

I have desires, *but I am not my desires*.

I have a mind, *but I am not my mind*.

Piero Ferrucci asks, 'Who is it that has been observing all these realms?'

And his answer?

'It is your*self*. The self is not an image or a thought; it is that essence which has been observing all these realms and yet is distinct from all of them.'

Piero Ferrucci is a psychosynthesis therapist. Psychosynthesis theory and many of its guided meditations are the legacy of Roberto Assagioli, an Italian psychoanalyst more or less contemporary with Freud whose dissatisfactions with psychoanalysis came with his perception that Freud's worldview was mired in human misery and paid too little attention to human beings' big existential enquiries: Who am I? Why am I here? What is life for? All questions which, in various ways, affect most strikingly how we judge what and who matters in our lives, and how we go about getting what we think we want and need.

Ferrucci's description — of self as an essence which observes all our realms: body, feelings, desires, mind — helps in understanding that self is not the same as ego. Ego is the centre of consciousness, the 'I' with which you function in the world. It is the most reasonable part of you, probably the part of you that goes to work and smiles in shops and helps children and old people to cross roads. In less public moments your ego may be locked into battle with your instincts, which are called the 'id', the untamed part of you, or the part of you which is out of awareness because it is unconscious.

Freud suggested that 'The ego is that part of the id which has been modified by the direct influence of the external world. In its relation to the id it is like someone on horseback who has to hold in check the superior strength of the horse.'

Freud's description suggests a tussle between instincts and so-called civilised behaviour which demands constant vigilance. This is probably not the case. Freud's metaphor becomes most useful when you think about how you may sometimes act in ways you can hardly recognise as 'yourself', or when you feel pushed to do something which seems to be in opposition to what you should do or would normally do, and when you remember that this is much less likely to happen when you are out in the world than it is when you are *at home*, literally in your own home, or when you are feeling sufficiently 'at home' with someone else to let your guard down.

Those murky areas of unplanned or even unwelcome desires, of unreasonable behaviour, of dramatic feeling and of wild inconsistencies are the emotional landscapes you tread with your intimates, those people with whom you are least protected by the reasonableness of your ego, surprising them, sometimes shocking them, and often surprising and shocking yourself.

And who is it who is being pushed to surprise? Who is it who is acting in ways which seem to have no precedent or reason? Or, alternatively, who is it who feels buried beneath the weight of other people's demands, needs and expectations?

Again, it is your self, the very self you cannot pinch or point to or even quite describe, but the same self nevertheless whom you want others to love, cherish, understand and respect.

Cherishing an inner reality

Those people who have a sense of self have an inner reality, something virtually as precious as life itself because it markedly affects the ways in which you experience yourself and relate to others. A sense of inner reality gives someone, or maybe stems from, what Jung's colleague, Marie-Louise von Franz, called 'solid ground inside oneself'. This is such a wonderfully useful way of talking about self that I want to share her thought in full. *'The experience of Self brings a feeling of standing on solid ground inside oneself, on a patch of eternity, which even physical death cannot touch.'*

Von Franz's reference to a 'patch of eternity' will not be meaningful for everyone, but her evocation of that 'feeling of standing on solid ground inside oneself' makes sense for many people.

When you have that solid ground, it is possible to trust yourself, probably to love yourself, and to be ready to reach out and trust others in relationships of greater and lesser intimacy. When you feel shaky inside, self-trust and self-love are hard to come by. Alone, you may experience feelings of 'not having' and of self-blame, rather than solitude. Reaching out to others may be more like searching for a crutch than the giving and receiving of love. Reaching out to others may even be retaliatory. By that I mean, someone whose sense of self is precarious may only be able to reach out in order to hurt. In that person's worldview his or her actions are defensive (I'll get you before you can get me). Their effect, however, is to push away the potential relationship which may be that person's best chance for healing.

People with a sense of inner reality will, for all that, find themselves acting and reacting in ways which are sometimes unpredictable or inexplicable. I am not suggesting a still (or stagnant) reality. They will also be affected by how other people judge them or react to them. But they are not dependent on the power of others to offer or withdraw 'status', 'acceptance', 'love', 'meaning'.

- They can choose whether to be with other people.
- They need not shrink from contact with others, nor are they compelled to be with someone else in order to know that they are alive.
- They can choose to be alone without feeling condemned to loneliness.
- They know that they are someone.
- They are free to take themselves largely for granted.
- They are who most of us would like to be! (*And can become.*)

This dual capacity to feel true to yourself and to take yourself for granted slips and slides in most people's lives. I know that is true for me. But in some people's lives it is a capacity that seems largely absent, sometimes with tragic results, for without a reasonably secure sense of self you will not feel safe on the 'inside', that mysterious, unlocatable place where heart and mind, dreams, emotions and thoughts tumble together in ever-changing emphasis.

Kristina speaks for many others when she talks about her 'performances', her way of being with people.

'I am always watching to see if I am amusing enough, quick enough, well-informed enough. Enough for whom? Enough to shut people out from knowing that, all appearances to the contrary, I think I am a joke that isn't funny. If they knew how small I felt inside they could never like me. There doesn't seem much respite. Even with my family I keep up the jokes. They are all in various stages of despair and madness, but the crazy bit is that none of us ever mentions this. From the outside we look like any other fairly well-off family. Or we believe we do. Eat, drink, prattle, gossip, be entertaining. Those are the rules of our family and I can't break them.'

Without a reasonably secure sense of self you may be uncomfortably defended on the inside ('I don't care what anyone thinks of me, the whole world can go to hell.'). Or you may, like Kristina, be especially vulnerable to what happens on the 'outside'. What your spouse, your boss, your neighbour or even a stranger might think or feel about you can overturn what you know but perhaps do not trust about yourself. *This is because your sense of gravity, your sense of personal power, is somewhere other than within yourself.*

Without a reasonably secure sense of self you are likely to experience a need to cling to identifying hallmarks (IBM employee, whiz at mathematics) or to entrenched emotional patterns ('Life is a bitch. Who can I blame?') or even to belief systems which offer a framework of meaning yet may be potentially entrapping.

Without a reasonably secure sense of self you may find it extremely difficult to say what you think or even to know what it is that you do think, feel, want or need. Acting, thinking and feeling only in accordance with other people's desires may have become all that seems possible for you.

Without a reasonably secure sense of self your relationships with other people may feel overly important, or perilously unreliable. Rob's pain and bewilderment describe this. Here he talks about the breakdown of a five-year relationship with Maggie.

'I really don't know what went wrong. I thought things were going well, then suddenly Maggie tells me she can't take it any more and that she doesn't want to go on seeing me. Even worse than losing her is realising that I was oblivious to whatever it was that was happening.'

What Rob feels devastated by, but is unable to put into words, is that his knowledge of what was going on with Maggie was limited by the knowledge he has of himself.

Wondering about his own inner life has never been part of Rob's agenda. *Who am I? What do I want? What is my life for and about?* are not questions Rob has ever framed, even to himself. How could he, then, keep in touch with what was happening in Maggie's inner world, that very place that he had once yearned to reach?

This is not to blame Rob, a good-natured man who might have turned away from such questions for no worse reason than that they would have seemed to him irrelevant or even self-indulgent. Yet they are, without doubt, among the most relevant and the least self-indulgent questions people can ask of themselves.

This is because it is not possible to know other people better than you know your own self. Your capacity to feel for and with other people — a capacity vital to intimacy — is limited by the extent to which you are able to feel for and with your own self. This is not selfishness. As you will see through the varied experiences shared in this book, it leads away from selfishness and anxious self-absorption toward that lovely, desirable capacity to take yourself, rather than others, for granted.

A sense of permanence in your life

It is your sense of self which also contributes significantly to a vital sense of permanence in your own life, as well as to a consciousness that you are living a life which is like billions of other lives, and is also unique.

Yet even the luckiest among us is unlikely to experience this sense of self as something constant. You do not grow up, find or establish a 'self', and have that experience of self, or confidence in it, for the rest of your days.

There are people who seem to enjoy a life relatively free of self-doubt. But there is no special moral advantage in that. People who have been pushed by circumstance or constitution to question who they are and what their place is in the world, often under really tough conditions, frequently have a richness of vision less apparent in those whose lives have been freer of inner conflict. Such richness of vision may not make their lives easier. On the contrary, it may make those people uncomfortably alert to how much they have in common with other human beings. But my own biases push me to say that such lives can seem more fully lived.

Whether your sense of self comes easily or is hard-won, you are likely to feel more *yourself* in some situations than others. Your sense of self will probably be harder to contact at times of stress or extreme conflict than during periods of emotional ease. You will almost certainly feel more yourself with some people than with others. At times of major upheaval — death, birth, the end of a relationship — your sense of *who I am* may be especially hard to locate.

In my own life I am aware of how crucial and how difficult it has been to bring closer together a sense of self which I expressed on the outside — the me other people saw — with the way I felt on the inside. I understand how painful it is to have an existence on the inside (in the way you experience yourself) which markedly differs from the way you are perceived.

For years as a child I allowed myself to believe that I was not living my true life. I believed, sometimes, that I would wake up and find my real life waiting. And the pain of that childhood sense of inner unreality — of utter powerlessness — has come back to me in adulthood.

For several years during my twenties I had a recurring, deeply disturbing dream in which I found out that my mother (who died when I was eight) was not really dead but was in hospital and needed me to save her. In the dream I would find the hospital, even find the ward, but with heart pounding and fighting the most appalling feelings of panic, I would race up and down the ward, desperate that I would not recognise her, and that by not recognising her I would betray her, fail to save her, and fail to save myself from the unending grief of missing her.

A decade later I gave birth to my second child, my daughter Kezia. She was born seven weeks prematurely and as she was too immature to suck she was taken from me to the intensive care ward where she was to be tube-fed. Gabriel, my son, was then only fourteen months old, so I had to go home, leave Kezia at the hospital and hurry between home and hospital attempting to be with both children at once.

The ward she was in offered skilled medical care, but took no account of the distress of separation in either the babies or the mothers. Each time I went there Kezia's crib would be moved to a different spot, so on top of my panic as I went up in the lift that she would no longer be alive (although she was in no danger of dying), I had the additional, shaming panic that I would not recognise my own beloved little girl.

The day before I acted and took Kezia home, I went to the intensive care ward — heart pounding with fear as usual — and could not find her. In response to my desperate questions as to where she was, I was casually told that she was in the 'boarding ward'. In a state of grief and rage that she and I could be treated in this cavalier way I eventually located the ward and once again had this utterly calamitous fear that I would not recognise her, that if I didn't recognise her I couldn't have her, would never have her, and that because of my failure she would not have me either.

I did find her, and with a rush of joy recognised her. But seeing her lying in a cot lined up with the cots of other 'boarded babies' — which meant babies well enough to leave intensive care but not strong enough to go home — and feeling the loneliness or utter abandonment of those temporarily motherless infants, I believed that I had to act to change the reality. I had to take Kezia home. Which I did and, eventually, after several months of screaming, she recovered, blossomed into the most enchanting little girl, and I survived, but not without cost and unforgettable memories of how quickly one's vital sense of solid ground within can almost disappear.

A split between the way a person feels on the inside and the way she or he appears on the outside is usually maintained at considerable cost, with increasing feelings of meaningless and decreasing feelings of choice. Such a pattern of splitting is likely to be set in place when there has been a trauma which the child is not encouraged to recover from or speak about so that what the child is feeling on the inside is given no legitimacy of 'mattering' on the outside. Inevitably, then, inner and outer become unbearably divided.

I think this is what happened to me. My mother's death was a double loss. Not only did I lose the person who was herself still my world, I also lost the only person who could possibly have understood what I was feeling, who could have 'read me between the lines' and sensed that my wildness, my wilfulness, covered terror and extreme sadness.

A similar pattern, splitting the way a person feels on the inside from the way he or she appears on the outside, can be established when the child's family cannot attune to who their child is, but insist on behaving toward him or her as the child they want, rather than the child they have. It can happen too in a family that has strong views about how a child 'should' behave, and even what kind of person the child 'should' be.

Some people do adapt to these requests for conformity, but when there is a strong sense of *who I am* within a child or young person, and this does not conform to the family ideals, the struggle for a coherent reality can be awesome.

The price for being one's own self is often the loss of love and approval, which is simply too high a price for most people to pay. On the other hand, the price of conformity is also high: loss of an authentic sense of self; loss of authentic relationships with other people; anxiety or neuroses which speak of deep conflict.

For me, getting older, having therapy, writing my books, and most of all becoming a mother to my two exhausting, healing children, have lead to a much closer 'match' between my inner and outer selves. But it is not always reliable. Sometimes quite ordinary situations will tilt it/me out of balance. What I might feel at such times could be variously described as ungrounded, uncentred, or out of place. What it adds up to are feelings of extreme anxiety or emptiness which make me want to flee from other people and turn in to take care of and restore myself.

Occasionally, for example, when I have been asked to speak in public — something I am used to doing — I have been left with a sense of having been almost literally scooped out on the inside. I think it comes about when I allow myself to feel invaded by other people's expectations of me *so that my own sense of inner reality is lost.* (What I want is lost in the confusion of my expectations about what other people want from me.) Or perhaps it is when the experience itself uncomfortably fragments me: when I know that who I am presenting is *seen as me*, but is not more than one rather artificial aspect of who I am.

Casting the net of memory further back, I vividly recall feeling quite unable to go into the cafeteria at university (the hub of all social life) unless I was with someone. I imagined that if people were to see me alone they would think I had no one to be with, or that without someone else *I was no one.* And I couldn't bear that. Of course it was impossible for me to realise that everyone else's self-absorption was as great as my own and that they were probably far too worried about their own self-image to damn me for mine! It was also impossible for me to work out that while I was standing there waiting to be judged, I was leaving behind what I knew of myself: *that like everyone else I am someone*; that I am not friendless nor unlikeable. Those facts, well known to me, dissolved in the face of what I imagined others might think of me.

Those experiences of my outer and inner selves not 'matching' demonstrate how a sense of reality within is not something that everyone can easily take for granted. What they also show is how harshly most of us judge ourselves when our sense of self (our sense of our own uniqueness and value) is waning or out of touch. *At just the time we need to treat ourselves with patience and compassion we strike the most painful of blows against ourselves — from within.*

We do this largely through creating fantasies of how we appear in other people's eyes. 'Everyone must have thought I was completely stupid.' 'They were only nice to me because . . . ' 'I can never go back there. I'm sure they must hate me.'

Those fantasies rarely reflect accurately other people's judgements, for *when your inner sense of reality is shaky, your own internal judgements of yourself will be infinitely more severe, and more damaging, than those of your externalised judges could ever be.*

There are people whose self-confidence seems impossible to dent. But self-confidence is not necessarily confidence that one has a sense of self. (Beware the person who always has 'the answer'!) Self-confidence may mean confidence in a set of *attitudes* which can add up to not much more than your always being right and my always being wrong.

Attitudinising, posturing, emphatically dividing right from wrong are generally the props of someone with little interest in their own inner life, and little capacity to be empathic. Grandiosity, possessiveness, envy, jealousy, attention-seeking, prejudice, single-mindedness and self-absorption: these are all clues not to a strong sense of self, but to the defensiveness of a weak, fragile or unknown self.

All of us would fall into some corner of this sin-bin from time to time. How could we not? We are creatures of conflict, of ambivalence, often wanting two or more contradictory outcomes at the same time. It is when these symptoms are flagrant that they preclude rewarding self-with-other contact. This is because they almost literally stand between a person and their capacity to tune into what someone else is feeling — *and to care about that* — a capacity at the very heart of intimacy.

Separate selves relating

A reasonably steady sense of self allows you to know yet something else of tremendous value: that you are like other people, but you need not be overly muddled up with them ('Tell me what you want, I can't read your mind.' 'I am sorry you're sad. I can be with you in your sadness knowing that it is you who is sad and not me.' 'I am angry and wish you were dead.' *I know I cannot make this thinking happen.*).

This differentiation from other people need not be part of your conscious thinking. It may often be known only at the level of sensing or feeling. What it translates into is a vital and vitalising security that *I am alive not because you tell me that I am*, and that I am a worthwhile human being, *whether or not you are able to believe it*.

As dependent as most of us allow ourselves to be on other people's opinions — or what we imagine to be other people's opinions — taking to heart that insight can be astonishingly liberating.

It supports your awareness that you have a right to be alive in your own way, and that your relationship with yourself is more intimate and more knowledgeable than anyone else's experience of you can ever be.

A comfortable sense of being at home in your own life gives you something else of great value. It allows you to accept most differences in other people as generally unthreatening ('Gerry's the silent type; I confide in my girlfriends.' 'When Chris is in a bad mood I stay away.').

This easy acceptance of difference is, however, likely to vary greatly with the degree to which you feel 'muddled up' with someone. By that I mean confused about where you end and the other person begins; about whose needs should take priority or who the needs 'belong' to; about what is being felt and on whose behalf ('We have to get married before the baby is born. My mother is insisting on it.' 'None of my family know that I'm gay. They wouldn't want to know.').

I have a vivid memory of a mother telling me how dismayed she was when her three-year-old daughter wanted to flush the lavatory without her mother's help or inspection. The mother experienced this as a severe jolt. She was being told by the child that she did not own what emerged from the child's body and she felt rejected because she was having difficulty *experiencing that child as a separate person.*

Such muddling up of emotions, needs, even thoughts, is likely to be most disruptive in relationships where there is most at stake. Sometimes the muddling up can become so tormenting that a total separation can seem like the only solution. In fact, feeling horribly muddled may be the single greatest cause of relationship breakdown.

Virginia and Jim appear to be the model of such confusion. Virginia believes that she carries the feelings in the relationship for both of them, and that her worst problem is that Jim won't acknowledge this or try to comprehend what a burden it is for her. Virginia describes how this dynamic operates.

'Jim never admits it when he's upset. I hear myself shouting at the kids for no apparent reason and then he roars at me and weeks later I might hear that such and such has happened at Jim's work and presumably he was distressed about that. But I am the one who lets out his damned feelings for him. I don't know if I can take much more of it, especially because when I try to talk to Jim about it he yells at me that I am imagining things and that if anyone is crazy it must be me.'

What Virginia is angry about, but also finds hard to put into words, is Jim's lack of self-responsibility, a direct effect of his lack of self-awareness.

Responsibility for others is crucial to living an emotionally mature life, but so is the capacity to acknowledge and take responsibility for one's own thoughts, feelings and actions: the effects they are having on others; the effects they are having on your own self.

Most of us are vulnerable to feeling at least somewhat muddled up with the people we depend on, like spouses, parents, or colleagues at work, or people we feel responsible for, like our children. This feeling of one self being muddled up with another — a feeling often experienced as irritation, claustrophobia, boredom, frustration, anger — is a complicating but often unrecognised force in intimate relationships.

At my local post office I ran into Serena who is trying to protect her daughter Lisa from making the same mistakes she did by marrying the wrong man. Serena complains that she gets abuse instead of gratitude from her daughter. 'I only want to help her,' says the exasperated mother. But Lisa, who still lives at home in a dependent relationship with her mother, and who has not begun to find her own path toward maturity, is experiencing pity and impatience towards Serena, as well as uncertainty and lust for the fiancé her mother dislikes, and a lack of confidence that she can separate from her mother except by marrying. In this turmoil, anger is, for the younger woman, the easiest emotion to identify and express. She does not yet have sufficient sense of self or self-awareness to realise that much of the conflict comes from *differing needs at war in her own head*. Her mother makes an acceptable target for her anger, just so long as Serena is prepared to go on standing in the centre of the firing range.

When Serena declares that she has had enough, and that at forty-five it is time she gave up emotional spoon-feeding, she will be acting with love to free her daughter. Lisa may not have enough self to choose to be free. She may marry Mr Unsuitable and live unhappily ever after, blaming mother every day. Or she may not. Serena will go on caring, but as long as she believes that her daughter can legitimately claim it to be her mother's fault if things go wrong, the two women will remain in a self-and-other muddle, which adds up to a limiting relationship for both of them.

Without a reliable sense of self, relationships may feel dangerous: you could easily be overwhelmed, entrapped or even lost. Without a reliable sense of self, you may also be inclined to fall for the seductive illusion that greater and more desirable than an I-self is a we-self. This doesn't mean that you are choosing intimacy. It may mean that you don't trust that you have enough self to stand alone. (Maybe two of us partial types can become one more satisfactory whole?)

Couple relationships can encourage that kind of thinking or, rather, in coupledom you can more easily give up wondering what you are thinking, whether you are thinking, and asking that crucial question: *Who is doing the thinking?* Instead you can distract yourself with the mighty task of telling your partner what she or he is thinking, feeling, wanting and needing. As one half of a couple it is incredibly tempting to give up exploring who you are in order to tell your 'better half' how she or he must be *as a pre-requisite to your being happy*.

It may not be spouse-blaming. It could equally be boss-blaming, government-blaming, education-blaming, parent-blaming, and so on. Variations are countless on the your-fault theme. This is because it is generally a great deal less threatening to our illusions about ourselves to appoint someone or something outside ourselves as chief barrier to our fulfilment, rather than taking on the rigorous challenges of emotional self-responsibility.

Because our societies place such enormous emphasis on coupledom, it is easy to understand why a we-self can seem like the best possible protection against loneliness. You breathe out and I'll breathe in, and never again will we have to breathe alone.

But we-ness which disallows solitude, which denies the two separate existences of linked people, can readily topple whatever sense you might have of a reality which is your own. As well, we-ness has an insistent way of becoming claustrophobic, at least for one partner — perhaps the healthier of the two.

The we-self can also be called the *adapted self*. Many attempts have been made to discriminate usefully between a true self and an adapted self which has also been called a *false self* (by psychoanalyst and paediatrician D.W. Winnicott); a *pseudo-self* (by family therapist Murray Bowen); an *idealised, conforming self* (by psychoanalyst Alice Miller); and an *as-if personality* (by psychoanalyst Helene Deutsch). What this term adds up to is a description of someone who is attuned to messages from the outside, rather than trusting in or having much sense of their own inner direction.

Such a person may well display characteristics which are highly praised in our communities. She (or he) may be loyal, compliant, intensely co-operative. She may be an excellent employee or the most devoted member of a religious or secular institution. Equally she may be a rebel, but have chosen to rebel along well-trodden lines. (There is nothing essentially self-expressive about being a thug, an addict, a drop-out.)

A person who has the characteristics of an adapted self may be happy enough. Yet they lack some human freedoms which we hold dear: the freedom to know one's own mind; the freedom to speak one's own mind; the freedom to be true to one's own self.

Adapted self behaviour can also be part of the life of someone who feels overly 'together', who would claim to know him or herself inside out. Of that kind of adapted self, analyst Harry Guntrip suggests: 'The more possible it is to predict consistently what a human being will do, the less of a real person he has become.'

Lorna's story seems to demonstrate this.

'I started to fail at school and in reaction to my father's disappointment I took the mother role in the family. I took over from where my mother couldn't cope and tried to get recognition in that way. I became mindless and it didn't matter what I did in terms of school work because I just saw myself as filling in time until marriage. I had no vision of myself after marriage. During those nearly twenty years of marriage I lost any sense of self. Leaving that marriage was finding that self again. And to me, finding that self is connected with me as a child, rather than the silly and artificial person I became, the conforming person.'

Every one of us displays some degree of adapted self behaviour when what we may want or feel has to be set aside in order to function co-operatively in a crowded society. This may mean biting your tongue when to speak your mind would give offence, or putting up with behaviour which irritates you or which you may even despise, or going to an alienating job year after year to provide for your family.

Those kinds of adjustments, even when they involve minor dishonesty to your own sense of truth or justice, may not be harmful to your sense of self.

What does seem to matter is whether, in addition to this tolerance (or pragmatism), you are capable also of acting, thinking and speaking on your own behalf; whether your sense of gravity remains within yourself or whether you have an unresolved need to lean on other people, or be leaned upon by other people, *who may seem to have more power over your life than you have.*

Then the need to discover ways to be true to yourself becomes very urgent indeed. Until you know *who it is* who is acting/ thinking/feeling/dreaming in your name and through your body, then contact with others will be as far out of reach as contact with your own self.

The goals of self-discovery are attuned to life.

When you feel real to yourself, whether you are alone or with others, and when others seem real to you even in their differences from you, you can count yourself lucky or blessed.

Remembering who you are

A sense of self is not a sacred entity coming to you in some mysterious way. It is very much affected by the world in which you live. Each of us is shaped by genetic/biological tendencies, our general view of the world, our personality type, our level of energy, our intelligence, the economic or social position of our family of origin, the psychological health of that family, the prevailing national and cultural norms, our religious and social background, and so on.

Still, there are some notions about the self which we can mutually identify and understand. Analyst D.W. Winnicott does so with wonderful simplicity.

'The life of a healthy individual is characterized by fears, conflicting feelings, doubts, frustrations, as much as by the positive feelings. *The main thing is that the man or woman feels that he or she is living his or her own life ...*'

If you picked up this book because you want to improve the quality of your relationships with other people, then this persistent emphasis on living your own life may seem like an unwelcome digression. *But it is the place to start.*

Living a life that is your own does not imply any lack of awareness of others. On the contrary, it is people who have some real sense of being alive from within who can emotionally afford genuine awareness not only of their own special person — who may be experienced as not much more than an extension of their own needs — but of many other people.

It is when someone has little or no sense of inner security, and little or no knowledge of what they are feeling, that they will have difficulty knowing what other people are feeling — and even greater difficulty believing that other people's feelings matter.

I found it fascinating to discover that much of that sense of being alive inside yourself comes from having a continuity of memories *to which you feel entitled*. Remembering *who you are* seems crucial to your being able to relate to other people without defensiveness, callousness or sense of unreality. This is because your reality is internal. It belongs to you.

After more than twenty years experience as a therapist David Jansen has concluded that recovering memories through therapy significantly helps a person to develop a sense of identity, individuality, uniqueness and meaning — all of which may add up to a sense of self.

People without memory do not have that sense of inner reality. They do not have self-acceptance. They are lost, until their memories can be found. Remembering who you are, you can largely take yourself for granted — you don't need to get up in the morning, look in the mirror, and ask your reflection who you are in order to get on with the day.

Stress can, however, affect that comforting sense that it is your own life you are living: a life that is largely of your choosing. This is partly because stress, or the dramatic circumstances which often provoke stress, can remind you how vulnerable you are. Death, disaster, the sudden loss of hope, can throw someone into the air and the landing can seem a long time coming.

In times of stress you are generally living in the present or the very immediate past. You are likely to be engulfed by feeling, unable to look back and recall times of distress which you overcame. When things are really bad, you are also unable to look forward to a time when the pain or stress will be more tolerable. This is entirely appropriate, even healthy, when the stress is acute. It is less healthy when it is a way of life.

At times of great happiness you may also let memories of the past slip away. You have been married five times already, but this time 'it is different'. You have been remade, entirely in the present!

Science fiction and horror movies seem to understand how important memory is and have variously exploited the terror of the lost soul: the person who does not know who he (or she) is, where he has come from, or how or if he belongs. It's a terror which most of us can tune into in some small way, and recoil from.

Understanding the links between self and memory, and writing in *The Observing Self*, Arthur J. Deikman explains that the phenomenological basis of the word self 'derives from four domains of experience: (1) thought, (2) feeling, (3) functional capacity, and (4) the observing centre'.

Deikman goes on: 'Memory, which applies to all four domains, convinces us of our continuity in time.'

Yet we must also ask, *who is doing the remembering?*

Krishnamurti saw 'the little man within' — a somewhat sexist description of self — as being composed *entirely of memories.*

Ken Wilber adds to this enmeshed portrait of self and memories: 'What you now feel to be the inner observer reading this page is nothing but a complex of past memories... the very feeling that you now exist as a separate entity is itself based entirely on memory.'

Talking to my friend Astrid I was given a perfect example of how vital those links are between memory and sense of self. Astrid is a teacher whose mother died when Astrid was ten. Her father, a doctor in a German country town, remarried quickly. His new wife was a forceful, possessive woman who ran rough-shod over Astrid's feelings and, presumably, her grief.

Through most of her adult life Astrid has had difficulty feeling that she has that deep sense of belonging which arises from within and travels with you. She has found it especially difficult to believe that she ever belonged in her own family.

At the age of forty, and faced with the imminent death of her father, Astrid saw a therapist. The few sessions have made a dramatic change in her life.

'I was telling Ellie, the psychiatrist, that as a child I used to eat in the kitchen with the housekeeper. Ellie thought this was awful, but I didn't. I think I rather enjoyed it. Then Ellie asked me more about those meal times and whether I felt the dining room was out of bounds for me and I explained to her that I was free to run to the dining room and to help myself to special things from their table and take them back with me to the kitchen if I wanted. The point was, in response to Ellie's interest I regained memo-ries of a time when I was free to run to and fro in the house, to insert myself into my parents' company if I chose, and was certainly not punished for this. I rediscovered that I was rela-tively free within the household at that time, and I was instru-mental in my own behaviour. *I was deciding, and I was belonging.*'

That recollection has been vital for Astrid. She now knows that there was a time when she was *in place* and that the difficult years with her stepmother lie on top of that but have not entirely blotted it out. With a sense of continuity — of memory — back to that stronger time, Astrid feels much more alive in the present, and faces the future with positive expectation.

2

Locating your solid ground

'Real from within' and 'on solid ground inside yourself' are easy phrases to use but they may not be so easily recognised as part of someone's everyday experience. Sooner or later the question arises: is the having of a sense of self something else at which we poor, fallible human beings can fail?

The short answer is no.

If 'real from within' or 'solid ground inside' are not part of your vocabulary of experience, you are not doomed to lack a sense of self forever.

A lack of inner security is developed in relationship with others or as the result of the lack of satisfactory relationships with others, especially during the crucial years of infancy and early childhood. That is one of the most basic concepts of psychoanalysis because those are the years when events are not analysed and rationalised, but hit at the guts — and stay there.

However, this same configuration — relationship with others — also has the potential for unequalled pleasure, growth and learning. And this includes discovering that for all but the most severely damaged of us a way can be found towards that important sense of inner reality.

This does not happen by changing the past. That isn't possible. It happens through coming to understand more about the individual dynamics of your own history; through discovering then rediscovering how the past is affecting you in the present and, as crucially, through a shift in attitude to what happened in the past which can, like Astrid's memory of childhood mealtimes, transform your present and your future for the better.

Sometimes these shifts in attitude happen gradually and naturally. Sometimes more concentrated efforts are needed, with the support of a therapist or committed friend, or perhaps a fairly determined process of self-enquiry. *What is needed as a starting point is a sense, no matter how tentative, that your own life is worth some attention, and that your own self is worth discovering.*

At the heart of any change in attitude is knowledge. Not simply knowledge at a cerebral level, but knowledge at that deep level when something strikes you with real force in the emotions and body as well as in the mind *because it is what you have been needing to know.*

'The relief I felt was just enormous,' said Penny to me, 'when I came to realise that I had gone way beyond the limits of my parents' experiences and emotional understanding and that I did not have to repeat the kind of limp, emotionally draining family life which they accepted and even promoted as normal. I do not feel angry with them, nor pity either. I just feel grateful that good luck and determination have driven me to find out what had been going on and to refuse to accept that.'

Penny is a large-hearted woman in her late sixties who wept as she said, 'We were taught to honour the commandment *Love thy neighbour as thyself*, yet the real message was Love thy neighbour and neglect thyself. Loving yourself amounted to selfishness. But now I know that the commandment should really be *Love thyself, and then you can love thy neighbour*. But it has taken me most of my adult life to realise that.'

Life with mother

The nature of someone's relationships with others — whether their 'tone' reflects compulsive neediness, involuntary isolation, or relatively satisfying flexibility — is largely determined by the development of a sense of self. Or by the absence of such development:

- The person who can trust that she (or he) is living her own life is able to interact with others without feeling either defensive or painfully needy.
- The person who feels real inside can be alone without fearing that she (or he) will cease to exist, either in her own mind or in the minds of other people. She knows that when she is not with the people she loves she can still be 'held' by them and is real in their thoughts. She knows too that when she is alone she is not alone with no one, but is alone with her own imagination, thoughts and feelings, experiences and memories. In short, *she is alone with her own self*.

It's an impressive list of outcomes, but who has this feeling of living their own life or of reality within, and how did they come by it?

The capacity to be comfortably alone flows from satisfying experiences of being with someone else. What's more, satisfying experiences of being with someone else fuel a continuing capacity to be alone, without feeling adrift or lonely.

It is exceptionally useful to understand this simple insight. Many people who find it hard to be alone blame or despise themselves (or know themselves so little they do not realise that they can't be alone but fill their lives with work, people, noise, booze or drugs). Yet lacking the capacity to be alone is not a moral crime; nor is it a life sentence.

What is called for is retrieving some sense of what being with other people was like — what *attachment* felt like — especially during the years of infancy and early childhood. Until those experiences of attachment are at least partially understood, it is difficult to make sense of why aloneness might seem threatening or entrapping.

When things are going well for an infant, the mother stands in for the parts of the infant which are helplessly immature, and comforts the infant through the stages of learning which teach the child that although need is felt within, it must be met from without. With this comes a crucial learning that 'within' and 'without' are not the same place, *just as self and other are not the same person*.

The next giant step for the infant is to experience through trial and error that it is possible to be separate from the person to whom he (or she) is attached *without losing his sense of attachment*. In other words, the child can have his internal experiences of the person even in their absence, just as the caregiver goes on having experiences of him, even when he is not there.

It is not difficult to see how acquiring this sense of confidence — that you can have someone even in their absence — will colour your adult experiences of intimacy and solitude, your feeling that you can or cannot get enough of someone; your feeling that you are alone with or without your internal experiences of the people who are important to you.

A very young child can only believe in what is present. When the mother of a toddler goes out of the room and the child screams, he (or she) may be screaming as a way of saying, 'Don't go'. He may be screaming because he has no power to stop his mother going unless he screams harder and longer and his mother cannot bear it. But — and here is the rub — he may be screaming out of an uncomprehending fear that the mother who is disappearing is disappearing forever and, worse yet, that she is taking with her their shared sense that he is Someone. Without her presence assuring him that he is Someone, he may be No one. This threatens total oblivion.

The 'peek-a-boo' games common to childhood allow a child to learn to express and to master his fear that someone who has disappeared *will not come back*. And eventually, when things go reasonably well for the child, something else is also learnt: even in his mother's absence, he goes on existing.

A child does not need to have suffered the experience of a genuinely disappearing parent to fear that without his mother's belief that he is Someone, he will be No one. It can be demonstrated by children whose parents are almost constantly present and almost as constantly devoted.

From our own adult fears we catch glimpses of that infantile panic: that there will be No one, and that if there is No one, then I, too, am No one. My anxiety at the doors of the university cafeteria was a re-run of that panic.

We can even speculate that a child's fear of darkness may not be a fear that the darkness hides a scary Someone, but that in the darkness there is *no one at all*.

Times of crisis show this most poignantly.

When the abandoned lover screams 'I can't live without him', she is screaming her fear that in place of a sense of self — which is an internal experience — she has borrowed an identity from outside herself. This is not something she can control. Her belief is that the man, or their relationship, has given her an identity. In removing himself, he is taking her identity-self away. He is not there; she is not there.

Having a reasonably secure sense of self does not free you entirely from wondering what will happen if you are suddenly alone, or are alone for too long. Nor does it free you from needing other people. On the contrary. Most of us long for feelings of sustaining connection. Problems arise not through wanting or having such connections, but from believing that without those connections in the present you are no longer 'alive', or that without those connections you are not whole or worthy of life.

The infant's inner or psychic development is just as phenomenal as his or her more obvious physical strides. Before the first year of life is over the child who has begun life as wholly dependent is already beginning to develop a capacity for concern for others.

At only eighteen months old a child is capable of creating separate images of mother and child, enabling the child who has received 'good enough' care to call up an image of his mother in her absence; so that if his mother is not away for too long, and if the care the child gets during her absence is loving, his mother can go on being a 'good mother' even when she is not there.

That marks the beginning of the vital capacity to have some-one even in their absence, a capacity which can transform the adult-to-be's experiences of both intimacy (I am with you. I can have 'enough' of you) and of solitude (I am alone with my thoughts, my memories, my experiences — *to which I am entitled*).

Yet even when all has not gone well in infancy, a person is not condemned to loneliness or to unsatisfactory relationships. Life, fate, luck, good will all provide opportunities to retrieve a sense of connection to your own self and to others. My writing this book, and your reading it, are testimony to that.

Equally, things may go well in childhood, but nevertheless the adult can lose his or her sense of steady ground within and feel tossed into terrifying chaos with little or no sense left of *who I am*.

A disappearing body, a disappearing self

Rebecca is a young woman who came close to ceasing to live her own life, provoking an emotional crisis which seriously threatened her physical as well as her emotional existence.

She was twenty-two when I talked to her, and the events she describes had taken place two or three years earlier. Her gifts for self-analysis would have been unusual in a much older person. From a young woman, they were startling. For weeks after our talk I found myself hearing her dry, attractive voice in my ears or seeing again her animated, mobile face.

Rebecca has lived most of her life in London. She comes from a talented Jewish family and is the youngest of three adult children. Her story powerfully conveys this complex idea of how one's sense of self can wax and wane, and then — with help, and luck — be found again.

Rebecca told me, 'I have always been very conscious of wanting to be an individual and wanting to be treated very individually, and that makes me a spoilt person. I don't think I ever was just one of the children. I refused to eat as a baby and my mother tells me she would cry over my cot. It's part of her story of being a mother that I cried and screamed a lot.

'Of the three children I was always the one who screamed so loud that in the end I was the one who Dad would allow to go right into bed between Mum and him because that's where I wanted to be, right in between Mum and Dad, and the other two weren't allowed in bed. Dad refused it. He said, "I want my independence from children. When I sleep I want to sleep." But I got in there. That's why I didn't want to go to school, because I was no longer allowed to be an individual.'

In her later teens, Rebecca went to Jerusalem to study music.

'I didn't speak much Hebrew and I didn't get on with the Israelis much. My world was very small. My boyfriend and I saw each other every day for two years. We lived a separate life and we got closer and closer, separate from the world around us. At first we had Israeli friends, then we had European friends, and then we had each other, and in order to compensate for that lack we did develop the most incredible intimate life. For example, having dinner was not just having dinner. We might pretend we were in an Indian community and that everything was Indian. Another evening it would be something different. It was as though to compensate for our lack of world we brought the whole world into our room.

'I became incredibly disconnected from the outside world and I could no longer communicate with anybody except this person.

'The fantasies were not childlike. It felt like being warm in a cave; it felt wonderful. My boyfriend not only shared that capacity for fantasy; he created it. We used to build mannequins. In a way it is quite a sad picture because what we did was we created people.

'We were supported by the State of Israel. We lived in a beautiful flat. We were quite poor, not at all rich. We were both studying music and we went less and less to school and stayed more and more at home. We got into this thing: you can do everything yourself. You don't need anyone else.

'He was a jazz musician. I gave up singing classical music and started singing jazz, which he taught me. It was one more way of controlling that personal aspect, bringing me in. In the end it wasn't intimacy, it was possession. I just gave me to the relationship. The relationship became me. There was no difference.

'When I came back to England I was quite shell-shocked and completely destroyed. We had eaten each other up and I could no longer function socially. I couldn't talk, I couldn't speak to people. Every public occasion was a complete nightmare for me. It was really that I had lost all sense of myself.'

Rebecca entered what she calls her 'anorexic phase'.

'This was very much about self-denial, about lack of control. Basically I had so little power at that time the power came to do with internal power over myself and becoming obsessive about not eating, and losing too much weight, losing my period, emptying myself out. I was like a spaced-out person, puritanical. Everyone had to be perfect. I had completely the wrong idea about myself. I can see that now. But at the time I was very lost and had definite ideas about what I wanted, but they were totally misplaced really.

'I did disappear. I really did disappear. At the time it was more about losing control — having lost control in the relationship with the man in Israel and wanting control over something for myself. It was also about not having control in the outside world. Two things: losing the world, giving myself to this guy. And what did I have left? I had my own body. And that's what I dealt with.

'I felt that I couldn't be with people. I didn't want to be alone but I couldn't be with people. Because I didn't look right, or it wasn't worth it, or it wasn't deep enough. Having had a very intense relationship with someone, I wanted to be on my own.

'I found a flat in a working-class area with a culture all of its own. I had my sister living three flats away, and it was fantastic. I painted my flat and I got such pleasure. I did everything myself. And when it was finished I sat down and I had a computer and I started writing. It went brilliantly for about a week. And then I sat down and could hear everything.

'I could hear the train as it went by. I could hear the man in the street. I could hear the woman downstairs coughing. I could hear everything.

'So I got up and walked around and made myself something to eat. Something that didn't agree with me, probably made me instantly feel spotty, and then I could smell gas. And then there was a smell of corpse. I could smell a dead body in that flat. It came from under the floorboards and suddenly this place which I had created became revolting. I couldn't bear it and there was nowhere to escape. I went outside and there were these people. Old women pushing pushchairs. Young women looking like old women with chip butties [sandwiches] in their mouths and five children. And not a good place to buy food. Everything was dirty, dirty, dirty. I would clean up, and it would be dirty. And all this; I could no longer work because everything was interrupting me. And all this space, all these rooms.

'I had three rooms all to myself and my thoughts were just bouncing over the place, were just rolling out like a carpet and to nowhere. I couldn't catch them. I couldn't catch my thoughts and enclose them because everything was disturbing me and all the disturbance was like banging around this place. And that's how I felt. My sister was very busy with her work and wasn't around. I felt shut in the flat by the outside world which was grey and disgusting and then slowly, slowly all the furniture came into one room until I was surrounded. I squashed myself in until I couldn't breathe any more and so eventually I rang the gas man and I said to him, "I can smell gas in my flat and it's giving me a terrible headache and I'm getting spots and please will you come?" And he said (the place was called Downs Court), "What do you feel?" And I said, "I feel sick. There's a smell, it smells of death. I can't bear it."

'He tested it. He said, "There's not one trace of gas. Not one trace."

'I said, "But I can smell gas. That is gas."

'He said, "Listen love, there's three things. Either you've got Downs Court-itis and you should get out of here. Or you're pregnant, and that's why you're sick. Or you should go and see my mate, who's a mentalologist."

'I was so shocked by what he said that I burst out giggling. Because, of course, he was absolutely right. I should have gone to his mentalologist.'

That era in Rebecca's life has a positive ending. When she and I spoke later she was able to say that she had moved far enough away from her obsessional anxieties — provoked by her gradual disappearance of self — to a state where she can eat fairly normally, where she has a lover she is comfortable with, and a relationship with her own self secure enough that she can afford 'not to think about what I am so much'.

Rebecca might enjoy Gestalt therapist Fritz Perls' remark: 'If you feel comfortable in yourself, you don't love yourself and you don't hate yourself, you just live.' For the goals of selfhood are several-fold (and different for each one of us), but they do not include self-obsession.

From the safety of self-knowledge, trust and acceptance, you are well-placed to know that you are your own safe place which you never entirely leave, to know that you are your own safe place to which you can consciously and willingly return.

Replaying the past

Rebecca's crisis of existence was provoked by a series of intense events which in their dramatic combination threatened to submerge her. A more constant story of little-self or no-self is likely to come from someone who is stuck in the past, unconsciously attached to what he or she has not had in infancy or early childhood: to a state of *not-relating* with warmth and confidence, to a state of *not-feeling* trust. Such a person is relatively incapable of acting with spontaneity or out of what Alice Miller calls 'self-esteem based on the authenticity of one's own feelings'.

Alice Miller, through her writing over the last decade, has had a good deal of influence on how people think about childhood and its effects on the adult the child becomes. Here she is stating what could be repeated by almost everyone who works where human need or misery is exposed.

'Over the years, my analytic work has included many initial consultations with people seeking advice in looking for an analyst, whom I saw for one or two sessions. In these short encounters, the tragedy of an individual destiny can often be seen with moving clarity and intensity. What is described as depression and experienced as emptiness, futility, fear of impoverishment, and loneliness can often be recognized as the tragedy of the loss of the self, or alienation from the self.'

You can't pick out those people through any distinguishing group of characteristics. They/we may be timid, withdrawn or self-questioning. But as you saw from that list of adjectives which described the weak or fragile self, they/we can just as likely be living an unusually confident life in the present, with very little reference to past events, with no time for introspection and no patience for those prepared to risk prodding at the big questions about life's meaning.

Tyro is a talk-back radio star who blasts his forthright opinions out across the airwaves five days a week to mass audiences. He prides himself on his extreme manliness and likes nothing better than to relax with the boys, usually persuading them to defy the anxiety of their wives and to stay out through the night drinking with him. Tyro is fifty-two.

Is it surprising to know that Tyro's own mother was largely absent through his childhood? He doesn't remember his anger with her. He regards her as a silly bitch and feels sure he and his brothers were better off without her. He does not remember his grief that she was not there when, like any other small boy, he needed her. Instead he persuades his men friends, 'the boys', to punish their wives — stand-ins for Tyro's mother — by staying out all night drinking. He exercises pseudo-power simultaneously over the boys, their wives, and the mother whom he believes he has exorcised.

Tyro would not like to be told that his behaviour is compulsive. Who would? He would roar with disdain if anyone was silly enough to suggest that he is setting up repetitions-in-reverse of childhood events in order to re-write an ending he could not write as a boy. Like the rest of us, Tyro wants to believe that he is in charge of his life. But it would seem more likely that past events are directing his life in the present.

Without awareness of his past, Tyro's initial theme tune plays on and on and on.

3

The beginnings of self

A convincing early memory of self comes from psycho-analyst Charlotte Wolff's tender, insightful autobiography, *On the Way to Myself*. 'Shortly before my third birthday I experienced something which made me think that at that identical moment of time I had been born to myself. It had been like this. After having been put into my cot for my afternoon rest, I was impelled to sit up, suddenly, apropos of nothing. An overwhelming emotional sensation went through my body and my whole being. I felt my own shape, I saw myself for the first time in my life; I looked at my body as if I was outside it. This was my first eternal moment... I had stepped into my life, and from then onward I was related to myself. I no longer belonged to my parents and my sister in the first place; I belonged first and foremost to myself.'

I love that phrase: *I belonged first and foremost to myself*. It is not a statement of self-absorption. On the contrary, it seems like a declaration of exceptional integrity. Yet for many of us, overwhelmed by orders as to who or what we should be *so that others will love us*, the chance to belong to our own self can seem woefully far from reach.

From the very beginning of life many people struggle to find or maintain a sense of self from within that is different from the pseudo-self demanded from without. Children frequently have their tentative sense of inner reality invaded, abused, belittled, denied or even destroyed, all in the name of love.

The right which so many parents believe they have to 'know' more about their child than the child knows about his or her own inner life and feelings — or to value what they know above what the child knows — has its echoes in many adult-with-adult relationships where the wonder of one self reaching hesitantly toward another is entirely lost as one self plunders the inner space of the other and uses what they find to shore up their own sense of insecurity. And, again, done in the name of love.

From the very start of your own life you were vulnerable to messages about how you 'should' be. These were passed on explicitly and unconsciously by those you loved and depended upon. If the messages told you how you had to be in order to be accepted, and if this was far from the *who I am* you longed to express, your experiences may have alienated you from your own self, resulting in a feeling of being only half-alive, or as though you were alive in someone else's life, rather than your own.

Such a fate is not rare; it is one of the most common tragedies of our time.

The intense delicacy of our need to please, our need to love, our need to be loved, is made much more poignant when the drive toward relationships which exists in all human beings is even partially understood.

It was psychoanalyst Melanie Klein's insight that from birth a child is not just feeding from but is also relating to the breast, that part of his (or her) mother which to the tiny infant means Mother.

Klein's fellow Freudians had regarded the infant child as auto-erotic, wrapped up in complete self-centredness. But, had this been the case, the infant child would not be as dependent as we know him to be on the emotional caretaking from his mother, on her capacity to engage in a relationship in which she carries her child's sense of self for him, reflecting back to him that he is Someone. Through her loving attention she assures her infant that he is someone who matters. What's more, she lets him know that she is aware that *her being there for him also matters*.

This mutuality of mattering has a real impact on how a child will experience intimacy in adulthood. *You matter to me, and I know that I also matter to you.*

Without that bond of both people knowing that they matter to each other, *that they are wanted as well as wanting*, the infant/child/adult will have considerable difficulty developing self-love and self-acceptance. And without self-love, without self-acceptance, there can be little or no capacity to love others *and to feel worthy of being loved in return.*

Having someone in their absence

- 'Taking mother in'
- holding an image of her through her absence
- believing that her absence will be replaced by her presence.

These are immensely important developmental tasks which must precede a child developing what American psychologist Lillian Rubin identifies as an 'independent, coherent and continuing sense of self — a self that's unique and separate from any other... one that knows an "I" exists irrespective of what happens in a relationship'.

- 'Taking your loved ones in'
- holding an image of them through their absences
- believing that their absence will be replaced by their presence.

These are also extremely important tasks in adult-with-adult relationships, but are not always or easily reached.

Virginia remembers, 'When I was first in love with Jim I could never seem to summon up a picture of him in my mind, at least not as a whole person. I felt quite ashamed, almost as if it negated my love for him. I'd remember bits, like his eyebrows or mouth, or even something he had said, or the way he carried his jacket flung over his shoulder. Or I would remember the smell of his jacket. But I could never seem to get the whole man. I'd have to slyly consult one of my photos of him to get his image to return to me. It wasn't so much that he was threatening in his absence as somehow irretrievable. For me he was literally dissolving into pieces unless he was actually with me.'

This phenomenon — of experiencing or remembering someone in 'bits' — is remarkably common and usually quite unnerving. It is a symptom of anxiety, perhaps of extreme conflict: about taking someone in, about 'having' someone, about that person being real to you, about your being real to the other person, about the relationship itself being something you want or can 'have' or want to be able to take for granted.

A response to this anxiety may be to demand more and more of the other person, perhaps physically through sex, or sometimes through talk — a demand to be listened to, or a demand that every last thought should be shared. Yet when this kind of unsettlement is disrupting from within, enough is rarely enough.

When it is the other person who is not doing enough, or when situations outside yourself consistently do not provide enough, the dilemma is not one of not enough other; it is a dilemma of not enough self, or not enough trust and security in your feelings of self.

Psychosexual development

As an infant and child you went through, or failed to go through, various stages of psychosexual development. These stages go on resonating in your adult life, and nowhere are they more apparent (nor are you more infantile!) than in the ways in which you make or resist contact with other people, and especially those with whom you share your bed.

Freudian analysts call these stages oral, anal, phallic (Oedipal) and genital. With more 'couple' or relationship emphasis, they can be called the stages of undifferentiated merging, symbiosis and separation. Fairbairn called those same stages breast, mother, adult partner.

Getting to that last stage, with two people genuinely regarding each other as *adult partners* who exist other than in relation to their mutual neediness, is a considerable achievement and a worthwhile goal of intimacy.

I have already suggested that you can have comfortable experiences of being alone only when you have taken in nourishing experiences of togetherness. In very much the same way, you pass through each of the psychosexual stages of development *only through experiencing it richly enough.* ('Enough' may, of course, be a matter of individual temperament, rather than any kind of absolute.)

If you do not pass through one of those stages by having enough then, theoretically anyway, you will be stuck. This leads to jokes when you clean the ashtrays even as other people are lighting their cigarettes (you are anally fixated), or when you stuff your mouth constantly while never ceasing to talk (you are orally fixated, of course!).

Looking at these developmental stages as a kind of progression suggests the 'stage-by-stage firming up' of a personality until individual identity is achieved with, one would hope, maximum choice as to when and how the ashtrays should be cleaned, the mouth filled or emptied — and with the phallic stage's Oedipal conflicts satisfactorily resolved. That means that you would have a clear sense that you cannot possess your opposite sex parent but that one day, because you have learned to identify with your same-sex parent rather than wanting to kill them, you will find an opposite sex person to take your desired parent's place between the sheets!

But is life ever that predictable?

Daniel Stern is a contemporary New York child psychiatrist and academic who has rocked several boats by arguing against those schematic divisions of psychosexual or psychosocial stages. Stern is convincing when he argues that we move from developmental stage to developmental stage *without* leaving stages behind, as the Freudian and post-Freudian models have over-diagrammatically suggested. I interpret this as thinking that we add on possibilities to our repertoires of behaviours and responses, but those we learned earliest on are still with us — and can be provoked as different aspects of our self come forward.

Murder, for example, can be interpreted as an act of infantile rage that the world is not as the child-within-the-adult wants it to be. Yet presumably some people are capable of murder, and most of us are capable of murderous rages, *and* of behaviour which would be regarded as 'normally' controlled and considerate of others, behaviour which has its origins in later stages of our development.

In our closest relationships this potential to skid back and forth through various stages of our development can be embarrassingly obvious. The image of the formal dinner party comes to mind, with guests arriving and behaving as they should, with hosts as gracious as expected, yet over several hours and with the help of several bottles, emotions can erupt, wild words can pass between fast-moving lips, bodies can shift and change in their habits of connection, and lives can be altered forever.

Symbiosis: fact or illusion?

Stern also offers the radical point of view that infants do not go through a symbiotic phase in their experience of mother. He believes that from the very beginning the child is developing a concept of self and other.

This has real significance as you think about intimacy because it substantially challenges the notion that the merging many people long for in intimacy, or romantic/sexual love, is a return to the merging of earliest life when mother and infant were as one. Not so, says Dr Stern.

'There is no confusion between self and other in the beginning or at any other point during infancy ... There is no symbiotic-like phase. In fact, the subjective experiences of union with another can occur only after a sense of a core self [which forms between the ages of two and six months] and a core other exist.'

Freed from the traditional view of symbiosis, I think we can usefully speculate that what has been called a longing for merging or symbiosis may be rather more like a longing to be free of conflict.

That conflict is a constant part of life is hard for most of us to accept. Yet how you experience conflict, and the torment of ambivalence, utterly affects how you live with yourself and others.

The traditional view of heaven as a conflict-free zone tells us a great deal about the perils of living on earth with our own unquiet, conflict-driven minds, and alongside our fellow human beings who fail so frequently to do what we want.

The traditional view of the ideal relationship as conflict free packs a similar punch. Perhaps the illusion that we were once without conflicts — and could be again — is too precious for humans easily to abandon.

There is another aspect too. Longing for symbiosis or merging could also be a longing to have our needs recognised and met as they were in the pre-verbal period, through mother 'knowing' what we could not express.

In intimate relationships this is frequently a crucial demand: that you will know what I want without my having to tell you; that you will be able to anticipate my unspoken thoughts and even my unformulated desires; *that you will appreciate my complexity better than I can myself.*

And when you fail to do this? That can feel to me like you have failed to love.

My conversations with two cheerful, dependable people gave me a striking example of this need to be understood without words.

Margaretta and Tomas have been a tightly-knit couple for fifteen years. They both came from large families where there was little attention paid to the individual needs of each child. They brought to their marriage what they now regard as low levels of self-knowledge and concomitantly low expectations of emotional understanding.

Still they have 'moved with the times' and are now aware that they have legitimate needs which are not material or physical. They complain (separately) that they want something more. But what is this 'something more'? Why does their partner not give it (instinctively, naturally)? More to the point, why can they not ask for it?

Part of the reason is that Margaretta and Tomas *want to be understood without words.* That is part of loving in their view. But there is more to it.

If they risked articulating those needs — needs which reach in to their most protected, vulnerable experiences of self — they would risk the potential pain of those needs not being met, and of their being left with nothing but their vulnerability exposed. (They would be worse not better off.) Also, by articulating their needs, even if they found themselves able to do so, each is dramatically emphasising that they are not 'Marg and Tom the couple', but two separate people, *each of whom is being asked to help the other.* This exposure of difference also feels like a risk too big to take.

Had I been working with Margaretta and Tomas in therapy, I would have wanted to find ways to support them to find more sense within each person that he or she could stand alone, and to push a little further into the background the we-self of their marriage which had replaced being 'one of the kids' in their large childhood families. This would greatly improve the quality of their relationship with each other and also *how they experience themselves as individuals*. Indeed, the most satisfying intimate partnerships do seem to be between people who have a clear sense of individual self and who, in their connections with others, are able to differentiate between:

- self and other (You and I are two different people — connected but not 'the same')
- past and present (I feel upset about this now because it reminds me of when ...)
- inner and outer (I am miserable — the world is not necessarily a miserable place)
- thought and feeling (I think your behaviour is ghastly; I feel hurt and angry).

Each self then has a real sense of *who I am, what I want, what I feel, where I am going*, closely affected by concern for his or her partner's welfare, but not overly muddled in that concern.

Loss of self or no self at all

The very idea of such clear differentiation is so attractive you might want this security all of the time. Yet I wonder if that is really possible. A lack of coherence, a temporary loss of self, even a sustained feeling of being frighteningly out of touch with your self: these all seem to be very normal experiences, usually as an outcome of conflict.

I can feel like this when trying to make decisions about what might be 'best' for our children, and at the same time I am trying to keep some grip on what might be acceptable for me in those aspects of my life not directly concerned with parenting. To the simple question, 'What do you want?' I might have no access to a simple answer.

I know that I will be helped if I can:
- identify my conflicts
- order my priorities
- make a decision.

I can also remind myself that unresolved conflict often brings with it powerlessness or even despair, and that what is called for is compassion and patience.

But — oh surprise, surprise — there are times when none of what I know intellectually helps one bit. I remain confused, no matter what I 'tell myself'. And that seems most likely to happen when there are issues too loaded with emotions from the past to be lightly unburdened through rational means. So, I have to accept that uncertainty is sometimes prelude to a new period of risk, to fresh and welcome insights. And sometimes that it is prelude just to more uncertainty.

Fiction provides a useful illustration of this temporary loss of self phenomenon. Catherine Hillery, in Isabel Colegate's novel *Deceits of Time*, is very much the competent Englishwoman whose social class, nationality and sense of the order of things all appear to be in place. Yet none of this protects her from the anxiety that she has 'little idea of what might be the "real" Catherine Hillery'.

'Catherine Hillery, widow of a professional man, down to earth, competent, independent, amused, Catherine Hillery who wrote biographies, went to the theatre, had sons, grandchildren, friends, trenchant views on everything under the sun, seemed to have disappeared, dispersed upon the wind, scattered like ashes on the forest floor beneath the Wiltshire trees. On what errors, on what illusions had she constructed the ramshackle system of connections she thought of as herself? There seemed now to be only a kind of alarm system, functioning without a central control, pumping out signals of distress, confused messages about primeval dangers. At night she sat up in bed with a thumping heart. By day she made herself odd little meals to try to curb her indigestion or sat heavily in a chair, between sleeping and waking, always listening. In the evening she made lists of things to do for the next day, but when the next day came she did not do them.'

You may well recognise yourself in that subtle powerful description of a temporary loss of self, which may more usually feel like bewilderment, uselessness, dreariness or a loss of direction, rather than a loss of knowing *who is doing the directing*. Such a loss is always painful and usually frightening. It can lead to a sense that one's whole inner world is crumbling and away from feelings of self-acceptance, and the good comforts of being able to accept others.

But, awful as it is, such wavering of self, such loss of self-acceptance, cannot usefully be compared to the experience of having no reliable sense of self, of almost entirely lacking inner direction, purpose, meaning, and with that any real sense of anyone else mattering.

Most of us use the term *narcissist* to describe someone we perceive as self-absorbed. Such a person is likely to over-value their own specialness and to be relatively oblivious to the specialness of anyone else, other than as the object of their gratification. Such a person is likely to see things only from their own point of view. He (or she) may even be somewhat paranoid, imaginatively centralising himself in any drama which even remotely affects his life.

The narcissist of common parlance will also be relatively incapable of listening to what is actually being said, and of responding to that without bringing the conversation around to himself. (Your fascinating story will never provoke questions or requests for more details. Your story will inevitably remind him of the time when...)

Such a narcissist may not be a narcissist in the sense that term is used in a psychiatrist's office. And such a narcissist, given a dash of self-awareness in there with the self-absorption, can make real changes in his or her perceptions and thus his experience of the world. Those 'narcissists' may well have come out of families in which they did not get enough attention, *or attention in the way they needed it*. But there are others who are worse off.

In Kafka's story, 'Conversation with a Supplicant', his hero says, 'There has never been a time in which I have been convinced from within myself that I am alive.' Kafka's supplicant is completely dependent on other people to experience him as alive. But can he trust their judgements? Probably not.

Trust — that crucial component in the comfortable experience of self — is unlikely to be part of the emotional vocabulary of someone who is unconvinced from within that he or she is alive. It is this state which is called infantile or pathological narcissism.

It would seem that the not-having of self, the not-having of feelings of warmth and connection, has reached epidemic proportions, at least in Western countries. Christopher Lasch, Alexander Lowen, Philip Slater and Alice Miller are some of the writers who have looked at narcissism not only as an individual emotional disablement, but also as a double-edged societal problem (a problem *produced* by our societies; a problem *for* our societies). Each writer's views differ, but they more or less agree that narcissism is not too much self but, rather, not enough self, and certainly not enough authentic and spontaneously expressed feeling.

The narcissistic adult is not one who has been 'spoilt' by too much attention, but someone whose life has been spoilt because those who cared for him in infancy and childhood were unable to see or know who he was, and respond to that. Instead they saw a reflection of their own needs, or someone who intruded upon their needs.

We return to that bleak picture: that without being lovingly recognised and cared for at the beginning *from the outside*, it is difficult to learn to know that there is someone *on the inside* (your own self) who can learn to be self-and-other caring.

Alexander Lowen — founder of the therapeutic approach called Bioenergetics — suggests that the narcissist's strongest expression of feeling will be 'irrational rage and maudlin sentimentality'. This reflects the profile of people who need to deaden feeling and cultivate 'sensation' through substance abuse.

According to American writer Richard Sennett, the clinical profile the so-called narcissistic person presents is that 'of feeling dead inside, feeling that one is worth nothing and seeing nothing worthwhile outside'.

We have surely all had experiences that reflect the model of our inner world being mirrored by the outer world. At the most simple level, when we are feeling joyful we are most likely to attract smiles; when we are feeling lousy we are sure to have a fierce argument with the waiter who has tried to short-change us.

The person who is stuck with responses dictated by infantile narcissism is responding to the outside from a *tone* of emptiness on the inside. And until something fairly major happens on the inside, the outside will remain self-fulfillingly empty.

Sennett again: 'The manifest content of such a distress is "I cannot feel"; the latent content, however, is that the Other, the other person or the outside world, is failing to arouse me. The statement of inadequacy is double-edged. I am inadequate; those who care about me, by their very caring become inadequate for my needs and are not really the 'right ones' ... The person caught in this bind feels that those who try to get close to him are violating him, giving him no room to breathe; and so he flees, on to the next person who is idealized as perfect *until he or she begins to care.*'

I have italicised those last words to emphasise the *danger* to such a person of vulnerability, the *danger* of intimacy.

What is also crucial in Sennett's analysis is his pointing to the dynamic of blaming the other when, hard as this is to acknowledge, *the lack is not necessarily outside oneself, but inside — inside one's own self.*

We are probably all inclined to hope when we are in a mess there is someone whom we can blame and someone who will save us: from loneliness, from the mess we have made of our lives, from the illnesses which plague us, from the spouse who bores us, from our single life without a life partner, from the job we hate.

We are in trouble with this desire when we are unable to see that while other people can bring insight and support (and trouble and pain) into our lives, no one can save us: *we can only save ourselves.*

The narcissistic person does not have the possibility to make this crucial recognition. Such a person has little inner reality and is doomed to crave affirmations from the outside. These can never be adequate in kind or number. What makes things worse, if you are caught up in the binds of no-self, you are likely to be mistrustful of the people who claim to love or admire you. *This is because it is impossible to accept the love of others until you love your own self.*

If others love you and you do not love your own self, sooner or later you must come to regard them as misguided, stupid or suspiciously needy. And eventually you will treat them that way. That will make it much harder for them to love you, and so your fears will be confirmed.

You were right. You are not lovable.

This does not mean that you are not great company, even charismatic. It is possible to be those things and to 'borrow' the feelings of lovability while you are sparkling. But intimacy, as well as solitude, requires a level of self-awareness and of vulnerability which exposes you — to yourself. Then the old audience must be dismissed and a new audience summoned.

Heinz Kohut was an analyst and writer who has become widely known for his work on 'self' issues. His theories on narcissism strike me as less satisfactory than more accessible writers like Lasch or Miller, perhaps because Kohut seems less interested than those writers in the social conditions under which infantile narcissism is 'learned' and reinforced.

For we do not acquire or fail to acquire a sense of self in a vacuum. Narcissism is the 'clinical ideology' of our time. We are all touched by it. The narcissist 'reads' the world only as it affects him or her. His cog is all that matters; the wheel can go to hell. Cooperation, connection, self-sacrifice: these are words the narcissist would laugh at.

The narcissist looks out to the world and sees reflected there his or her own inner world of meaninglessness, punctuated by people who can only be measured by the degree to which they are of use to him. The effects of narcissism — the plague of no-self, no-feeling, not-caring — threaten all our lives and the very survival of our planet.

But all Westerners, those who feel alive inside as well as those who don't, know it is quite ordinary to look at people in terms of what use they might be; to assess whether knowing them adds or detracts from your own prestige.

If I am a rich, old man then it is completely unremarkable when I borrow your young beauty and preen myself alongside you, and when, in return, you borrow my fat bank balance, and preen more lavishly because of it.

Our societies are built upon structural institutions which make powerfully felt judgements of inclusion and exclusion, praise and denigration, emphatically dividing the 'somebodies' from the 'nobodies'.

Few of us want to believe we are loved for our bank balance, our membership in a rock band, our Key West apartment, or our velvet eyes or perfect legs. Most of us want to be loved 'for myself'. But what does that mean? Who is that self to be loved above and beyond the trappings of personality, charm and possessions? Is that self even known to you? Can you stand to spend time alone with the self you want recognised, valued and loved?

The worst crime committed by the family that raises a child blighted by narcissism is that it cannot provide a buffer between home and the world. In such a family, the world of late twentieth century civilisation has been brought home.

Celebrating the Golden Age

In contrast to the rearing of the narcissist-to-be, the lucky infant is responded to with joy, pride, admiration. As the child learns its earliest skills, the encouragement continues. This is the Golden Age of infancy. An age which, not incidentally, will echo in adulthood during the honeymoon phases of a romantic relationship when inner as well as outer conflict is temporarily abated.

During the first and most important Golden Age, the child is more or less radiant in its appropriate grandiosity and the parents are blissfully unaware, if this is their first baby, that with the coming of opinions, will etc, it is not only the baby who will topple from omnipotence but also the parents who will discover, to use Fay Weldon's insight, how world wars start.

Infant narcissism is normal and desirable. Aspects of it — self-love, the wish to do the best by one's own self as well as by others — will continue into adulthood. Analyst Heinz Kohut has usefully introduced the term *grandiose self* and suggests that if this is met and responded to by the child's parents, it will lay the most reliable foundations for ambition and self-esteem in adulthood. And in satisfying adult relationships there will again be mutual idealising and admiration, with each person at least somewhat attuned to or reflecting back (mirroring, echoing) the other's inner state.

At about eighteen months, and certainly into the third year of life — the terrible twos — the child will be sufficiently separated from Mother to begin to have some idea that he or she is dependent (that an adult must do some things on his behalf, but is not always willing to do so) and that he cannot order his world entirely to his own satisfaction (although he will certainly go on trying!).

A child's gradually awakening understanding of how another person feels 'becomes an important factor', according to child analyst Selma Fraiberg, 'in governing behaviour, in restricting aggressive and destructive acts and words. *This capacity for identification is implicit in our concept of the civilized person.*'

The Golden Age is over. The quest for a human-sized self continues.

The child who does not have a Golden Age — perhaps because the parents are emotionally or largely physically unavailable, are aggressive or chronically depressed, or regard the child as an ornamental enhancement to their lives and not as a real person — is by now in some trouble in terms of future relationships. So, too, is the child who is so adored as an outgrowth of his or her parents (or of their fantasies) that he is not allowed to face and survive conflict and to discover that awareness of others is basic to emotional maturity.

Knowing what others are feeling

The vital capacity to know imaginatively what someone else is feeling, and to care about that, has its origins in parent–child interactions.

Each time parent and child exchange a glance of understanding, they are building up in each other — for this works for the parents too — a sense that each is experiencing something *which the other is capable of understanding*, although not necessarily admiring.

This is the concept Kohut calls mirroring. Stern makes it more subtle by calling it *attunement*: 'Interpersonal communion, created by attunement, will play an important role in the infant's coming to recognize that internal feeling states are forms of human experience that are *shareable* with other humans.'

And, I would stress, *are worth sharing*.

That formula is very much a part of adult intimacy: the glance that expresses more than words, the confirmation that what I am feeling, you can 'know'.

This desire to be understood without words is often associated with intimacy. A moment without words between people, when each believes the other is feeling as he or she is, can be astonishingly powerful. But it is also an aspect of intimacy which can lead to confusion or pain as you learn that while I may be able to understand what you are feeling, *I need not be feeling the same thing*.

That reminder of difference is hard for many people to accept, for if I feel something different from you, isn't this a threat to our relationship?

It is a considerable challenge to learn that it is possible to share an understanding of feelings *without having to share the feelings themselves*. This is because I am not you, and you are not me — a statement of fact which can become clouded in long-term, muddled-up relationships.

'The best hope of emotional maturity,' says Christopher Lasch, 'appears to lie in a creative tension between separation and union, individuation and dependence. It lies in a recognition of one's need for and dependence on people who nevertheless remain separate from oneself and refuse to submit to one's whims.'

It is a goal worth pursuing.

4

Reclaiming your power

From a therapy training film I saw while writing this book came a striking example of how difficult it can be to acknowledge one's own inner strength and direction and to remain in tune with that.

The film showed two twentieth-century therapy giants working (sequentially) with the same woman. One was Carl Rogers. His therapeutic approach was characterised by overt empathy with the patient, displayed through his measured manner, the gentleness of his probing, his willingness to show himself entirely on 'her side'. The other therapist was Fritz Perls, father of the Gestalt school of therapy. His approach was, by Rogers' standards, highly confrontational. Yet, of the two, it seemed to me that Perls took the woman more seriously and that if she came away helped at all, it would be Perls' work which would spur her — at least if she could ever get over the shock of having her defences challenged and exposed.

These therapeutic displays took place in the early 1960s. The woman's appearance was excessively 'feminine'. She smiled a lot, especially when she was describing events which had caused her pain. Yet she was undoubtedly courageous, presenting herself to world-renowned therapists as well as to the faceless thousands who might see her on film.

The problem she had come to discuss centred on her daughter, and on her own uncertainty about whether to respond honestly to her daughter's questions about the mother's sexuality. The patient was divorced and was having sex with men with whom she was unlikely to form a permanent relationship. She felt guilty about this, and her guilt to some extent masked conflicts she felt about her rights, as a woman, to make choices which went some way toward answering her own needs, and her duties, as a mother, to satisfy her daughter's and her own ideas about how a mother ought to behave.

As Rogers encircled her with warmth the viewer could see the woman disappearing and a little girl emerging. Rogers refused to answer the central question to which she persistently returned: would her daughter be hurt more by hearing the truth or by having the truth kept from her? He correctly insisted that she must find her own way to answer that question. But beyond that refusal Rogers seemed unable to resist being a father to her, a wise man who on that meeting could not fail to reinforce for this woman what society had already taught her: that 'truth' and 'answers' lie somewhere outside herself.

In my viewing of that film, Rogers' Wise-Old-Man stance inhibited her from finding an answer. In their interaction she remained stuck in the little girl/helpless woman modes she had been encouraged to adopt. As long as she was stuck in those modes (learned, adaptive expressions of her self) Rogers was asking for the impossible when he pressed her to answer her own question. For in their actual interaction she was re-experiencing some of the most extreme conflicts of femininity: her desire for autonomy and her fear of it; her need to be self-directing and her need for approval; her need for comfort for the 'little girl' who was alive in her (and reinforced by the little girl who was her daughter), and the comfort that she wanted, as a woman, and believed she could find most readily through sex. And all this in the early 1960s when there was comparatively little context in which to explore this without the woman feeling her problems were due to individual failure.

Perls' approach was quite different. 'What's that smile about?' 'Why are you kicking?' 'Kick some more.' 'Who are you kicking?' 'What are your hands doing?' 'Do it again.' 'Do it again!'

The woman was rarely able to finish a sentence, and certainly the viewer got far less of the story than during her session with

Rogers. But the issues of maturity versus infantilism — of leaning on someone else versus finding her own centre of gravity — came out much more strongly and, in reaction to Perls' attacks, a fighting woman emerged who inspired more confidence than the little girl evoked through Rogers' quiet gentleness.

This account is not given to suggest that most of us would benefit from confrontation. Human beings generally need to feel thoroughly accepted before they can tolerate confrontation. And Perls, as a man who could seem to be bullying a woman younger and less privileged than himself, inevitably made me uncomfortable. Nevertheless, most of us would benefit from being taken seriously, and Perls did appear capable of doing that. More specifically, he appeared to believe in the woman's potential strength and inner-directedness and was interested in reaching a real self glimpsed behind her learned, self-limiting feminine behaviour directed toward pleasing others.

After all, the issue could never be whether he could solve the problem for her, at least not without more problems coming to take its place. What Perls could do was to take as his subject matter the camouflages which prevented that woman from getting a grip on her issues. He did this by literally pushing her to exaggerate the physical signs of her inward conflicts in order that she might bring repressed feelings closer to the surface, and recognise the self issues which lay behind the apparent helplessness of her central question.

In recognising them, she may have been able to do something, or accept that the price of doing something, making a change, was more than she wanted to pay. Inaction is also a decision.

When Rogers and Perls looked at this patient, each 'saw' a different woman, created in part by the internal spectacles of his own experiences and prejudice. We can reasonably suppose that the woman also saw herself in what amounted to mirrored reflections. 'Society's view' would be mediated to her through the public culture of her time and place. Her daughter's 'view' — and her view of her daughter's view — would be hinged tightly to prevailing notions of decency. Through her male lovers whom she didn't love we can suppose she saw herself as 'sexy', 'fast', perhaps unmarriageable.

She would have existed differently again in the eyes of the man who had been her husband, and in the we-self view of her family who probably regretted the breakdown of her marriage, and questioned her chances of re-establishing a worthwhile life.

And where was she in all that? Who was the self who was not aspects of her identity: mother, daughter, lover, divorcee, suburban shopper? Who was the self who was not her self-denigrating thoughts, who was not her needs (to please others, to satisfy herself), who was not her desires (to feel loved, attractive; to have her questions answered)?

Who was the self who might have an answer for her of far more value than an outsider could offer, however 'expert'? Did such a self exist for her?

We cannot know.

What I do know is that the more fragmented you feel, the less you are able to choose; and the more tightly contained you feel, the less you are able to acknowledge that you have choices.

You and I do not escape similar choruses of voices and judgements, at least not unless we are cursed with the most isolating grandiosity. And each voice and judgement acts on us, affects us, jars us, *because* conflict is part of the human condition, and *because* we are not the unified beings we would like to be. This is why it is possible to be brave and good in some areas of our lives, and petty and calculating in others. Perhaps it is why it is possible to be a facilitating, effective therapist, even while driving your spouse to the wall.

The power of self-encouragement

Alfred Adler is the person to whom we owe that useful phrase 'inferiority complex'. As with every other theoretician, hindsight gives us many chances to pull apart his work. Nevertheless he did have some insights which thread usefully through this book.

Adler agreed with Freud that the first six or seven years of life are crucial in setting the emotional course for adulthood, but he differed from Freud in that he stressed *consciousness* rather than *unconsciousness* at the centre of personality. In effect, this would mean that you are affected by past events but you are not necessarily ruled by what you have repressed and cannot remember or control. Thus you have the potential to experience intimacy and solitude in ways which are flexible and rewarding — *even when your earliest experiences were far from ideal*.

Adler maintained that you have the possibility of making conscious choices, and of acting with more self-determination and self-responsibility than Freud's view would suggest. This is because Adler regarded your early experiences as less important in your adult life *than your attitude to those events*.

The truth in this matter cannot be absolute. There are too many variables, including temperament, genes, environment, opportunity, and so on. It can, however, be predicted that the ill-effects of problems proceeding from the very earliest period of an infant's life may be most difficult to overcome, although the Adlerian view of self-encouragement nevertheless holds.

Adler's faith in the attitudes we can choose to develop in adulthood and in the power of self-encouragement is not the same as the big business of contemporary 'self-realisation' (which itself should not be confused with the much harder-to-win 'self-knowledge'). So-called therapists who suggest that over the course of an expensive weekend you can be bullied into discovering that all impediments to happiness lie within you, and that you can 'choose' to be master or mistress of your own success, are naive and exploitative.

Adler acknowledged that there are biological and social conditions (and I would add political to that list) that very obviously limit us. Emotional privilege has also not been shared out equally. Nevertheless, between the devil of 'instant enlightenment' and the blue sea of despair, Adler's view does allow you a good deal more power than you may sometimes feel you have.

Adler's goals were directed towards individuals gaining self-knowledge and with that a capacity for self-encouragement. I was strongly reminded of the importance of this when talking to Rosie who, like many of us, functions well at work but less well in her private life. She has been married twice and has had several other major affairs. All these relationships have ended badly.

When we talked she returned repeatedly to one theme: how after a very short time in a relationship she begins to feel the need to press her male partner to reiterate why he is attracted to her — even while knowing that her insistence on this is making her less attractive. She judged her own behaviour ridiculous, and in our discussion about how she experienced herself she jumped on Adler's useful term 'self-defeating'. She described her own self-defeating behaviour, recalling how she feels compelled to ask to *hear* her lover's affirmations of her so that she can temporarily assuage her own lack of self-acceptance.

Yet, of course, her demands have driven her lovers to distraction, and then away. And also, she offered, 'I would feel increasingly unsure whether they meant what they were saying, or were saying it to shut me up. So that even if my husband or lover was being charming or loving or expressive, I would plague him with questions about whether he meant it!'

Rosie's first step towards self-encouragement has been to accept her essential aloneness. With that she wants to come much closer to knowing and trusting her own self, knowing now that someone else cannot make up for that hollowness of self which has frightened her in the past.

'I have had to learn to bear being alone, because wanting to be with a lover had become an addiction. Taking any kind of grip on myself could never happen while I was hooked on getting some man's approval.'

Rosie believes that choosing to be alone, and consciously labelling her aloneness as self-chosen solitude, is part of a long process to help her learn to listen to her own deeper opinions of herself, rather than to the clamour of self-denigration which had been the usual surface noise in her mind. She also hopes that time with her own self will allow her more sense of who she is in her own eyes, rather than who she is in the eyes of others.

When a person feels that she or he exists only in the eyes of other people, then she or he is virtually a slave dependent on the vicariousness of others' judgements. Rosie wasn't willing to go on being a slave. But she could exercise this choice, and acknowledge that she had some choice, only because she is not profoundly damaged. When someone is unable to build up from even the smallest patch of solid ground inside, then 'choice', 'will', 'courage', become very hollow words indeed. This may not be a matter of failed or successful nurturing only; we undoubtedly have variable natures also. And sometimes even the most skilful and loving help does not seem to be enough.

Leaving your self behind

Vogue has a view on the question of self: 'You are what you wear and how you live.'

Mercifully, this is likely to be even less true than most definitions. Nevertheless, in the acquiring of *self-acceptance*, what you wear, how you live, who you live among and *how they see you* can provide powerful messages that are hard to deny. We are all deeply and continually affected by the ways in which we encourage or fail to encourage ourselves and the ways in which we experience others' judgements of us.

'For many of my people,' writes South African exile, activist and singer Miriam Makeba, 'the message begins to sink in. Day after day we are treated like dirt and told we are inferior. It is drummed into our heads. First, your self-respect disappears. You begin to hate everything that is black ... When you begin to hate yourself, you look at someone who is in your own image and you don't have any love for him, either.'

It is useful to bring to mind that our judgements of others (and theirs of us) are inevitably matters of opinion and prejudice — for or against — and are also, and sometimes quite unsubtly, displays of how little or how much we have been able to accept ourselves.

The less we know and have come to accept ourselves, the more harshly we will judge other people, and the more adamantly we will believe we have a right to judge other people. Sometimes this goes along with an infantile lack of self-awareness, an intolerance for difference and a smug, limiting complacency which can be hard for others to take.

For others the harshest judgements turn in on themselves. Faith Reboin explains this. 'Accepting myself as a lesbian grandmother has required me to look closely at my own self-image and develop a willingness to change it. I discovered within myself depths of self-hatred, misogyny, and homophobia that I had not realised existed. These ugly attitudes, fed by four decades of messages from the outside world that old women and lesbian women are not desirable, normal, interesting, active, and acceptable human beings, were ironically a part of me — an aging, lesbian mother. I had first to acknowledge these untruths as part of my beliefs about myself in order to let go of them. Even letting go of such destructive attitudes is difficult, strange as it may seem, when change feels so risky and the status quo is, if nothing else, familiar.'

You come to the discovery of self in the company of others.

You gain self-awareness alongside others.

You are vulnerable to the environment around you.

Rich, power-filled men may seem advantaged when it comes to self, and to be running in a different race when it comes to self-acceptance. And there is no doubt that questions about self and life's meaning are easier to contemplate when you feel *entitled* to be Someone.

But beyond self-esteem, which can be not much more substantial than icing on a cake, I cannot be convinced that understanding self, or expressing self, is inevitably easier for those who are rich, powerful or stereotypically male. On the contrary, serious wealth and the pursuit of power frequently demands shutting out an awareness of the needs of others, or even an awareness of the reality of others, to a very dangerous extent.

To be locked into a belief in your own superiority is as limiting as it is to be persuaded to accept your inferiority. It is not as physically or socially uncomfortable, but the psychic malaise of conformity, meaninglessness and no-self crosses class, race and gender boundaries.

It may take a loss of what a person is most identified with to push them to discover a self which is not bound by inevitably limiting identifications.

I have a big salary, *but I am not my big salary*.

I have a gorgeous face, *but I am not my gorgeous face*.

I have won many prizes, *but I am not my prizes*.

I have a rich husband, *but I am not my rich husband*.

I have a Mercedes Benz, *but I am not my Mercedes Benz*.

The better you know your own self, and the more you can trust yourself to act with minimum conflict and good will, the more easily you can afford to be aware of others. That kind of security allows you to discover that deep connection is enhancing for your sense of self. More than that, connection with others leads to greater knowledge of *who you are*.

But if it is through *connections* between self and other that you most deeply experience your own uniqueness, does this call into question the distinctions between self and other which most of us learn with such difficulty, when we learn them at all?

Let me move rather slowly toward considering this point.

We commonly use expressions like 'I was carried away' or 'I completely forgot myself' to recall situations when we felt as though we were leaving our own selves behind in the experiencing of something which is transporting. Music is probably the best example. But a room where meditation takes place can have the same effect.

The experience is enhanced by the conscious or partially conscious awareness that we are *sharing it with others*. They may be in the concert hall with us or simply assumed — as other music listeners at other times. This feeling of unity with other human beings is something which comes almost as a jolt of recognition when the experience is over, when we 'return to ourselves' once more.

Some people are able by example to bring into question the separations between self and other. Gerhard Adler, a Jungian analyst, describes a seminar with Jung which shows this exactly.

'The seminar had been full of exciting new ideas and thought. I had felt deeply touched and stirred by all that had been said. With me on this morning there had been two close friends; together we left the Clubhouse in the Gemindstrasse in silence and concentration. I was the first to break the silence, saying "Today he has truly talked about myself and my crucial problems and answered all my unasked questions." I shall never forget the almost indignant response with which first the one then the other friend contradicted me. "But no, he talked about *my* problems." "Nonsense, it was exactly *my* questions he answered." We broke off and looked at each other, realizing that a man had talked to us out of the centre of his being, and therefore from such a level that he included all our individual personalities and transcended them.'

Mystical writers from various traditions support this view. This quote is from the Hindu scripture *Bhagavad Gita*:

Passed beyond the pairs...
For he that is freed from the pairs
Is easily freed from conflict.

The Buddhist text *Lankavatara Sutra* says, 'False-imagination teaches that such things as light and shade, long and short, black and white are different and are to be discriminated, but they are not independent of each other; they are only different aspects of the same thing, they are terms of relation, not of reality. Conditions of existence are not of a mutually exclusive character; in essence things are not two but one.'

And in the Gospel of St Thomas, Jesus says,
When you make the two one,
and make the inside like the outside,
and the outside like the inside,
and the upper side like the under side,
and in such a way that you make the man
with the woman a single one,
in order that the man is not man and the
woman is not woman...
then you will go into the kingdom.

It is an exhilarating paradox. You make your discovery of self in the company of others.

Through someone else's belief that you exist, and have a right to exist in your own way, you begin to find your solid ground within.

From that place of inner reality you are able to reach out — perhaps even to forget yourself temporarily — to make contact with others.

Being with others allows you to go on learning *who you are*.

Feeling safe about *who you are*, you can afford to appreciate others' differences, as well as the ways in which you are alike.

Knowing *who you are*, trusting *that you are*, you can also be alone. Not in a state of defensiveness against others, nor in a state of loneliness, but knowing that you are alone with your own self.

And who is that self?

Someone with memories and experiences of others.

PART TWO

Women and men

'When you meet a human being, the first distinction you make is "male or female?".'

Sigmund Freud

5

A girl or boy?

No woman gives birth to a baby. She gives birth to a girl, or a boy, who will grow up to be a woman or a man.

Descriptions of birth experiences sometimes tell us that the parents remained momentarily oblivious to the child's gender. But that is not usual. Birth attendants almost always announce the sex of the child even as she or he emerges: it is a crucial piece of information which will have profound effects on the way that the family relates to the child, how others see the child, and how the child learns to know who she or he is. This will, in turn, shape the ways in which the child-become-adult comes to express his or her self in solitude and with other people.

Whatever or whoever your self is, it is mediated through a body which signals female or male and, for most of your life, through characteristics of behaviour, emotional response and attitude largely associated with that body. Gender is difficult, perhaps impossible, to escape; nowhere is this more true than in our closest and most self-revealing relationships.

Of course, whoever you are, you are something more than a product of your gender conditioning. The moment in history in which you are born; the conditions under which you are born; the place where you are born; the attitudes of the parents who raise you: these all indelibly shape *who I am*.

Biology plays a major part, as does your personality type, your will and your individual sense of inner reality and freedom. You may feel locked into society's expectations for someone of your gender. You may experience yourself as someone who is choosing your own way of being. You may be in a sexual relationship with someone of your same gender. You may have swapped the usual gender roles with your opposite-sex partner. But in your expression of self you are unlikely in any really significant way to transcend your gender, or even to find it psychologically useful to do so. In fact, contrary to two decades of counter-conditioning, it can seem that gender is a vital aspect of self-definition and that 'transcending your gender' may be a somewhat shaky goal through most stages of your life.

What seems more realistic is knowing that it is an inner sense of security and flexibility that offers you the opportunity to *encourage in yourself* the attitudes, feelings and responses that most appropriately express who you are, without too much regard for whether these conventionally match current gender stereotypes.

This can be part of your life-long processes of self-and-other discovery, but it is rarely a route to androgyny. You do not become more masculine if you are a woman who feels freely entitled to tap into the bank of what has been called masculine and take what is most useful for you. You do not become more feminine if you are a man who throws off 'the tight pants of masculinity' — to quote Michael Kaufman — to explore what seems to belong in the realm of women.

What changes with this kind of freedom is not your gender *but your self-definition of what that gender means*. In other words, you are re-defining appropriately for yourself what it means to be a woman or a man at each and every stage of your life. This can be wonderfully liberating when it comes to self-and-other relationships.

There is a clear analogy here with Daniel Stern's observations about infants: that they do not pass through stages and leave them behind, so much as *add on* behaviours as different developmental stages are reached.

You are likely to act out 'male' or 'female' in a way that is most appropriate for your unique expression of self when the functions of gender knowledge have been largely served. This is because through most stages of your life *your gender-knowledge is an essential aspect of knowing who you are,* even while it has the potential to be entrapping.

It is possible to take this potent idea a little further.

The stages of human development can be mapped out as having the potential to progress from:

- a vital need to know who you are in terms of gender (child self behaviour) to
- acting out that gender or rebelling against it in ways which are partly biologically determined and partly socially constructed (adapted self behaviour — which is most of us, most of the time) to
- behaving, thinking, feeling, dreaming, acting, responding in ways which feel true to your own self whether or not this fits conventional expectations of your biological gender (true self behaviour).

Yet any notion that you could express your gender entirely freely would be, I think, illusory. Most of us are too deeply subject to the gender messages all around us. But even holding flexibility as a goal is worth something. It would significantly affect the compassion and freedom you might allow yourself, and would also free you up from limiting prejudices about how other people should or ought to behave.

'Wanting to be myself' is a theme that comes up repeatedly when people have a chance to review their intimate relationships. When it comes to gender, however, many of those same people feel locked in, not because they want to be but because their expression of gender is not something they have particularly thought about, or considered in its appropriateness for this goal of being *who I am*.

Anna's story illustrates how a conventional and unconsidered experience of gender limited her potential to be her own self, and how a changed experience of *who she is* enhanced her capacity to be her own self.

Anna runs a successful business recycling waste products. She is fifty-five, extremely fit, gives lively parties, and has the enviable appearance of a born optimist.

'I am always aware that people will find it hard to believe that it is not a blessing to be born beautiful. Or at least, it wasn't for me.

'My mother was also beautiful and in her day that really counted. She married well and I think she regarded her beauty as her major asset in keeping my father devoted. She was probably right. So, her attitude to my good looks was proprietorial at the very least. She had produced a beautiful daughter — clever her! She wasn't envious, at least I can't recall that, but she certainly pushed me to make the most of my looks in an unswervingly feminine way.

'I went to university but did rather badly and then got a series of silly, well-paid jobs I liked well enough at the time. I married twice and in my second marriage I had two children rather quickly.

'Then my husband died, just at the point where I was beginning to get to know him, when the children were that bit easier. I was devastated. We hadn't had a perfect marriage but I remember feeling that a chance for something more substantial had been snatched from me.

'Anyway, I threw myself into the Merry Widow role. I wasn't very old. Not much over thirty. And then a year or two later I had a stroke. It was awful. I thought that I had died. Except if I was dead why could I hear the children making so much noise, behaving like monsters, when I couldn't speak or say anything to them?

'I was hospitalised for ages. Mother had already died and friends had to rally for the children but I felt weepy and incredibly unsure that I would survive or really that I wanted to.

'It took me ages to ask what my prognosis was. They muttered a great deal but I deduced that something had gone wrong with my face. Much more than my face, my left side was badly affected.

'Well, with a lot of support I managed the full Douglas Bader bit — you know, gallant little woman makes great recovery. It wasn't just that I was gallant. I had so much help as people were inspired to help me as I was so young (and once beautiful) and had kids on my own, and so on.

'After a year or so, I regained most of the mobility I now have, and then I had a breakdown. I lost the power of speech again! It was absurd. But off I went back to hospital, this time to an expensive private clinic where I got bugger-all help and the offer of rather too many pills.

'But what happened, with astonishing good luck, was that I

met a woman who had lost a baby and had had a breakdown. She had a boring, self-centred husband and that hadn't helped. So we teamed up and talked ourselves out of our misery somehow.

'When we got out she left that husband and came to live with me. We had a sexual relationship for a while and it was great, though it fizzled for both of us almost as suddenly as it had started. However, the friendship didn't fizzle and we went on living together and my children loved her, and she them.

'Some time during this saga I assessed my looks. They were still there, but were, as the expression goes, a "shadow of their former selves". I had depended on symmetry and didn't have that any longer. The funny thing is, though, it was such a relief because what had also gone was the set of feelings that went with such a face.

'What were they? God knows exactly, but *feminine* feelings, soft, pretty feelings. Maybe unconsciously I had thought I must reward all that admiration by being the womanly kind of woman my looks suggested.

'It was not that I stopped being soft and even pretty inside, and I was certainly very warm during that love affair with Pat. What had gone was a sense that my outside had been made to please and that my insides should match up or I would cause people distress instead of pleasure.

'I still want to please. I still want to be liked. But it is now much more on my terms. I run this business in a way which suits me and it seems to suit the others who work here. I enjoy being the boss, but don't very often feel the need to be "bossy".

'For some years now I have lived alone and I'm still loving that. I am having a terrific *affaire* with a free spirit a good deal older than I who is another source of inspiration. This person is over seventy and we have the most marvellous sexual relationship I've ever had.

'I am not going to tell you whether my lover is a woman or a man because one of the great bonuses is that this is not a determining factor. Of course how I relate is affected by my lover's gender, but it is not any longer primary. Sometimes I am astonished by this myself, yet it also seems like the most natural thing in the world and you really wonder why people make such a fuss about who is gay and who is straight.

'It all seems a long way away from the world of my girls school and Mother's manicured parties. I am sure my mother did her best, cultivating the beauty of my perfect little face, but the exhilaration of being my own person inside and out is an indescribably better "prize". I can recommend it!'

You might be asking: Is this woman's life too good to be true? Has her expression of self in intimacy and in solitude come to an almost unbelievably perfect balance? When I asked her that Anna laughed.

'I still dribble occasionally, especially when I am tired, and that tends to distress me, despite my best efforts not to care. I have also had a ghastly menopause. But those factors don't stop me feeling like myself, nor do I allow them to push me into timidity in my relationships with other people. When I choose to be alone or find that I am alone, it's not because I feel "not up to it" or any need to hide away in order to recover from the world. After all, my sense of who I have every right to be encompasses that dribble and the embarrassment which goes with it, and the hot flushes, and the right to say I want to be on my own, without apologising for it. No, I'm not too good to be true, but I am incredibly lucky and awareness of that usually keeps me joyful.'

Anna has not reached some unreal plateau of 'personhood'. She is no less a woman than she ever was, but that series of major events allowed her to break out of the mould of being other people's Anna to become her own Anna. In other words, what she seems so clearly to be describing is a journey from being an adapted self to someone who, in her public and private expression of gender, feels very much more like a person true to her own self.

Who am I? What do I want? Is my life as I would like it to be? These are all questions Anna can answer with relative confidence.

6

Landed with your gender

Adapted self is a shorthand way to describe someone whose behaviour is limited by a conscious or unconscious belief that opinions from the outside hold more weight than whatever information the person has on the inside about his or her own self.

It is not 'other people' who must bear this lack of inner power and the inward uncertainty that goes with it, but most of us who are in a continuous state of 'adapting' with more or less sense of reality. This is because in order to be acceptable to others you and I are likely to believe — with good reason — that there are ways in which we 'should' or even 'must' behave. Problems arise when this looms so large that you lose contact with what is going on inside yourself: when you do not know quite who you are, what you want or what you are feeling.

If life on the inside has felt unreal for a long time, change comes to seem impossible. This is hard not only on you but on everyone around you, for then your sensitivity to emotional self-and-other questioning — so vital to your capacity to be responsive in intimacy — will shut down beneath a blanket of self-pity, anxiety or numb certainty.

People who are self-absorbed are suffering from too little rather than too much self. People who over-value what other people think about them may give every appearance of caring a lot about themselves. They may even be painfully turned in upon themselves, but because they lack much or any sense of inner direction, often this self-obsession produces not much more than a fairly chronic sense of helplessness.

I am not in charge of my life. My life is not as I want. I did all this to please other people. Who will save me from myself?

There is also a fairly vast army of people who claim not to care a toss what other people think or feel about them, and not to need anyone other than themselves. Such an attitude does not allow them the luxury of comfortable times of solitude, alone with their known self. It arises not from an authentic sense of inner freedom but from a stance of hostility, usually born out of anxiety and self-defence (Mother, father, the 'world' have not nourished me, so why the hell should I pay attention to you?). Hidden behind an 'I don't care' attitude is often a screamingly sensitive emotional core, much too sensitive to risk exposure. Analyst Margot Waddell's observation helps make this thought clear: 'Beneath a thick skin is usually a very thin skin indeed.'

If you (or your nearest ones) experience yourself as landed with a fairly narrow version of masculinity or femininity, this may be just one part of the complex story of your adapted self, but it will markedly affect how you experience, or avoid, intimate relationships.

You cannot know other people better than you know yourself, nor allow other people freedoms that you do not allow yourself. So a limited perception of your own gender will also limit what you are prepared to understand or tolerate about other people's choices.

If you have spent a good deal of your life snuggled tightly into a gender role, other people's attempts to 'break out' may feel dangerous to your sense of inner order. They may arouse disturbing feelings of anger, perhaps against your family or even against yourself, that the belief you hold that a woman must behave like this, or that men must not feel that, is an attitude only, and not an inviolable truth.

Almost literally through clenched teeth, Roger said, 'I was taught all through my boyhood that I must not cry. Even my mother insisted on it. I learned not to cry all right, but as an adult man I have had great difficulty feeling sadness or being able to bear anyone else's sadness. Often what I feel instead of sadness is anger or contempt which are, apparently, more acceptably manly emotions than genuine sadness or grief. I feel crippled by those childhood injunctions and bloody angry about that.'

Roger may indeed feel crippled, but he is among the lucky ones. That he has recognised the limits put on his emotional expression and wants to fight against those limits suggests that he is comparatively liberated from his adapted self corset. He sees quite clearly how the past is affecting his life in the present. That does not mean he can throw off his past simply by wanting to do so, but he is aware that changes need to begin with himself. With those changes in train, the responses of other people toward him will also change.

Many people take their gender for granted. And given the state of confusion that so many of us live in, being able to take some vital aspect of life for granted can seem like a welcome relief. Yet while there are very obvious generalisations you can make about women and men — which will probably be more right than wrong — it is possible to regard the expression of gender as potentially fluid: something which can reflect the individuality of a person's changing experience of him or herself as he or she moves through life.

Anna's story showed that, and as I continued my interviews for this book I became increasingly aware that gay men and lesbians could be seen as having a head start when it comes to considering what gender means to them as an expression of self.

Theo is a scriptwriter who was active in gay politics through the 1970s and 1980s. He points out, 'If you grow up in a particular culture and are another way inclined, you have to re-learn everything. That's a luxury. Like other gay men, I was raised heterosexual and, like everyone else, defined myself in relation to the norm, which is male. Heterosexual men are the centre of the world. They don't have to define themselves. They never have to take a measure of themselves. Everything revolves around them. The gay boy knows that he is by Norm's standards inadequate, but that can become an advantage. Some people are destroyed, but if you can get through it, it gives enormous strength.

'When something happens to a heterosexual man in later life — perhaps if his wife leaves him — he has no way of coping. He has never had a chance to define himself, to be an independent being. The macho behaviour of Australian men, for example, actually masks a very juvenile set of attitudes. The hen-pecked man never leaves mother. It's a declaration of independence in a funny sort of way to be gay. Feminists accuse homosexual men of being as misogynist as straight men. That deep down they fear women. But I have never felt that.

'I've experienced relationships between gay men and women, and gay men and gay men as much closer and more productive in intellectual ways than the sexual warfare you see in married couples.

'Heterosexuals often fall into the trap of expecting all their emotional needs to be met by the other person. Gay people have more experience of that *not* being the case.'

American poet Carl Morse backs up Theo's point of view: 'The gay child who does not look around does not survive.'

Theo's freedom from the illusion that someone else will meet all or most of his emotional needs emphasises a crucial point. When you limit yourself along gender lines you have to look to the so-called opposite sex to take up the slack, whether this is explicitly emotional (Who will feel my feelings for me?) or covertly emotional (Who will fix the bathroom shelf for me?). And that is often a fruitless search, or a search that insists the other person provides those aspects you do not want to develop or recognise in yourself.

No matter how difficult it may be, it is infinitely more vitalising to attempt to develop in yourself *the qualities you need in other people*.

Even partial success will mean you are taking responsibility for your own self, and gaining greater knowledge of your own self. It will also mean that you can approach others on steady feet, rather than as someone lurching towards the crutch held out by a potential or actual 'other half'.

This is not to denigrate the joy of complementarity in friendships or sexual relationships. What bliss it is to discover that your cooking is appreciated and that you are never called upon to do more in the garden than admire it. How delightful it is for me to know that the bills are in order, and for you to know that the front porch will, eventually, get painted. How pleasant for us both to know that you enjoy my exuberance, and I feel steadied by your calm.

But those kinds of divisions of physical and emotional labour are more appropriately made according to temperament, inclination and experience than along gender lines. In fact, whenever I think back nostalgically to the ideals of the 1960s and 1970s, to the goals of transforming the world and ourselves along with it, I am soothed by remembering that increasing numbers of people are benefiting from just that insight.

Expressing your gender

In your intimate relationships, and especially in your intimate sexual relationships, you may be no less stereotypically male or female than human beings have ever been. Or you may be eager to break out, only to find that you are struggling to make things work with a partner who seems to be demanding that you should be more narrowly masculine or feminine than is comfortable for you.

Joyce is twenty-nine and has been living with Guy since she was nineteen. She says, 'Guy has had every opportunity to become the ideal New Man. He has great parents, went to a liberal school, works as an accountant for an environmental group, yet at home he increasingly behaves like a ratbag macho male. He expects me to pick up after him both physically and emotionally and to fit in with whatever mood he is feeling. I want a different kind of relationship to that, but short of leaving Guy I just don't know how I'm going to get it. I can't understand where the hell he is coming from.'

Where Guy 'is coming from' is hard to know without exploring what he is getting out of treating Joyce like a functionary instead of a separate self. But Joyce's painful cry is typical of women and men who find themselves landed in almost exactly the kind of male–female dance they had sought to avoid. The world is, after all, supposed to have changed. But has it?

Gender is not self-evident. Without understanding a good deal about its functions and the support it gives you in establishing and maintaining a sense of self, as well as the ways in which it can be the worst restriction on your expression of self, it is difficult — perhaps impossible — to unravel many of the problems of intimacy and many of the hurdles to rewarding times alone.

You learned who you are in terms of gender in very early childhood. Most of us took up those lessons with astonishing ease. Indeed, this writing could not have existed with its present emphasis had not Joanna Ryan pointed out to me how difficult it is to make children behave in ways they resist, and how relatively easily most children acquire or come to demonstrate 'ways of being' remarkably congruent with their biological gender. Joanna made this observation as an analytic psychotherapist, and also as the mother of a son who has a good deal of comfortable contact with men, but lives in a largely female household.

Emancipation from sex-role stereotyping has been part of the social agenda for at least 200 years, but while women's place in the world of paid work has certainly changed dramatically, and some men are now actively questioning the old divisions between the public and private spheres, it would seem that when it comes to the deep feelings which create self-image, to people's inner experience of themselves as women or men, boys or girls, not very much has changed at all.

Why can I step into kindergartens and find small girls bathing their plastic 'babies' or quietly drawing inside while the boys loudly defend the universe in the playground outside?

Why do so many girls need to be encouraged to risk falling and tumbling, to rejoice in their exuberance and strength? Why are they often keen to help with the 'packing away', or to do tasks which make other people's lives more comfortable?

Why is it that most boys by the age of three or four are able to identify some games as boys games and to know (correctly in my view) that many of those dramatic, imaginative games are more fun than what are defined as girls games, but are 'too rough' (incorrectly in my view) for the girls who are no smaller or less dexterous than they are? And why is it that so many girls accept this, playing their games around the edge of a large playground, while the boys dominate the desirable centre space that literally gives them room to move?

Why is it that the six-year-old boys in my story-telling class seem compelled to interrupt, roll on the floor or crack silly jokes to draw attention to themselves, or insist on their often violent subject matter to get the group to admire them, while the six-year-old girls listen to what I am saying, listen to each other, and respond to that? Or, worse yet, why do those same lively, intelligent girls sit passively waiting, enduring the boys' interruptions as though it were their fate to do so?

This behaviour already shows striking differences in priority about who or what matters, differences which will have major effects in adult life when the time comes for those girls and boys to try to get their needs for relationship met, and attempt to meet the needs of someone else.

Some of that difference does seem to be socially constructed, largely through the unthinking stereotyping responses of adults.

Twenty years after the second wave of women's liberation began to hit our shores, my daughter briefly believed that she would look 'more beautiful' (her words) if she went to kindergarten in a dress rather than in the shorts or pants she usually wore. She believed this because she heard the young female staff praise the girls for their clothes: 'Such a pretty dress, Shona!'

At three years old, canny Kezia observed how much the girls enjoyed this praise. She did too. She learned that beauty and decoration are rewarded. She also believed that beauty and decoration are female prerogatives.

'Boys can't be ballerinas,' Kezia assured me. 'Boys are bums.'

But the stereotyping responses of adults do not fill in the entire picture. There are aspects of children's behaviour which remain mysterious and which lead me to believe that some gendered behaviour comes from so deep within it is tempting to call it innate.

Fraser Harrison is a British writer who uses his own life as his subject matter. Here he writes as a father, offering an account which is unusually subtle in its observations about his two children, Tilly and Jack, and their relationships to dolls. Jack is the younger child.

'He has always had a huge collection of soft toys and doll-figures, and he sometimes lavishes on them the same kind of domestic attention as Tilly does on her dolls ... He also derives much infantile comfort from them and he too never sleeps alone. But, apart from his bears and other furry toys, which are treasured purely for their security value, the doll-figures he really likes, such as his A-team manikins, all have some heroic quality to them. They are miniature, possessible versions of super-human beings, all masculine, with whom he identifies, and whose extraordinary powers he borrows in fantasy. They are relics of the true cross, fetish objects whose magic converts him into an irresistible, all-powerful god. In other words, he looks up to his toys, worshipping them as shadows of the charismatic superman he longs to become. For this reason he never objects to his soldiers, robot-monsters, knights, spacemen and so on being referred to as toys. They are just that to him, for the word *toy* does not diminish their magical associations.'

And what is the power relationship between Tilly and her dolls?

'Tilly looks down on her dolls. The process is the same, but works the other way round: by being babies her dolls make her omnipotent, whereas if they were mere dolls, she would be no more than a little girl... Tilly's fantasies are concerned with imposing power through relationships, rather than muscular strength. Her caring and nurturing games, which hold no inter-est for him [Jack], are the means of manipulating her little court of babies, all female, according to her absolute whim.

'As a baby herself, her attitude to other younger babies was always warm and very patronizing... She would often come up to me holding out her doll and pointing to it. "Baby, baby," she would repeat again and again, until I acknowledged it and agreed that it was indeed a baby. This frequently enacted ritual seemed to confirm her own existence and importance, and she would signify her pleasure by closing both eyes, giving me a kind of slow-motion, double-barrelled wink.'

'Counter-sexist' childrearing

Over the last couple of decades a significant number of parents have tried to raise children along counter-sexist lines, tackling with vigour and imagination some of the 'social constructors', only to find that anyway they are sharing a home with a skateboard warrior who refuses to cry or a young person in pink who offers to tidy up after her filthy younger brother.

Have these parents failed? Can they blame TV?

Another friend and wise professional, Wiebke Wüstenberg, listened with enormous patience to my professional and maternal rumblings on this topic and then used her careful observations of West German pre-schoolers to emphasise my seeing that: *learning the meaning of your gender at a specific point in history and in particular kinds of societies plays a crucial part in learning to know who you are.*

This cannot be underestimated. Perhaps the expectation of such parents, that children could be young 'persons' freely choosing from a range of socially desirable behaviours, is simply unrealistic. Perhaps this denies the considerable force of biology. Perhaps this would also deny the child some of the pegs she or he needs to hold onto in that crucial learning *who I am* ('I am Michael, and essential to my Michael-ness is that I am a boy.').

I am *not* suggesting that being a secure Michael needs to mean being macho. I would view that as learned, adapted self behaviour, almost certainly reflecting the conscious or unconscious needs of the parents for the child to fit into a gender stereotype. Nor does feeling securely male preclude Michael from enjoying, and being encouraged to enjoy, activities which have traditionally been regarded as feminine, nor expressing feelings conventionally regarded as sissy or unmanly. For we are still discovering what being male, being masculine, can add up to for any individual Michael.

We are also only at the beginning of discovering what being female might mean to any individual Mary as female educational, vocational and social opportunities slowly expand to meet girls' varied needs, and family expectations slowly change to allow each Mary to discover what she needs.

What I *am* suggesting is that each young Mary or Michael will absorb the messages all around them about what a female person is and what a male person is — *as well as what kind of adult they are in the process of becoming* — and will take some of these messages as their guides in the early years of childhood when *who am I?* is a question that is absolutely central to their psychological development.

This point does need emphasising: gender can be a trap; it is also a crucial aspect of the establishment and grounding of a sense of self. Indeed, Robert Stoller in his pioneering work, has been tremendously convincing that 'core gender identity' — the sense that *I am a girl* or *I am a boy* — is essential to healthy development and that children who do not know clearly that they are female or male are in deep trouble when it comes to establishing a reliable sense of self, and with that the capacity to relate satisfactorily to others.

Core gender identity gets established early, around eighteen months to two years old. What can be called 'masculinity' and 'femininity', Stoller sees as coming later (probably not much later). That could probably be described as the more variable behaviours and attitudes a child learns to attach to his or her sense of 'boy-me' or 'girl-me', attitudes which are very specific to time and place and which may well belong in the adapted self basket, especially if they are directed toward pleasing others and winning their approval, whether or not this feels true to a child's own tentative inner reality.

'My father never asked me what I wanted,' Fazal told me with sadness. 'It was completely beyond him to imagine that what he wanted for me might not be what I wanted for myself. School, sport, wife, profession: Dad knew it all. There was to be no possibility for failure. There was to be no possibility for deviation from the path Dad set out for me. For sure I managed to be Dad's boy, but not to be my own person — not that, not ever.'

In laying the ground for the next generation to have satisfying experiences of solitude and intimacy, the goal need not be that Mary swaps with Michael and plays games that tutor her in the art of controlling her own feelings and suppressing her awareness of others. Nor that Michael swaps with Mary and is praised for bathing baby, while not also being praised for lively, assertive risk-taking. The goal may be much more modest: *to raise children who are as unfettered as possible by previous generations' definitions of gender*, especially when these have the dreaded ring of certainty around them.

Similarly, when laying the ground for yourself to express your gender more freely, keeping in mind those distinctions between male and masculine, between female and feminine seems especially useful.

Even the most liberated adults generally enjoy some activities traditionally associated with their gender and display attitudes and feelings likewise 'typically associated'. This does not mean that you are fatally adapted! It may mean instead that you are redefining feminine, while remaining securely female, or redefining masculine, while remaining securely male.

Children's enjoyment of 'typical' activities and their display of 'typical feelings' may go significantly beyond pleasure. They may serve as an essential function in learning how to be internally steady in an unpredictable and unsteady adult world.

It is nevertheless interesting to speculate who child-Michael might be, and even how adult-Michael might experience himself in situations of solitude and intimacy, when enough Michaels begin to think about their gender, rather than taking masculinity for granted.

Theo's remark that 'Heterosexual men are the centre of the world. They don't have to define themselves' points to the ways in which outsiders from the male-majority culture can see men as limited by that 'centre-of-the-world' attitude which points not to a well-developed sense of self, but to a fragile, out-of-touch self bolstered by the trappings of self-importance.

This limitation is most obviously seen as a lack of awareness of others. But that lack of awareness demonstrates someone who is also out of touch with his own inner world, even when his self-absorption dominates his life and his worldview.

It is safe to assume, for example, that the father who knew best for his son Fazal, even until Fazal was a mature man, had never allowed himself the luxury of self-questioning and self-awareness. Shut off from his own feelings, propped up by his certainties, any attempt by Fazal to locate and express his feelings and to step off the path his father had laid out would have been consciously experienced by the father as insulting and irrational, while unconsciously it would have profoundly disrupted the inner conflicts those certainties were in place to protect.

Restricting destructive feelings

A child rarely learns, perhaps never learns, to restrict his or her destructive acts and words without an understanding of 'how another person feels'. This does not mean that you need to be feeling what I am feeling. It means acknowledging that I can feel the same pain you do, and the same joy that you do — and believing that my joy and my pain *matter.*

Selma Fraiberg has specialised in psychotherapeutic work with economically disadvantaged families. She believes that understanding how another person feels is 'a special quality in human intelligence'. She defines that quality beautifully, as 'the ability imaginatively to put oneself in the place of others'. This capacity to put yourself into someone else's place, to know imaginatively what that person is feeling and to care about it, is vital to any meaningful experience of intimacy. Without it, you are simply one self sucking on another self, one self using other selves for whatever it is they can give you.

Along with the capacity to know what someone else is feeling — an aspect of intimacy worth returning to again and again — exists an equally vital capacity: to step outside yourself. This allows you to observe your own behaviour with relative detachment, judging not only how it is affecting your own self, but other people also.

These twin capacities are available only to those people whose sense of self is alive from within: who can trust that they exist comfortably enough to be aware of others; who can trust that they exist safely enough to be flexible and capable of change.

Men have, in general, greater difficulty than women do in stepping 'outside themselves' in order to observe themselves. They also, in general, show less facility for putting themselves into the place of others, to think with the mind of another person, however briefly, and to restrict their destructive acts and words through understanding how another person feels.

Could it be that as outwardly directed as men in general are encouraged to be, their sense of solid ground within themselves, and the awareness of others which comes with that, is often neglected, leaving them heavily dependent on the judgements of others, especially those they regard as more important than themselves?

After all, if men in general could *imaginatively* experience the effects of sexism and racism and militarism, and economic and ecological exploitation, could they continue in such numbers to sustain or even promote them?

And if men in general could imaginatively experience the needs and desires and love a young child feels, could they stay away from their own children in such numbers?

That some men are capable of deserting their children, and of promoting systems of exploitation and divisiveness, is part of a complex story of violence which is affecting all of our lives. That story may express infantile rage that the world is not how those men want it to be, or it may reflect a mask against feelings of vulnerability that those men cannot risk acknowledging.

But there is another aspect to this story also, and that is about a loss of connectivity, a loss of the capacity to put yourself into the place of someone else and to know imaginatively what that person is feeling. *And to care*.

The absence of that capacity is very dangerous. It is an absence of awareness of *who I am* in relation to the rest of the world; it is an absence of feeling safe from inside *that I am*. The absence of that capacity is certainly not part of the psychological make-up of all men, but it is a most dangerous theme of masculinity.

Masculinity is not a universal experience; nor is it desirable that it should be. Yet in the minds of many men it wavers between the universal, the supreme (different — and better) or the so obvious that discussion seems irrelevant.

Jonathan Rutherford offers a pertinent assessment of men in British Left politics who have 'made a problem of feminism and gay politics and ignored the issue of heterosexuality and the problem of men'. What he describes about Britain reflects the situation elsewhere. He emphasises: 'Heterosexual men remain unquestioned.'

Meanwhile the 'problems' are seen as belonging to women, racial minorities and gay people; or even that women, gays and racial minorities *are* the problem! Rutherford points out that this triumvirate 'is written and spoken about as though they were distant planets orbiting men's sun'.

It may seem wonderful to take your gender so much for granted that it can be forgotten. Yet what can actually be forgotten is only gender supremacy, which takes itself entirely for granted.

Questioning your gender, and uncovering how it affects your expression of self, does not need to lead to a breakdown of what you cherish about being female, or male. On the contrary, it may mean reinforcing a sense of maleness or femaleness, while tossing out some inherited garbage.

Perhaps we need more Michaels to become Garths. Garth Baker is a New Zealander, born in 1957. Writing in *One of the Boys*, he spoke up most eloquently for his 'maleness', while also showing that he is free from the bondage of conventional masculinity.

'All I can figure is that men have a unique vigorous energy that women don't. I've come to regard it as a spiritual thing. The yin of "yin and yang": a pure power that is peaceful, generous and Good with a capital "G". Of course far too often it is mistaken for, or misconstrued as, aggression. When I was young maleness seemed aggressive to me and I shied away from considering myself male. Being manly was something other boys did... Never in my wildest dreams did I imagine I would be a man who sews clothes, climbs mountains, wears pink and still reads Biggles.'

Conditions for change

It may not be possible to make substantial changes in what gender could mean when even women and men who have taken up relatively progressive views on gender roles still divide out fairly traditionally when they become parents, at least in terms of emotional caretaking.

Is this because our children *need that*?

Henry V. Dicks, an analyst who worked for many years at the Tavistock Clinic in London, is the author of *Marital Tensions*, a book which remains influential in its close examination of marital and family relations. In 1967, Dicks saw man's sexual identity 'linked as a rule to his implicit readiness for action, by which he achieves economic security and social-occupational status ("has standing"), and is somebody to be reckoned with outside. The woman's identity is typically linked with cherishing, nourishing, maternal functions towards *his* children for *him*. Few marriages,' Dicks claimed, 'can endure when these primary biological tasks are completely denied, or even if some of the secondary roles deriving from them are too flagrantly reversed.'

Could it be that this continues to be true, at least for the early years of childrearing when the discovery of self and gender is inextricably mixed, and when physical and emotional continuity between parent and child lays the foundations of love and trust that will give the child his or her best chance for emotional well-being in adulthood?

It is a position which many non-parents will decry as hopelessly reactionary and traditionally confining of women. I must say that I baulk at Dicks' notion of raising '*his* children for *him*', but I am convinced that every young child needs the committed, constant love of someone capable of meeting his or her needs and that this person — usually mother — herself needs the loving support of at least one other adult if she is to manage this awesome, incomparable task without going under.

The child who gets consistent, stable nurturing from the outside learns to be self-and-other nurturing on the inside. It is not only the individual who benefits, it is all the individuals who make up human society.

Analyst Harry Guntrip passionately supports this thought in a quote that I regard as one of the most important in this book.

'If human infants are not surrounded by genuine love from birth, radiating outward into a truly caring family and social environment, then we pay for our failure toward the next generation by having to live in a world torn with fear and hate ... The importance of security for babies and mothers outweighs every other issue. If that is not achieved, everything else we do merely sustains human masses to struggle on from crisis to crisis.'

Avoiding that awful outcome — of being shut in with fear and hate instead of being open to others — flows on from feeling reasonably good about your own self.

The person who has relatively little sense of self, and therefore little possibility to be genuinely aware of others, is likely to make and even to need sharp divisions between people. Such a person fears difference, yet sees difference everywhere. This is especially dramatic when the inner psychological conflicts, which difference disturbs, are unknown to him or her, and shied away from.

Robert Seidenberg is a psychoanalyst whose bleak view is that, 'In the unconscious of men as found in psychoanalysis, there is a deep-seated fear and loathing of women... it is the loathing of *difference* that encourages and maintains the male homosexual culture from which females are regularly excluded.'

By homosexual *culture* Seidenberg means the world of men, from which women are largely excluded. More hopefully Seidenberg adds, 'The "fear and loathing" is permitted and encouraged by a million social forms... [but is] not inevitable.'

If you accept that loathing of difference is 'not inevitable', then you can take the steps necessary to undermine the dulling certainties of those million social forms.

How can you do this? You can encourage *in yourself* a vital flexibility of perception which mocks the dualistic thinking (right/wrong; black/white; woman/man; rich/poor; deserving/undeserving) upon which racism, sexism, and social and economic exploitation depend for their (non)sense.

Such flexibility comes out of acknowledging the infinitely flowing mutuality of self and other, lived out in a world in which illusion and reality are very close neighbours indeed.

If you are lucky, it is possible to hold many ideas in your mind at once, even contradictory ideas. At nine years old, Sydney poet and philosopher Jonathan Wilson-Fuller showed how this works. He said, 'Like most boys I like toy wars and water guns. Toy wars are okay because you can't hurt anyone. You can't even blast out a tree. Toy wars are fun. With water pistols you get wet, with real wars you get hurt.'

Flexibility of perception can lead to encouraging in yourself an openness on all fronts — physical, emotional, intellectual, spiritual — that denies difference and defies the practices of exclusion.

Does that sound puny? Encouraging flexibility, encouraging openness: can this really effect change?

It can if you accept that fear of difference and loathing of difference cannot flourish in an open mind. This should not imply someone without opinions or values. On the contrary. An open-minded person might question what 'value' talk of values has, while my value as a human being is less than yours because of my gender, colour, religion or class.

An open-minded person knows that fresh information is constantly available as you move through life, and that opinions can change with that new information, or with a new perspective on old information. You (the open-minded person) also know that it is possible that you and I might have different opinions and that perhaps neither one of us is 'wrong' or indeed 'right'. Your open-mindedness means that you are not threatened when I hold an opinion different from yours, because *you are not me and I am not you*, and also because you can distinguish between your opinions and your sense of self.

The most simple of examples occurs to me. An open-minded person may say, God exists for me. A close-minded person may say, God exists (or, God does not exist). The latter stance invites argument, defensiveness, maybe aggression: wars waged in the name of God. The former stance allows for difference, deflects fear of difference and punctures the certainty which loathing of difference demands. Who knows, it may even lead to increased insight.

A closed mind makes absolute sense to those who possess it (apparently), but it is a prison and is always under threat. That is why its 'rights' and the 'rightness' of its position must be defended with force and brutality when propaganda fails. I guess that it is from this fate that most of us are seeking to save our children.

As important as flexibility of perception, and certainly not separate from it, is a recognition that as adults continue to loosen up their range of self-expression, which would include expressing their gender honestly, children will also experiment across a freer range of gender expression and benefit from a more straightforward release of their feelings.

Some boys *are* crying without embarrassment on behalf of others as well as on their own behalf. And they are not ceasing to be boys.

Some girls *are* acting on their own behalf, even shouting on their own behalf, as well as on behalf of others. And they are not ceasing to be girls.

This may add up to more people being able to:
• know imaginatively what others are feeling
• share internal feeling states
• step outside themselves to observe their own behaviour.

What it does not add up to is raising children in whom gender lines are blurred so that naming yourself as a boy or a girl is irrelevant.

Would that even be desirable? I do not think so.

7

The first eighteen months

Your childhood does not determine your adulthood, at least not if you even half agree with Adler that you have the power to be 'self-encouraging'. Nevertheless, it is in childhood that patterns are set which will markedly affect the way you experience your own self, and therefore your capacity to have rewarding relationships with others.

The human capacities for love and learning are rooted in what is called the oral or sensorimotor period of development: the first eighteen months of life. Freudian theory offers the view that deprivation at that oral stage, especially during the first year of life, can lead to severe personality problems. These may bring about an inability to form intimate relationships *because other people cannot be trusted*. This leads to rejecting the loving approaches which others may make because the person has learned that needing is too risky.

What incredible sadness that apparently simple sentence conveys: *needing is too risky*. And this has profound resonances for all of us in a world where being 'open' to your own needs and the needs of others is frequently equated with being naive, if not downright stupid. (Being open to others is a distraction on the road to self-promotion and individual success.)

Yet being yourself with other people, and knowing that you are in your own good company when you are alone, are experiences that are available *only to those people who can be open*, who can afford to be vulnerable, who can trust themselves and who can, in general, trust others.

Peter works for an airline. He is gregarious and self-aware yet the issue of trust is not one which he can readily explore. He told me, 'I have sex with lots of men. They are not my friends. They are bodies that I can connect with. I have friends too. Many of them are women who have given up on straight men, and who can blame them? Sex and friendships don't go together for me. Nor for a lot of straight women either.'

The capacity to trust goes back for each of us right to the beginning of life, to the quality of our earliest connections with mother. But father too plays, or fails to play, a central part, perhaps especially for boys and men.

Separating from mother, connecting with father

Sean Cathie works as a priest and pastoral counsellor. He has collected some of his thoughts from his own experience of what it means to be a man, as well as from his work with battering and abusive men, and has woven them into an article which neatly asks, 'What does it mean to be a man?'

In Cathie's view 'The boy-child cannot easily make [his] transition into an identity of otherness from mother if he has not had sufficient experience of at-oneness with her.'

He is saying that if the child has not felt securely *attached*, then getting 'unattached' — separating from mother in an appropriate way — will feel difficult and dangerous. The child's sense of self will feel threatened and defensive. In short, it is extremely hard to 'give up' and 'move on from' what you have not satisfactorily had. This echoes the movement I have already described through the psychosexual stages: until you have enough of what you emotionally need, *you cannot feel that the experience is yours* and is part of your inner life.

Cathie asserts, 'A serious lack in the maternal provision undercuts the move into a masculine identity.'

This transition into 'otherness' (other from mother, separate from mother) is widely regarded as the linchpin of maleness.

However, it is not just mother who is important. Cathie also believes that 'If father, the representative of separateness, is absent or experienced as hostile, this can be a further hindrance to making the transition.'

Men, thinks Cathie, 'need to have a clear enough sense of their difference from women to be able to relate to their female partners autonomously, without violence, and without passivity'.

He means, in my reading of it, that if you have not had enough 'mother' to be able to let mother go, then you will hang on to her or the idea of her, expressing this attachment through reactions which are uncomfortably ambivalent or perhaps hostile or overly needy of those standing in for mother: probably women with whom you are in any way intimate.

That sense of otherness or separateness from mother is made much easier through satisfactory experience of identification with father as 'the representative of separateness' (someone who is safe to turn to). This kind of male-with-male identification helps men to feel secure enough in their masculinity to avoid its excesses in relation to other men — fighting, baiting, disrupting — and to avoid its excesses in relation to their own selves, allowing themselves no feelings of genuine tenderness, but only self-pity.

A positive identification with father also enables a child — and this is as true for girls as it is for boys — to take in a sense of a world existing beyond the dyad of mother and child, and to feel that in this world 'there is a place for me', while learning that this 'place' is won through some mastery of the rules of social conformity. Along with this can come release for the child from potential unconscious and later conscious fears that she or he must take care of and protect mother, because there is no one else to do so.

Of course, the adult support person in mother's life need not be father, nor even male, to 'rescue' a child from such feelings: successful lesbian motherhood has shown that. And, increasingly, the mother's place in the paid workforce teaches the older child that a world exists outside the mother–child dyad, and that 'there is a place there for me'.

What is less easily replaced by a mother alone or by a mother whose closest relationships are exclusively female — or, indeed, by those many mothers whose male partner is physically or emotionally absent — is positive identification with a loving father or a consistently interested male figure. Such identification dramatically reduces the possibility of men or male authority being perceived by the child as threateningly or actually punitive. Without that positive identification, a child may develop into adulthood with a victim or 'combative' posture in regard to the world, rather than leading with a sense of his or her own inner authority.

Learning what gender means

As a mother, I find it easy to agree with Daniel Stern that it is not the dramatic events which teach a child who she or he is. Stern has produced evidence to show that it is the everyday interactions which count, the flavour of the continuous flow of interaction, as well as the mother's beliefs and fantasies, even those which are unconscious.

The 'flavour' of those first experiences of intimacy will resonate in the tone you bring to your adult experiences of *who I am*: of *who I am* with others and of *who I am* when I am alone.

Your posture towards yourself as a woman or man, and your posture toward others — the kinds of judgements you make when you see 'man' or 'woman' — will also have roots way back in your forgotten past.

Beatrice is an opera singer married to Jacob, her childhood sweetheart, about whom she speaks with exceptional tenderness.

'I can't help myself. I have to take care of Jacob. When I am living at home I can't go off to a performance without being sure that he is OK and that he is well fed. Food is extremely important for me. I cook more than I would if I was not away singing so much, not less. I also make sure that the house is immaculate and filled with flowers. I like to choose the very best on small things, like the best flowers, the softest possible toilet paper and the nicest smelling soap. I wonder about this sometimes, as though I must be a bit of a wimp, and certainly Jacob doesn't expect it or wouldn't complain if I stopped. But I can't help myself and I don't actually want to help myself. I like the way I leave things behind me when I walk out of my front door.'

During the second year of your life you had received enough messages to let you know that you were a girl, or a boy, and to understand that this meant you would grow up to be a woman or a man and to have some idea of what being a woman or a man would mean.

Much more important than the lessons of what activities girls and women can do and what activities boys and men can do (those are important enough, but are largely the 'femininities' and 'masculinities' specific to time and place, and therefore malleable) are the lessons you were already taking on board about how you related at a psychic (internal) and physical level to the two most important adults in your life: your father — or his absence — and mother — and her presence.

Mothers and daughters

If you were a girl-child, you learned that you were *like* mother in gender. Your gender identity — your sense of being safely female — began to develop out of this sense of 'being like', of continuity with mother who was your first love.

Out of your identification with your mother came the unfolding process of identifying in yourself qualities which were, if you were both lucky enough, central to her mothering: acknowledgement of others' needs, self-sacrifice, expressiveness, nurturance, joy in loving, protectiveness.

From her, if you were both lucky, you had daily tutoring of the most natural and unforced kind in what it means 'imaginatively to put oneself in the place of others'.

In adulthood, feeling connection to other people may be part of feeling all right for you. Perhaps, like Beatrice, you cannot walk out the door and forget the people you are leaving behind; instead you express your feelings by leaving behind you reminders of connection: food, flowers, soft toilet paper.

Feeling connection is a life-enhancing quality, but to women especially it may bring boundary problems which can severely mar your experiences of closeness and intimacy. You may not easily distinguish your needs or feelings from those of other people. You may sometimes lose track of what you want in your efforts to discern what other people want. You may be more dependent than you would like to be on others' opinions of you.

You may regard differences of attitude or experience as potentially threatening and defend yourself against them. You may be unable to confront others and to say what is on your mind. (Will he or she still like me if we disagree?)

You may be able to put yourself in someone else's shoes without much thought or difficulty, but you may also want to *be* in someone else's shoes more often than your own.

Along with taking up mother's nurturant qualities, you may also have breathed in her ambivalence about the effort it takes to care for others and what it costs in loss of self to have little energy left to take care of herself ('I never had a moment to myself. From morning 'til night, I worked for you and your father.').

In other ways too your mother might have experienced her femininity with ambivalence. Her attitude to her intelligence, her looks, her desirability, her emotional competence (holding 'everything' together, while doing 'nothing' but staying at home): these may have been marked by rebelliousness or by acquiescence. You may have observed that she revered Dad, or manipulated him. He might have been a 'good man' or not 'man enough'. There might have been no partner at all, but just the 'lost one' or the 'better-off-without-him one', or the 'longed-for one'.

The atmosphere of gender relations in your household of origin will certainly have had its effects on you, whether it was reinforced by general cultural patterns or carried on a tide against such patterns.

As a girl you probably received as many prohibitions as encouragements. Being a girl was 'natural' enough, but being a good girl — an acceptable girl — was something which mother taught and father judged. Being good meant making other people's lives easier. And not demanding your right to be different.

Pleasing others in order to be praised as 'good' is the essence of adapted self femininity. *All the power is on the outside; none of the power is experienced on the inside.*

The promise society gives the good girl is that she will be cared for: by the affection and approval she meets from her fellow citizens and, most of all, by the decent man who will be her husband. In popular depictions of her life there will be a cosiness to it, an aura of intimacy, and not much likelihood of loneliness, the dark side of solitude. She will always be surrounded by other people, because in anticipating and taking care of their needs, she is surely taking care of her own. Isn't she?

Being highly tuned to the way other people see her, and taking her cues as to her own self-value from this, can make the bravest of women inauthentically childlike, and create in her a fear of abandonment she is probably unable to acknowledge.

It may manifest, however, in her clinginess, 'bitchiness' or manipulative behaviour, in her obsessions with her body and looks or her desire to be constantly and obviously useful.

This fear of abandonment is not part of society's overt promise to good girls. It is the hidden cost of placing their 'centre of gravity' outside themselves.

And is the price worth the reward? Will a good girl's experiences of intimacy be rich, or her moments of insight as to *who I am* experienced in times of solitude? I doubt it.

In our communities the dangers for the good girl are in losing touch with — or never getting in touch with — desires which emerge from her knowledge of her own self and are not a reflection of the needs and desires of others. The good girl I am referring to does not dare to initiate. She does not direct her own life. She acts out roles which others have proscribed. And often with the awful fear: *have I got it right?*

Literature can offer countless examples of the good woman, but these are sometimes less telling than those where, arguably, it is not the good woman who triumphs.

In his hugely popular novel, *The French Lieutenant's Woman*, John Fowles created contrasting portraits of two women, linked through their involvement with the same man. These are particularly revealing about the fate of Ernestina, the pretty, acquiescent young woman to whom Charles becomes engaged, but whom he eventually dumps in favour of the fatherless or father-free Sarah Woodruff, the 'immoral' French Lieutenant's woman.

Ernestina ('delicate as a violet') has done all that she has been taught to charm Charles and have him love (protect) her, but she is made to appear ridiculous, manipulative and so 'light weight' that her feelings can hardly matter when contrasted with the 'heavy weight' passion of Sarah and Charles.

This novel is conventional in its implications that happiness will be found with and through another and that being alone is a bleak alternative, and also in its posing of the women almost entirely in their relationships to Charles. But what those women represent as contrasting types is of potential interest.

For Charles, as for the reader, Ernestina the 'good girl' signifies a life of decency which is both reassuring and stifling. Even her name 'belongs' to a man and is a diminutive of the 'real thing'.

Sarah, by contrast, represents a level of freedom Charles would be unable to discover on his own. For Ernestina, the world of fathers and the law, and the actual presence and righteous anger of her own father, are the only resources she has when she wishes to get her revenge on Charles for his abandonment of her. She wants to take from Charles his claim to be a 'gentleman' and his right to the 'decent' life which she represented. She wants to deny him the protection of conventionality, because conventionality has failed her. The girl-woman she has been taught to be has no power of her own, not even Sarah Woodruff's power to escape into solitude with some sense of autonomy intact.

And Sarah, the woman of depth, whose 'real' feelings are acknowledged by Charles on behalf of the reader — does she get what she deserves? Is Charles what she deserves? Is he anything but a quite ordinary man who follows his desires for self-gratification with somewhat greater than usual energy? Charles has 'fallen in love' as much with an image of himself which Sarah has stirred up for them both as with the qualities he associates with Sarah, with the look, sound and smell of her. Sarah has taken him 'out of himself'. Who will put him back?

Few women, perhaps none, are entirely 'good' for we are always in motion, even when we are attempting most strenuously to remain infantilised, girlish, pleasing. Nevertheless, because the imperative of goodness has fallen heavily on female children, it is worth considering whether the demand on women to be pleasing — rather than real — has lessened.

I do not perceive that external demands have changed a great deal. Even the youngest girls at school are rewarded for compliance rather than initiative. But the internal voice bidding a woman to be good is, I think, less of a shout and more of a whisper than it was, if only because there are now so many more ways in which women can discover *who am I?*

Your way of discovering *who am I?* may be very different from mine, or from the women who tell parts of their stories in this book. Yet we may also share some ways of being which are recognisably late twentieth-century female.

These 'ways' are not absolutes. I do not believe that women are a neat group of conformists or even a group at all. Heaven forbid. Nevertheless, there are characteristics *more likely to be found* in the behaviour and attitudes and emotions of a woman than in those of man, and the generality of those attitudes and that behaviour has significant effects on the ways in which you judge yourself and others when you are alone, and when you are, or are wanting to be, intimate.

These characteristics can be read as both positive and negative. Some of them can be seen as having come out of a sense of likeness, at-oneness with mother. Some can be seen as coming out of the maturing girl's differences from (and longing for understanding from?) her father.

A woman is likely to:

- feel incomplete when she does not have close relationships
- find it difficult to compartmentalise her life (forget the children when she is at work; forget the fight when her partner leaves the house)
- use her primary relationships rather than her work as her measure for self-acceptance
- see her mother rather than her father as largely responsible for problems in her family of origin
- blame herself when a relationship or interactions with other people are not going well
- value friendships with other women
- find it difficult to tolerate differences of opinion in close friends
- believe that his role is to initiate and her role is to respond
- believe her male partner's opinions and experience carry more weight than her own
- protect her male sexual partner from unpleasant 'truths'
- protect her male sexual partner from his emotional inadequacies
- wait a while before getting into another relationship, should she and her partner split up
- feel children and home are primarily her responsibility, even when she and her partner are both doing paid work
- need solitude as a time to be self-caring

- doubt her entitlement to solitude
- have difficulty distinguishing thought from feeling
- feel insecure about her personal appearance
- feel relatively free to risk being no one important, without feeling that she is no one at all.

Mothers and sons

If you were a boy-child, then before you were two years old you had begun to learn that you were *unlike* your mother in gender. Your gender identity depended on that difference. Feminine was what you were not; femininity was what you were different from.

Girls' gender sense developed out of being *like*, your gender sense developed out of being *unlike*.

Being unlike your mother may have made you angry. The qualities you most loved about her and needed most from her ceased to be qualities when you expressed them: they would have marked you as a 'sissy', a not-boy.

How were you to make sense of the world when some of the feelings this confusion aroused in you — sadness, loss — were also feelings you were not readily permitted to have?

Not much of that process of disidentifying with mother remains conscious. Such profound feelings of loss could threaten to overwhelm your early sense of self and so you would have largely repressed those feelings as you learned to disidentify from her. ('You don't want to be a mummy's boy, do you?' And even if you did — whatever that means — you would need to be an uncommonly brave boy to admit it.)

Mother was needed, loved and loving, if you were both lucky enough. You valued the extent to which she empathised with you, nourished you, nurtured you. Then mother had to be renounced. Better by far to be Dad's boy than to be Mum's.

And what were the compensations for renouncing mother? For surely there were many.

Canadian social scientist Michael Kaufman suggests that the boy 'claims for himself the activity represented by men and father. At the same time he steps beyond the passivity of his infantile relationship to his mother and beyond his overall sense of passivity (passivity, that is, in the sense of feeling overwhelmed by desires and a frustrating world).'

Having stepped beyond the passivity of the maternal circle, what happens next?

Kaufman again: 'He embraces the project of controlling himself and controlling the world.'

Whew! *He embraces the project of controlling himself and controlling the world.* Is it any wonder then that young boys toss each other to the ground, roll around and roar, pretend to be slime beasts, He-Men, Hercules or Atlas, and keep the makers of monster toys super-rich? Is it any wonder then that grown men have their gaze fixed beyond the garden gate, with little time left over to deal with the world of home or the muted demands of their inner, hidden world?

As a man, your relations with women will take at least some of their tone from this early childhood period. Biologically, spiritually, intellectually and emotionally, you may be drawn to women in friendship and in love. But the warnings will continue to ring: you should not be like them; you need to show them who is 'in charge' — and that it isn't mother.

What complicates the conflict is that, while you (or maybe only other men) consciously understand that being a man gives you more power than women in general have, unconsciously you remember your mother having enormous power over a very small boy. And it is possible that your mother did not always use that power well or wisely.

You learned relatively late in developmental terms that father, or men, had power in the 'real world' outside your home, and that your masculinity cut you in on a share of that power — as long as you were unlike mother.

Yet at home the power your mother had to give or withdraw her love felt absolutely like the real thing. And it was. It was as much the real thing as power could ever be; *it dramatically affected the way you felt about yourself.*

As a man, years removed from the boy you once were, the unconscious memory of this power-wielding woman is likely to be a significant cause of any unconscious fear you may have of women. The fear is probably less of the woman herself than of those feelings (vulnerability, neediness, dependency, longing) that can be provoked by a woman or by her absence. These are feelings which, as a man, you should not have; which can, even, 'unman' you.

Misha, a highly articulate psychiatrist, told me that he is reduced to silence by the anger of a woman — a resentful, temporary silence, but silence none the less. He says that he has witnessed this 'speechlessness' (the not having of speech — an extraordinarily vivid re-enactment of pre-verbal intimacy) in other men when he has worked with couples and the woman has forcibly expressed her anger.

Men's need to dominate and control — coming out of their intense fear of being shut out — is frequently commented upon by women and pointed to as a major dampener of their ardour. It is much less often commented upon by men themselves, many of whom remain self-protectively unaware of this dynamic in themselves or in other men. However, it is a male writer who conveys this idea especially well. This short passage is from Paul Bryers' acidic novel, *Coming First*. Preston and Polly are the unhappy couple under Bryers' scrutiny.

'Whenever Preston encountered two women together — his wife, say, and a friend, in the kitchen — he suspected they had been talking about him only seconds before. They always had that kind of expression on their faces. The one who had been talking would look crafty, slightly pleased with herself, the other measuring, judgemental. Polly said this was rubbish of course. She said women had far better things to talk about, but Preston was haunted by fear of what they could have been saying.'

Women complain about this need of men to centralise themselves in any situation and therefore to dominate it. They complain about the inequalities of attention-giving in their heterosexual relationships. They complain about having to compensate for their partner's lack of meaningful intimacy outside their own relationship. They complain about their partner's emotional 'blindness'.

Some of this is understood, if not forgiven, when you have in your mind a picture of the pressures on a small boy to understand that he is not like mother and that her qualities are not for him to cherish and emulate if he is going to make it as a boy.

Some of this is even better understood if you envisage this same small boy needing to turn to father in order to establish self-love and self-acceptance, and finding, where father should be, someone who is rushed, unempathic, fearful and unmindful of his own emotions, perhaps bullying, perhaps entirely absent.

That combination does not make it easy to grow up to be an emotionally aware, responsive partner in intimacy. Nor does it make it easy to develop the qualities of self-knowledge and self-reliance which can transform being alone from an experience of loneliness to one of comfortable, self-accepting solitude.

Fathers and sons

'My father spent the weekend avoiding me. He talked to Katy and played with the children and occasionally talked to Miranda, his wife, but he wouldn't talk to me. This has been going on for as long as I can recall. I keep trying but with less and less enthusiasm. Katy and I cook him meals and we go for walks, but that's it. Since my book was published and I can no longer be a complete failure in his eyes, things have got worse, not better. It's as though to have any contact with me at all would be too painfully embarrassing for him. It is hard to understand.'

Adam had little contact with his father as a child. Nannies took care of him while his parents worked and pursued a child-free social life. Adam might reasonably have hoped that the strained, distant quality which had always marked his relations with his father would improve now that he is in his mid-thirties and his father approaches his seventieth birthday. But it would seem this is not to be the case.

If you were once a boy-child, you learned very early on, through many signals given to you by your parents acting on behalf of society, that to be a boy you had to adopt father as your model.

The problem was, though, you hadn't grown in father's body and hadn't fed from father's breasts. Perhaps father was not often there. If you were asked to identify with an absence, even more than with a presence, this probably made you angry; it should have made you lonely. It probably also confused you, and you may remember this least of all.

The discrepancy in power between the child and 'controlling' adult is enormous. We know that. What we do not know but can guess at is that the invulnerability and self-control *which to the child the adult appears to have* can make the child feel even less in control of him or herself than he or she may actually be. (The bigger you are, the smaller I am in my own eyes; the more certain you are, the more confused I am in danger of feeling; the more coherently you present yourself, the more fragmented is my experience of self.)

Kafka again provides a poignant image: 'There was I skinny, weakly, slight: you strong, tall, broad. I felt a miserable specimen. And, what's more, not only in your eyes but in the eyes of the whole world, for you were for me the measure of all things.'

In father's absence his 'control' and 'invulnerability' can become positively awesome. What little power he has in the outside world (outside the realm of women and children) is surely magnified in the child's perception of it, again making the child feel — in relation to father — small, insignificant, unsure, except in the child's fantasies that in the magical world outside he will eventually find a place, not just a place of work, but a place where he will be puffed up with whatever it is that makes father's life, interests and *time* so important. (*So much time for work; so little time for me.*)

That father's power is probably fake, vulnerable, hard-won and high-priced are concepts which father may avoid confronting, and is unlikely to share with his children. Father's power exists for his children. This can be a grief for all sides.

Kevin Ireland was born in 1933 in Auckland, New Zealand. He remembers coming home from his paper round.

'By the time I'd finished, the men would be coming home and the streets would be filled with shouts, slamming doors, terrible blows and the screams of children — all issuing from behind shaved lawns, the short back-and-sides hedges, the starched-and-pleated weatherboard bungalows... How are we to explain the brutalisation of our society except to understand that most of the men of my generation are the products of systematic thrashings.'

Why did these men act in such a de-humanising way? Why are some men continuing to do so?

Alice Miller's work would suggest that they are expressing what they themselves have learned and resisting what they cannot face: their own feelings of weakness. (She is not 'excusing' them by saying this, because she is unequivocally on the side of children.) Here is a tempering quote from Miller: 'Contempt

for those who are smaller and weaker is the best defence against a
breakthrough of one's own feelings of helplessness: it is an
expression of this split-off weakness. The strong person ... does
not need to demonstrate his strength through such contempt.'

These men are also acting out society's permission that men
can have power over women and children and that physical
violence is an acceptable way to express that power. Ireland's
briefer view is, 'Fathers bashed up their children — though more
often and more viciously the boys — for no better reason than
that they "Felt like it" ... We fail to remember because it was so
usual.'

There are enough, or perhaps nearly enough, recountings within
the pages of this book of positive feelings between men and men,
women and men, parents and children, to make it only just
necessary for me to emphasise that all men are not crippled by
masculinity. Some of the most loving and certainly some of the
most insightful human beings among us are, decidedly, men!

So what has gone wrong with those other men, those fathers
of Ireland's memories, the men of whom you are afraid as you
walk the streets at night, whose actual or incipient acts of
brutality affect all our lives?

It is possible to suggest that for the beating father (or the
verbally brutal father, or the denigrating father, or the drunken
father, or the sexually abusive father, or the contemptuous
father, or the too-busy-for-you father, or the absent father) there
seems to be a good deal of 'me', a great deal of ego and conscious
'I', but *there is probably very little self.*

Without a sense of self, there can be little awareness of you,
except as you fit in, or fail to fit in, with my worldview.

Such fathers, and brutal mothers also, appear to lack that
'ability to put oneself imaginatively in the place of others'. Shut
off from knowing what they feel about themselves, it is virtually
impossible for them to engage in any real way with the complex
feelings of other people.

It is not only in emotionally impoverished or child-abusing
families that emotional expression is censored and curtailed. The
imperative not to express rage or disappointment and to stop
crying (girls) or not to start crying (boys) is widely prevalent
even in the most loving households.

A childhood strewn with urging to constrain feeling means that boys-become-men will, like their fathers, be virtually unable to tolerate and empathise with others' pain, because their own pain is *something to be conquered, rather than felt.*

Fear of feeling is an awesome barrier to satisfying experiences of either intimacy or solitude:

- In solitude it is difficult to care for your own needs unless you know what you feel and also *that you can tolerate your own ambivalence.* Without that, the prospect of time alone may fill you with anxiety, self-pity or the dread of aloneness.
- Intimacy is not possible until you can, from an aliveness within yourself, express *who I am* freely, and can be with the other person as they express *who I am* without feeling the need to shut them out or off to protect yourself.

From this comes one of the most striking rewards of intimacy: through coming closer to others, you also come to know your own self.

- You cannot know other people better than you know your own self.
- Through knowing others, you increase your knowledge of your own self and, with that, your capacity to share feeling states with other people.

For males of any age it is not the most encouraging of pictures.

You loved mother but had to learn not to be like her.

You loved father, but he was more often absent than present and sometimes his presence was less comfortable than his absence.

Your knowledge of your mother's power was largely covert, if not downright repressed. This means that it is hard for you to identify its echoes in the present.

You were not encouraged to be aware of the emotional needs of other people, nor to learn through your relationships more about your own inner world.

Out of these variable peculiarities of your relationship with father and mother come a list of generalities about boys-become-men. Like the generalities about women, they can be interpreted as positive and negative.

A man is likely to:

- have difficulty listening to other people

- blame others rather than taking self-responsibility
- feel uncared for when he is alone
- collapse on being left
- compartmentalise his life with relative ease
- express anger more readily than tears
- use anger as a shield against deep feeling
- find it difficult to be intimate or even open with other (heterosexual) men
- measure people according to their 'differences' from him
- mistrust women
- put more effort into his work life than his intimate relationships
- gain his self-acceptance through his work rather than love
- replace his partner quickly should she leave him, die or be dismissed
- assume that small children are better off cared for by women
- find it difficult to empathise
- perceive he has more worldly (physical, economic) power than his female partner
- want his partner to recognise and tend his 'little boy' within
- believe that his command of rational thinking makes him more often 'right'
- believe that at times of crisis he should take command
- find it difficult to describe his feelings.

Does that list seem depressingly predictable? I looked for exceptions and found this poem 'How to Watch Your Brother Die'. In it Michael Lassell addresses the heterosexual outsider at an AIDS death:

Over coffee in the hospital cafeteria
say to the lover, 'You're an extremely good-looking
young man.'
Hear him say,
'I never thought I was good enough looking to
deserve your brother.'
Watch the tears well up in his eyes. Say,
'I'm sorry. I don't know what it means to be
the lover of another man.'
Hear him say,
'It's just like a wife, only the commitment is

*deeper because the odds against you are so much
greater.'
Say nothing, but
take his hand like a brother's.*

8

Patterns of childhood in Man

Maude is an American-born, London-based writer, a talented, sensual woman in her fifties, who talks here about her husband of ten years, from whom she was divorced some years ago. He is an artistic, 'sensitive', famous novelist.

'In the end I thought my ten years of marriage had amounted to nothing more than his T-shirts. It wasn't washing them I minded. It was *turning them the right way out*! Why did he have to take them off and leave them inside out? Why couldn't he turn them out the right way himself? That's an infinitely babyish demand. I don't like grown-ups behaving like babies. At the daily level of it, it is tedious, tedious.'

It is easy to understand Maude. It is not the turning or not-turning of T-shirts which could or should break a marriage, but the sense that one person has that someone else will take responsibility for this domestic detail, and for a thousand others like it, *on his behalf*.

Maude chose not to stick with the T-shirts. After ten years she felt she had been mother to a grown man for long enough. Did this affect Mr Maude? Apparently not. From Maude he went on to leave his T-shirts lying inside-out on some other woman's floor. Perhaps it did not occur to him that he could choose to leave behind his adapted-self, dependent behaviour and take responsibility for his own domestic security and, possibly, for his emotional security also. After all, he brings to his relationships his urbane self, his prestige, his money. In his worldview that is probably enough.

You may know men who are emotionally self-sufficient. You may be such a man yourself. Nevertheless, men's willingness to be cared for, and women's eagerness to collude, is worth consideration.

Whether it is women as a group or men as a group who are emotionally stronger is contentious. Men are certainly more likely quickly if not instantly to replace their wife or lover when the previous incumbent leaves, dies or is dismissed.

Yet there are also women who find it difficult or even tragic to live without someone to 'live for'. That is a somewhat different emphasis, however, from the man who needs someone to take care of him.

Maude again (in acid mood): 'Men seem to need to have someone taking care of them all of the time. They go from one woman to another without a gap. They don't seem capable of taking care of their own *bodies*, of their own *needs*. They never leave their wives to go nowhere, only to Someone. It's a safety net or something they can't do without.'

Maude and Mr Maude were both in their forties when their split came. Is it mere coincidence that among those couples young enough to be their children, couples I spoke to when writing this book, little seems to have changed?

I observed young men eager not to explore the world or to find their place in it, but to be in or remain in highly dependent relationships in which their bodily and emotional needs were the centre-piece of the relationship dynamic. And women, very young women, are apparently eager to go along with this, to take over from mother: caring, nurturing, ego-massaging, sexual caretaking.

At twenty-two Rebecca has this to say about her relationship with Paul. 'My relationship is very, very traditional. I find it comfortable. The different responsibilities we take on ... he does the washing of the clothes and the hoovering. When we have dinner parties I do the food, he buys and corks the wine. Girls my age have assumed women's rights. Saying you're a feminist ... I hear "group" in that and back away. It's a more individualistic atmosphere now. I never have felt the need to belong to a group and I think people are less and less attracted to those things. People move in couples more and more in my life.'

Mine was the generation which believed it was doing something about the uncomfortable ride on a 'bicycle built for two'. Yet the current generation of early twenties adults seems avid to clamber onto an emotional bicycle large enough to support only a very claustrophobic version of intimacy.

Of course, individual couples can seem very convincing in their pleasure in each other. That is certainly true of Rebecca and Paul. But as a trend it does strike me as depressing, suggesting a lack of confidence that one can 'stand alone' with many friends and with shifting, changing relationships in a more open stance toward the world than is usually achieved by a tightly-knit couple.

More understanding of what is going on does seem needed.

Women as caretakers

In infancy and early childhood boys are physiologically less mature. Child psychiatrist Sirgay Sanger claims that because of this, 'Faced with the threat of overstimulation [mother is experienced as too powerful, too intrusive or controlling], a boy will often tune out his mother and withdraw into himself.'

Even if this withdrawal is only partial, or is somehow resolved as physiological maturity is reached, it still does pose questions as to how men can stand the potential 'intrusiveness' of women taking care of their physical and emotional needs. More to the point, not only being able to stand it, but often demanding it of their female partners.

The answer may in part be that they (that you?) regard such tasks — physical and emotional caretaking — as being so 'natural' and having so little measurable value — except in their absence — that this care neither embarrasses them nor intrudes on their (on your?) sense of self.

Mr Maude, for example, is likely to see no irony in the fact that he can be praised for the sensitivity of his psychologically tuned writing and be capable of leaving dirty shirts, inside out, for his writer wife to pick up, wash, rinse, dry, turn right-side-out, fold and put away.

Caring for the body — what goes into it, and what goes onto it, what it is housed in, what will heal it or prolong its life — remains overwhelmingly women's work doomed by its nature to be visible to women and undervalued if not invisible to men except, again, in its absence.

When the body is the object of high drama, at moments such as birth, grave illness or death, it is elevated to men's attention. At less dramatic times, 'Man' rarely draws his primary sense of identity from the domestic sphere. *His sense of self is located in and dominated by the world outside the home.* This certainly helps him if he wants to become corporate vice-president; it does not do much about his T-shirts, and often it does not do much for his sense of self.

There is another factor, too, which emerged somewhat obliquely through a number of interviews. This seems to express the idea that the intensity and even intrusiveness which many men and some women associate with women and mothers is tolerable only when it is also *controllable*. When it is not controllable, then the kind of withdrawal that Sirgay Sanger refers to with infant males can seem to take place in adult males too.

Brendan is a Christian Brother in his forties. His father was a publican and his mother worked alongside. The children had to 'keep out of the way as best we could'. He recalls that they gave every appearance of being a united family, but as the oldest boy he was the unwilling recipient of his mother's confidences.

'What she actually told me was nothing very personal by today's standards. She was very modest and very discreet. None the less, I could feel this yearning in her and I had absolutely no idea how to deal with it. So I retreated from her. And I would say that although this life [as a Christian Brother] has worked out pretty well all right, part of the reason I went into the novitiate that early [he was sixteen] was that I couldn't cope with those feelings of my mother's. All that emotion just upset me.'

What upset Brendan was likely to be a number of things which certainly become powerful enough in their combination for a sensitive young man to feel that he had no choice but to flee.

They might include:
- a prohibition on the expression of his own feelings
- an unconscious fear of his own feelings erupting
- an unconscious fear of the binding effect his mother's emotions might have on him
- a conscious belief that women's emotions are dangerous *and* trivial
- a conscious belief that it was not his place to help: dealing with emotions is women's work.

It has to be said that men could not continue to be taken care of if women were not willing to go on being caretakers.

'Finn has been great since we had the baby,' I was told by one young wife and mother. 'He never complains if his dinner isn't ready when he gets home. In fact, he says it is really monotonous always to have dinner at the same time. I am so lucky.'

How should we understand that willingness of women to take up as a significant aspect of intimacy caring for grown men as though they were children? Or is it not willingness so much as need, duty or lack of choice?

There seem to be a number of factors, some of which have already emerged in this book. A narcissistic exchange is one possibility: the more important he is, the more important I, his helpmate, also am. Pleasure in caretaking, *power* in caretaking, a desire to be needed: these all play a part.

There are also economic components to these caretaking acts of love. While women continue to be paid less for their work, men's work will continue to be seen as having more value and taking greater precedence in most heterosexual households. This lesser valuation of the woman's time can lead to unconscious assumptions that valueless work in the home is less of a 'waste of time' when it is done by the woman. The fact that she already knows how to do it — because her mother has taught her — compounds the pattern.

Once the woman is at home looking after young children the 'naturalness' of her caretaking role can swamp the equal opportunities intentions of even the most enlightened households. *She is aware of what other people need and turning her back on that may be more than she is capable of doing.* And even when the woman rebels, she can quickly be accused of 'spoiling things for everyone'.

Few women do not believe that the tone of their household radiates from the quality of their emotional caretaking. When children are involved, this anxiety about the household's tone multiplies, making it easy to push women back into line with emotional as well as financial pressures.

And if her husband has been her 'career', then a wife must take care of him or fear getting the sack. That is not a pretty prospect when age as well as gender work against women selling their skills in periods of high unemployment.

Clinging mothers, disappointing sons

Maude is the mother of a son, now in his late teens. Her views on sons will not be entirely popular, or may not be popular at all, for although I do not believe it is in the least her intention to blame the 'evils' of masculinity back onto mothers, she does return to mothers some of the effects of their sons' behaviour.

'Probably it is a terrible thing we do to our sons. Having one myself I am capable of taking the blame too. And I saw my mother doing it to my brother. No matter how many times you strenuously make the effort to treat your children the same, there is something about binding a son to oneself . . . I had a friend who thought her son had some congenital condition which meant he would be doomed to grow up a midget, and she was *glad*! She said she was glad because it meant he would be with her forever and I had the feeling that this was one of those people who was telling the truth, not someone who was trying to be outrageous.

'There is a horror about the way that women cling to their sons. Perhaps to make up for all the disappointments in all the other men, they want to create the man who will not leave them or who will need them in just the right way.

'You keep bumping into men's mothers even if their mothers have been dead twenty-five years. They are shapes between you, except you don't know what's there. It is like a black hole, sucking something in. They very, very seldom can define it or even name it. Maybe it's a great fear because their mothers tried to pull them in so much they are afraid forever afterwards of other women doing the same to them. I feel that men are very, very frightened of women, by and large all of them. Yup! And you rarely meet an honest one who will admit it while he is loving you.'

Of course not every son is a disappointer; nor do mothers create sons on their own. On the contrary. If Maude is describing a situation as true for some other women as it is for her, then it needs to be remembered that women's clinging to their sons is no more important than the unconscious memory sons have of their need for their father. With this came their powerlessness to control father's absence and the pain they felt in the face of his likely inability to express loving acceptance even when he was present.

Some of this familial mix 'n mess continues to show up many years later as those sons-become-men continue to have problems feeling or expressing emotions, and as women continue to protect them by experiencing their feelings for them, a covert power exchange that can sometimes have disastrous results as two selves increasingly get 'lost' in each other.

Changing tactics

After a twenty-year relationship Yvette and Carl are proud that they are still together and can usually enjoy each other's company. They have changed their relationship considerably since their early days and are emphatic that sex-roles are *passé* in their household. Yet whenever Carl works in the kitchen, Yvette hovers and nudges, both verbally and physically. She crowds Carl until he can hardly bear it. He has asked her not to. She has agreed not to. But nothing changes.

Carl's father, Trevor, was a wonderful parent and Carl remembers him with tremendous affection. He also remembers that his mother could never quite resist putting Trevor down. Carl hated it and wondered why his father never exploded, why he wasn't 'man enough' to stand up to her.

In marrying Yvette who 'nags' and belittles him in the kitchen, Carl has not 'married his mother'. But Carl's reaction to Yvette's tactless interference can never be anything but highly charged. He is consciously irritated on his own account — as a man being bossed around by a woman — and he is unconsciously furious on behalf of his father who is now dead and will never have his chance to tell Carl's mother to shove off.

These two well-meaning people, Yvette and Carl, are re-enacting old dramas from their families of origin which dominate a specific interaction in the present.

That's clear, but knowing it is not enough to change things.

Carl could have the reasons he is acting/over-reacting explained to him, yet go on feeling irritated and tense. This is because his mind, like yours or mine, is capable of knowing many things that his emotions fail to register. Carl's memories, and a therapist's guidance in making sense of those memories, could give him helpful information about his parents, especially how he is 'carrying' something on Trevor's behalf which could now be dropped. (*He cannot change Trevor's experiences retrospectively, no matter how badly he might want to.*)

Yet despite this information Carl's 'nerves' might begin to grate in the same old way. His response patterns may be deaf to the new message. Carl wants to act differently, he wants to *feel* different, but next time he cooks Yvette hovers and nags and — bang — off they go again.

Yvette has all the right rhetoric about men taking their share of domestic responsibility. But, for all her talk and *conscious* beliefs, Yvette is behaving as though men have no place in the kitchen and cannot be trusted when they are there.

It could be that Yvette's mother had no source of power or self-acceptance other than her domestic skills. Perhaps she resented her husband hustling in on her territory and conveyed this to Yvette. After all, did she go down to the shop and take over her husband's business? Grown-up Yvette does have other sources for self-affirmation, but her sense of domestic territory and the attitudes which go with it echo those of her mother. Can she change?

As with Carl, understanding the history of her behaviour will help. But Yvette also needs to acknowledge that feelings are much slower 'learners' than thoughts. Her thoughts can, however, be her ally.

Yvette can make a decision that the conflict around this issue is not worthwhile. When Carl is in the kitchen she needs to stay out, or maybe she could discuss with Carl whether he wants to be in the kitchen at all. Perhaps she would do better to abandon the principle of equality in the kitchen rather than continuing to have these painful, pointless fights.

It may be that what Carl calls her 'bossy interference' will then erupt in some other area of their shared life. If this does not coincide with an old wound of Carl's, it may be easier to identify and find a creative way to circumvent.

It may also be that Yvette and Carl could, with good humour, examine whether assertiveness on Yvette's part is *defined* as 'bossy interference' by Carl (because his darling Dad encouraged him to think that way). Re-naming a behaviour more positively and less emotionally can be absurdly helpful. 'Bossy interference' could be re-named 'caring helpfulness' and may even come to feel like that.

Taking a step away from themselves and looking at their behaviour as 'representing' their gender — or as representing learned 'bad habits' that came out of their gender training — may also take the heat off the sense of *personal* strife Carl and Yvette both feel, for it seems safe to assume that part of what is riling Carl is the idea that his mother ought not to have been cranky and assertive, whether or not she was frustrated by full-time housekeeping or angry with the man who was maybe a less perfect husband than he was a father.

Carl is uncomfortable with memories of his father as vulnerable and he is uncomfortable when Yvette's nit-picking reminds him of his own vulnerability and maybe of her own lack of control. She has promised to stay out of the kitchen; she has failed to do so.

Carl would like to have seen his father as nothing but a hero. His mother disallowed that, not through her niggling, but through her husband's failure to defend himself.

In the kitchen he shares with Yvette, Carl's own anxieties and feelings of insufficiency about cooking (women's work) are mingled with those of his father. They are enough to handle without Yvette's interference. This increases his lack of confidence, and with that comes questions about his own manliness. Men can cope, can't they? Men can find solutions to problems, can't they? Men are in charge, aren't they?

In many significant ways Carl and Yvette are having a very different relationship from that of either set of parents. Perhaps the major difference is their awareness that there are more ways to behave than the 'right' and 'wrong' way. This awareness comes from the freedom they have to discuss these possibilities and the feelings that go along with them.

Old irritations and forebodings won't lose all their power through this airing and discussing, but they can come to look different when set in a broader context:

'I am behaving this way because...'

'I would like to behave in this way instead...'

'I think it would help me if you...'

'I think I can help myself by...'

'I know emotional habits can be slow to change...'

There is no magic formula for changing interactions between two people. Stress, habit, fear, internal conflict: these all play a part in securing you in your rut.

What does help is acknowledging what you no longer want; stating what you do want; and knowing that shifting the emphasis of your attitudes toward someone or something will certainly make changes in your feelings.

an as 'safe place'

and Helen's story may seen more dramatic, but these two le are also locked in to internalised gender stereotypes and ed self behaviour.

n and Helen have been together for ten years and Helen home for seven of those years. They have two children e now of school age. After that seven-year break, Helen ack to the paid workforce and has done extremely well. ary has quickly matched Tom's and she is getting more ay than either of them expected.

nust collect the children half the week after school and fed. And he is having to take telephone messages for though that were not enough, she has, he believes, itical of his opinions. No one has been much surprised om has taken up with Leonie, a perfectly lovely girl, who is twenty years old, sweet-tempered and not, as yet, professionally ambitious. No one, that is, except Helen, who finds herself feeling angry and very weepy.

When Helen rages and cries on her best friend Martina's shoulder, Martina wonders what else Helen expected. Men are well known, in Martina's view, for being unwilling to take second place to a woman.

If Martina is right, at least more often that not, why would this be the case?

Tom has stored away in his unconscious mind vivid impressions of the most powerful and needed person in his life: mother. She may have been an impeccable mother, fair to him and loving at all times — unless she was like the rest of us. But the dependency on her which he felt as a child is incompatible with the self-image demanded by adult masculinity; that is, the self-image of distance, rationality and self-sufficiency.

Tom (or Dick or Harry) *never wants to be that dependent on a woman again*. He doesn't want to be dragged back into a messy, unpredictable world of too many feelings, too often expressed. Surely adult masculinity has put an end to all that?

Helen has not been suggesting that Tom should be more dependent on her. On the contrary, as a wife and mother in full-time paid employment she had been relying on Tom to be less dependent, both emotionally and physically.

But the shift in the power balance of their marriage has been enough to stir up in Tom unconscious anxieties about how needy he is of Helen. *Her absence makes this obvious to him in ways that her presence could not.* Present, Helen could easily be taken for granted.

This need for Helen is churning around in his unconscious along with memories of his longing for mother, perhaps his longing to be like mother, as well as his acceptance that the price of masculinity was to be unlike her and like Dad.

But even if he couldn't be 'like mother' Tom wanted her there in a fixed place from which he could wander and to which he could return when it suited him to do so. Mother-as-home-base is etched deep into Tom's psyche.

Tom has never thought much about the pleasure it gave him to come home to find Helen warming the house. Now the absence of Helen-in-the-house upsets him more than he can express. And so, too, does the idea of an independent Helen, with parts of her life that are quite her own.

Within Tom's psyche an infant child lives on who, at the oral stage of development when the capacity to trust begins to develop, cannot conceive that mother, or those parts of mother vital to the child like her breasts, *have an existence separate from their connection*. The processes of learning mother's 'wholeness' and acknowledging the separateness of her existence are slow and intermittently painful for the child. They need to be accomplished with a great deal of loving support from the mother if this separation is not to be a part of the child's 'discouragement' from discovering a reliable sense of self.

Adult Tom genuinely believed that he wanted what was best for Helen. What he cannot bear, however, is that what is best for Helen is not best for Tom.

Tom does not have sufficient sense of a separate self — separate from Helen — to accept that his interests and Helen's cannot always be identical, may not even be compatible and that negotiation between two separate selves is needed. Instead he feels as hurt and as rejected as if he were still a small son needing his mother — a genuine and legitimate need — rather than a grown man who would enjoy his wife's caretaking, but who could with effort also survive and even benefit if their relationship included less caretaking by Helen of Tom and more caretaking *between* two adult people.

As Helen's willingness to take care of Tom has lessened, Tom's inner, unacknowledged feelings of infantilisation have grown. He is not aware of this. What he is aware of, as is everyone around him, is that he is exploding in outbursts of rage, often around trivial and seemingly irrelevant issues.

Tom may or may not be affected in the present by problems of trust originating in the oral period of his development. But what he is certainly demonstrating is regression to what is called the splitting stage of infancy, when the infant tolerated the variable behaviour of mother as he experienced it by splitting the idea of mother in two: the Good Mother does what the baby wants; the Bad Mother fails to do so.

The older child, and mature adult, is able to accept that *Bad Mother and Good Mother are, in fact, one and the same person, and can tolerate the implications of that knowledge.* Tolerating that knowledge precedes the capacity to acknowledge in yourself your own goodness and 'badness'. That capacity saves you from having to project all your 'badness' outside yourself and onto other people ('She made me do it.').

But there are echoes of infantile splitting in many adult-with-adult intimate relationships and that is exactly what is coming up with Tom. Kind Helen is now Helen the bitch, Helen the selfish, Helen the uncaring mother (of him or of their children?).

It is much easier for Tom to blame Helen for his genuine misery, rather than enduring his own feelings and trying to understand what genuine needs lie behind his rage and sense of injustice. It is perhaps easiest of all to set his own misery, and Helen, aside, to be consoled by young (just as mother was), loving (just as mother was), uncritical (just as mother was) Leonie.

But what will become of Tom — and Leonie, not to mention Helen, and Helen and Tom's children — when Leonie too comes to a point in her life when being mother to Tom is not enough, when she too wants to venture out at her own pace and leave Tom to warm his own dinner in an empty house?

'What will become of Tom' will depend on the extent to which he:

- can unravel what needs lie behind his knot of feelings
- can accept those needs as his own, rather than dumping them at Helen's door
- can learn that other people have needs as legitime as his own
- can learn that someone who is not meeting his immediate needs is not 'bad'
- can accept that another person's feelings can be different from his own and that *this is not a danger to him.*

'What will become of Tom' will also be affected by what becomes of Helen. If Helen can manage to acknowledge Tom's pain, without feeling dragged in to do something about it, Tom will be a great deal better off. Helen's instinctive reaction may well be to make things better for Tom by doing what he says he wants. But where would that leave Helen? Resentful, cramped, untrue to her self. And where would it leave Tom? In the same infantile, dependent state that has already caused them both much distress.

Taking another adult seriously, believing that another adult can and must look to their own issues and take care of themselves — even while being loved and supported — is central to any sustained experience of intimacy. But adult-with-adult relationships of this kind are surprisingly rare to find.

It would help Tom, as it would most of us, to accept that he is affected in the present by events from the past, but this does not make him weak or crazy. Nor is he doomed by those events.

Experiences of childhood, especially of the pre-verbal period of infancy, are felt at a level of intensity which as an adult you will never recapture and which you are likely to deny simply because your memories do not make those experiences consciously available to you.

It is the very nature of that intensity which makes your earliest memories unavailable to your conscious mind, and which makes them powerfully formative of the adult the child becomes, formative *because* they are unconscious, difficult to recognise from within and easy to deny.

Women and men: a doomed alliance?

For all the continuing problems and disappointments, friendships between women and men — which may include no overt sexual component — seem somewhat on the increase. It is interesting to speculate why. A partial lessening of stereotyping behaviour could be one factor, but probably more important is that women are in the paid workforce in ever-increasing numbers and variety of roles. This allows for some normalising of relations between women and men, and some opportunity to identify areas where common interest can supersede difference.

Mysteries, as well as fascination, do remain, however, especially when the breach between friendship and sexual intimacy is crossed.

Sebastian has had two wives and several other long-term lovers, sometimes concurrently. When interviewing him I found myself enjoyably disarmed by his willingness to voice frankly what most other men would mask.

'Women say things they want you to hear and expect you to say things they want to hear. They expect certain things you consider crucial to be put aside in the light of certain other things. I think it's impossible to function effectively with a woman in a relationship.

'Let me give you an example of what I mean. Lorrie and I, we have a business and we can't function as business people separate from our emotional life. We can't function socially separate from our emotional life. If we have an argument, we take that out with us socially.

'It will eventually be discovered that there is some fundamental endocrinological factor that makes women different. But I guess that their otherness is certainly a major element in their appeal. Women are very seldom boring. They are essentially much more varied than men. Within the range of one woman, she has much more variation.

'Women are the unknowable other. There's no way you can really meet the needs of women for anything, it seems to me. It's the struggle and the effort that is the satisfaction.'

Sebastian obviously enjoyed talking about women. When it came to talking about other men he appeared much less fluent.

'Men and I don't get on. The person I'm closest to is a writer I've known so long we can discuss things quite openly. He's inclined to be confessional so I've been privy to practically every experience he's had. I can be receptive without giving too much of myself. I have a major personality problem in that I'm so competitive I find it very difficult not to compete with friends.'

Sticking to the point — men — also seemed difficult for Sebastian. Soon he was talking about women again.

'Women, of course, are the worst competition. They can come at you from the direction you were not expecting. And they see through you.

'I'm not sure that I'd make a very good woman. I'm not sure that I would have the qualities. There are qualities women have that I wish I had, and they are inconsistent with being a man. Women have instinct, and base perceptions on that. I admire too women's single-minded persistence. The great libel of women is that they are somehow feather-headed — unable to sustain coherent thought. It seems to me the absolute reverse is the case. The third quality I admire is style. I'm not talking about clothes but a sense of personal vision about themselves: knowing that they wish to appear to be something and have the ability to make themselves look and be that. They can be mother, mistress, good pal, business person — whatever they want. And much more effectively than men can.

'Having a woman who wants you in her world is the greatest compliment there is. But you never really feel equal to it. You never really feel that you're at home there. There's always some trap. I mean, they never give everything, do they? That's the problem.

'Icy self-analysis is not my strong point. That's why I like the films of Howard Hawke. I remember in one of his films the psychiatrist is approached by Katherine Hepburn who is driving Cary Grant absolutely crazy and she says, "I don't understand, there is this man who keeps stopping me and trying to argue with me all the time." Feld nods and says, "Ah, yes, the romantic impulse frequently expresses itself in terms of conflict." Which is the whole basis of the movie! Always, at the end of Hawke's movies, some woman comes up and says, "Can't you two see so-and-so?" And the men look at each other and they think, "My God, it's true!" But it's always the woman who has to shake them, bang their heads together, tell them something. That element of the revelation coming from outside that illuminates relationships is one I'm very familiar with.'

Women envying men

Getting women to talk about men was never difficult. Without exception the women I spoke to — lesbian and heterosexual women — had strong views, even certain views, when it came to men. I was curious to know what it was they most envied men for and the answer came to be predictable.

'I envy them their ability to walk away and I envy them their choices once they have done so,' was Jasmine's view.

She went on to ask, 'What "fairness" can there be in heterosexual relations when he is burying himself in his work and I am at home burying myself in the pillow because I am so damned upset I can't get to work? And then, when we have broken up, you can bet your boots he has a ton of women to "choose" from, while I will be lucky to meet a couple of men a year I could be remotely interested in.'

Constance is a lesbian who works as an analytic psychotherapist. She sees men as 'much more instrumental and strategic about their relationships. They try to work out all the pieces so they can "get them together" '. Constance adds, 'I envy them the sense that they are in control and are dictating the terms. I know that they are *not*, but they are *very* concerned with control. I have also envied in men what I perceived as their capability of taking initiatives, making things happen.'

Recalling two decades of intense relationships with men she

said, 'I sometimes felt consumed by my emotions and felt that the men were not. That they could walk away from me or the relationship and more or less forget it while they were away. They could be absent from it, separate from it. I envied that. And that their work could be relatively unaffected by their emotional turmoils, I envied that too.'

Those feelings are echoed in Helen Garner's *Honour and Other People's Children*: 'In that moment she saw him separate from herself, forgetful of her, about to emerge whole into the outside world.'

The man's 'wholeness' and his 'separateness' are illusory. He is likely to be dependent on his female partner to 'act out' and make real his emotional self: yet it is an illusion that both women and men believe in.

This sense of separateness which women speak of allows, possibly, men to do what most women could not do: desert their children, fail to provide for their children, fail to show interest in their children. It also allows them to leave behind wives of several decades and to begin what they describe as a new life with virtually no backward glances.

Yet it is men, largely, who are so palpably *un*separate (or fused/confused) from their partners that what they perceive as their partner's acts of betrayal can arouse them to react with extreme violence or even murder.

That is partly an issue of control. When the woman acts in a way which disrupts the man's certainties — about how things should be; about who is in charge — he frequently acts with rage to protect himself against unwanted feelings of fear and vulnerability. His outbursts of rage may be far more energetic than his expressions of love have ever been.

But there is more to it.

Social philosopher Vic Seidler has some pertinent comments to add: 'Feminism has challenged men to develop more involved and personal relationships with their children. This can be difficult to achieve if we have learnt from our own fathers that we care through being a distant and respected figure. It can be hard to care in more personally sensitive ways *because we have learned to be quite insensitive to our own emotions and feelings*. [my italics]'

Seidler's insight will probably be illuminating to many women who have wondered, often with considerable pain, 'How could he do this to me?'

Perhaps he can 'do this' — which may be acting brutally or 'just' insensitively — *because that is how he has learned to act with himself*. For it is impossible to be more in touch with the inner reality of another person than you are with your own inner world of feelings. It is impossible to be more attuned to another person than you are to your own self. It is impossible to honour the complex self of another person more than you honour your own complexity.

Seidler goes on talking about men: 'Often we arrive home too exhausted, drained, and used up. Our best energies have been used up at work and we rarely hold ourselves back so that we have something to give when we get [home]. In this state it is difficult to face challenges from our partners...

'We learn as men that we can do anything if we put our minds to it and show will and determination. It can annoy us to discover this does not work in our personal relations for this is the only rationality that we know. It can encourage men to pressure their partners to organise childcare as if it can simply be a routinised activity. This will allow greater male participation without men having to face the difficulties they have in relating more personally and intuitively to the needs of an infant or child.'

Or to the needs of a woman, you could add.

Those splits, illusory but powerful, between separateness and connectedness, and between 'rationality' and emotional-intuitive responses, continue as stumbling blocks in many female–male relationships. So too does the outward-directedness of men, which can often lead to neglect and ignorance of their inner world, and the other-directedness of women which can often lead to a compulsion to live other people's lives for them, while neglecting their own inner reality.

The envy between women and men is not one way, of course. Martin expressed a wish that, 'Men could behave more like women in intimate relationships. Men have learned much more about intimacy from women than women have from men.'

Later he said, wistfully, 'I also really, really wish that whatever we have learned [from women] we could take into our relationships with each other and be frank without self-consciousness and self-censorship. It is very difficult to be intimate with other men, or even to own up to wanting that.'

Martin is a man who has taken to parenting in a full-hearted way. He is also — and I found this frequently with fathers sharing the care of their young children — the son of a divorced mother to whom he feels very close.

'My parents split when I was eleven. I had and have an intimate relationship with my mother. As the eldest I was privy to a whole lot of stuff, my mother took me into her confidence on family and financial matters, and personal stuff. I felt as if I was responsible, grown-up, and it made me feel very good about myself. The intimacy I had with my mother was something which helped my self-esteem and confidence. At school I had a lot of shit put on me. I came to puberty late, I couldn't play football. But inside myself I felt so much older, more mature, and thought, "*Fuck you*"'.

Meeting each other's needs

Jetske lives in Amsterdam and works as a writer and counsellor. She paused for a long time when I asked her if she thought women and men were capable of breaching the disappointments and meeting in a long-term way the other's need for intimacy and for separateness.

'I have rarely met it. I long for it. It's something I really look for and I have never experienced it. I have only experienced glimpses. I think it is possible. I hope so. I have an older couple in mind as an example. They are very different from each other, and still very interested in each other. They have a politeness and a definite concern about each other and the way each can develop away from each other. What they have is rare and very beautiful.'

9

Reviewing the myth of Mother

Feminist therapists Luise Eichenbaum and Susie Orbach predict that what our mothers give us emotionally 'forms the very essence of our personality'. Alexander Lowen, father-founder of Bioenergetics, believes that parents affect children just by who they are. And Jung warned: 'Parents should always be conscious of the fact that they themselves are the principal causes of neurosis in children.'

Those of us who are mothers may quake when we read these lines. Could Maude be right when she said, 'It's a terrible thing we do to our sons'?

Were *you* right all along to blame your mother-in-law for the pathetic inadequacies of your male partner's attempts at intimacy? Could she, should she, somehow have raised him differently so that he would be the caring, sharing, good humoured, sexy, adventurous person you wish him to be — the man you *deserve*, instead of the man you have?

Or could she not have raised a daughter who knew how to keep her mind on the matter in hand, as one of my interviewees put it, when pressed (not very hard) to express what he would most like to be different about his wife. That remorseless capacity to dredge up the past, to tell you what you think, worse yet, what you *feel and need*, when you know that you want nothing more profound than a sweaty fuck and a couple of drinks before returning to the *Business Review*: the source of that emotionality is now clear to you.

Oh mothers, couldn't you have done it differently, better, for all our sakes?

That question is, I hope, self-evidently banal. But it is lodged somewhere in the minds of most of us. Mother — whoever she was and whatever she did — is rarely experienced as having done enough, loved enough, been enough.

And if she did do 'enough', then her martyrdom will surely assert itself to let you know and make you pay.

I was sharply reminded of this when I was calling to arrange for my daughter Kezia to see her friend Amanda. Amanda's mother told me that she had her own mother staying for a few weeks. When I asked with some caution whether that was all right for her, she was astonished. 'It's wonderful,' she replied. 'I really love my mother.' Such unqualified pleasure in the adult–child–mother relationship is rare enough to jolt. Why should this be the case?

Because 'Mother' is much more than a real flesh-and-blood person. She is also the fallible human being upon whom is projected one of the most powerful myths that people have ever had to create.

The conditions under which 'Mother' exists and attempts to operate deserve our understanding.

Western society calls on and relies upon the idea of Mother, who must be personified by real women, to carry sentiments (real feelings) as well as sentimentalities (fake or masking feelings) which are largely debarred from the male-dominated public culture, for in the West, we do not adulate goodness or kindness. Our communities love winners, not people who remind us of our common humanity with those who are not winners.

The processes of socialisation which lead to this collective state of mind are captured in Philip Slater's *The Pursuit of Loneliness* which is, for this outsider anyway, a most insightful analysis of US culture. One of Slater's observations seems equally descriptive of other Western countries.

'Children are taught a set of values in earliest childhood — cooperation, sharing, egalitarianism — which they begin to unlearn as they enter school, where competition, invidiousness, status-seeking and authoritarianism prevail. By the time they enter adult life, children are expected to have largely abandoned the values with which their social lives began.'

Mothers, however, are required not only to teach those values to their children, but also to maintain them themselves. They are required to live them out in the face of a bundle of mixed messages about what they are doing and should be doing; about what they are and who they should be.

And while they are being 'Mother', those real flesh-and-blood women continue to be daughters of their own mothers, often longing for the idealised mothering that few if any of us ever really have.

To a considerable extent, you act out 'male' or 'female' in response not only to your own actual mother but also to what you perceive as your likenesses to and differences from the *myth of Mother*. In turn, this myth of Mother is shaped by and serves the purposes of the particular time and community in which you live.

Crucial to the myth of Mother is that she does not belong in the public sphere. That is where 'men's business' is carried out in ways still largely safe from women's 'interference'. (Women are allowed into the workplace, but occupy positions of power only in 'controllable' numbers. Too many women in positions of real power could too easily provoke uncomfortable unconscious memories of a small fragmented boy and a giant coherent mother.)

Mothers' entry into the world of paid work has been very recent. It is still problematic for many men and fraught for the women themselves who are struggling to juggle at least two jobs. The consequences of that double work burden remain incomprehensible to most men and to many women who are not themselves mothers.

The chasm between the public, male-dominated sphere of paid work and the private sphere of Mother and home is neatly illustrated by the political couple. Alongside most ambitious male politicians walks a visible wife, apparently willing to be interested in how people live, how they feel, to find out what 'ordinary people' want.

That *he* should learn to go alone into the public sphere taking with him any qualities he may have learned about caring for people in any meaningful way beyond vote-getting, is not yet a demand put onto male politicians by their political parties or by the electorates. And given the state of most political marriages, where the politician sacrifices intimacy to pursue his professional ambitions, he may be singularly ill-equipped to do this. Hence the need for the cooperative wife.

And what has this got to do with your experiences, and mine, of intimacy and of solitude? The short answer lies in those chasms between the worlds of 'private' and 'public', chasms that profoundly affect the ways in which you experience *who I am*, how you are with other people, and what you expect of other people, chasms the myth of Mother is intended to bridge.

You come home from work. The day has been tiring. The journey home has been impossible. Your head is filled with noise. Your body is fighting the fumes of pollution. Your self-esteem resembles nothing so much as a punch bag.

Who will make up for this? Who should restore you to yourself so that you can go back and face it all another day? And find some meaning to it?

Someone who at least remotely resembles the myth of Mother would be a good start.

But don't we all need her? Doesn't Mother herself need such an angel, for how easy has her day been?

And so we turn to each other, doing the best with what we have, but often carrying resentments that each of us is insufficiently consoled, cared for and restored.

You feel this consciously in the present, and you may well feel it at an unconscious level hanging on from the past. For there are few women who have ever been able to satisfy entirely the needs of their children, needs which can seem insatiable, even devouring, to the woman who is possibly their sole object.

While we continue to live in societies which tolerate constant physical and psychic violence, and profit from it, Mother and her domain, the private sphere of the home, are required to carry an impossible burden of balance.

Home may be the place where friends and family gather to enjoy a delicious, attractively served meal, then sit laughing and chatting in front of a fire until it is time for the friends to leave, laughing and holding hands, for the children to go clean and happy to bed clutching their teddies, for the dishes to be washed in a machine which never breaks down, and for the parents to stretch out in front of the dying embers to make gentle, relaxed and then more vigorous love until both have a satisfactory and simultaneous orgasm. Thence to bed and untroubled dreams.

But for women, home is frequently their major workplace, even when they are also in the paid workforce, and even when they share that home with an adult partner.

Home is also the place where acts of violence are most likely to be committed, where women are most likely to be beaten or raped, and where children are most likely to be abused.

And while acts of physical and sexual violence are overwhelmingly carried out by men against women and children, acts of verbal, emotional and psychic violence are carried out also by women: against their children, their partners, and in infinite ways against themselves.

How could it be otherwise?

Women are required by our communities to take on the emotional needs of men, of children, and to *add these to their own.* And this in societies which continue to show their primarily masculine face with public and pornographic denigration of women's gender, by their economic priorities which support constant war readiness, and by their unwillingness to take into their public cultures those values and attributes traditionally associated with Mother.

By these I mean a sense of connectedness, the expression of feeling, of compassion, an advocacy of cooperation rather than competitiveness, a willingness to be aware of others and to honour rather than denigrate their differences.

Those are the qualities largely associated with intimacy. Those are the qualities most of us seek in intimate relationships, but which many of us retain for the private sphere.

In the face of everything, some people do maintain those human values, more or less, and sometimes carry them into public life. The men who fail to do so are not rebuked. If they suffer any conscious pain aroused by a lack of continuity between the public image of masculinity and the private experience of being a man who is needy, dependent, vulnerable, then they usually keep that pain well hidden.

But those *women* whose embittering life experiences prevent them from being a refuge for others, or from being lovable, are mistrusted, even loathed. Some of our worst epithets are saved for such women: selfish, hard, whore, bitch. And why the anger? Is it because such women offend by making their unhappiness public, that same unhappiness they should hide beneath service to and for others? Or is it also that such women force us to consider how unevenly the burden of real and mythical Mothering, and intimacy, is presently shared?

Coming out human

It may be that you are imprinted in your genes to act out 'male' or 'female', and that the changes made this century will not progress a great deal further and will leave the majority of people somewhat dissatisfied with who they are and with their significant others of the opposite gender.

Yet it does seem to me that some hope lies in the many ways in which intimacy — and the knowledge gained through intimacy of what we share, as well as what divides us — does seem to be slowly creeping out of the closets of privacy.

In the early 1960s when family therapist and innovator Murray Bowen presented his own biological family to demonstrate his work — which revolved around people's need to find ways to become genuinely independent from their family of origin — he created a considerable stir in part because of the work itself, but also because of what he was prepared to reveal. The shocking thing he was doing was presenting his own family of origin and not an anonymous 'case'.

Bowen responded by writing, 'As families move from the compartmentalized, less mature world of secrets and foibles which they assume they are keeping under cover, and into the world of permitting their private lives to be more open and a possible example for others to follow, they grow up a little each day.'

How we feel about ourselves as women or as men; how we feel about people of our gender and of the other gender, are topics which are increasingly aired, often at a level striking only for its banality, but nevertheless bringing into everydayness some sense of what women, and men, are 'about', separately and in their varied relationships with each other, as well as what we might — women and men both — individually become.

The myths that say 'female' is this way and 'male' is that way are slipping somewhat in their hold on public consciousness. Mass communication has played a part; the congregating of people in unprecedented numbers in cities has played a part, and so too have advances in educational opportunities for girls and women, and changes in the work habits and workplaces for people of all emotional/sexual 'inclinations' who are increasingly aware that life is a long and complex challenge, and that this challenge is best met with knowledge, flexibility and optimism.

Romantic love is still big box office, but so was the hit movie *The Blues Brothers*. In that movie the female lead, played by Carrie Fisher, having threatened to shoot her once-beloved, falls once again for his big soft eyes. Half way through their smooching reunion he remembers what life is really all about, that she is not it, and he drops her literally in the muck.

The audience does not, for one moment, believe that she will stay there.

It is coarse slapstick. The boys get infinitely more laughs and action than do the girls, but it offers teenage viewers of both sexes a rather different view from that suggested by Debbie Reynolds — in real life the mother of Carrie Fisher — when she crooned, 'I hear the cotton woods whisperin' above,

Tammy, Tammy, Tammy's in love ...'

PART THREE

Solitude: Knowing your self

'The greater part of our lives is spent
with ourselves, no matter where or
with what other people we may live...
our imagination is the only companion
chained to us for the whole of
existence.'

Charlotte Wolff

10

What solitude is

Yot and I share a drive toward connection. We probably also share a hope that at least some of our connections will be loving. But, as you have already discovered, your connections with others can only be as rewarding as the connection you have with the only 'someone' with whom you live every moment of your life: your own self.

Being in good contact with your own self, welcoming time with your own self as you might welcome time with a friend: this makes being with others less essential (I can't bear to be alone) or perhaps less dangerous (I can't be with others. They are sure to hate me/find me out/ignore me/crush me.).

Knowing you can enjoy your own company is a vital precursor to being able to enjoy other people's company without feelings of panic or neediness. And valuing your own company precedes believing that you can *matter* to other people in much the same way they matter to you.

Your capacity for solitude, for feeling comfortable with your own self, exists on a continuum with your capacity for intimacy — being in good contact with others. This does not mean that solitude is a substitute for intimacy: *it is a different experience of your same self.* Nor should solitude be looked upon as some kind of training ground for better experiences of intimacy. It is, or can be, a unique source of joy, knowledge, ease and strength.

One of the great pleasures of solitude is that it gives you a chance to take a rest from seeing yourself through other people's eyes — or how you imagine other people are seeing you — and to discover more about how you feel on the inside about your own self. Self-knowledge and self-acceptance are as much part of rewarding experiences of solitude as they are of intimacy, especially when they lead to the capacity sometimes to take yourself for granted.

Yet the outcome of insight is not always pleasing. Stuart Sutherland, a British psychiatrist, recognised this when he wrote in *Breakdown*: 'I may have more insights into myself, but the insights have brought only pain, since I do not like what I see.'

Shelley works as a hairdresser and is with people all day, then goes out almost every night to bars or clubs to rage into the small hours. She makes much the same point, 'I can't spend time by myself because I am always bored. What am I bored by? Me, of course. I light up when I am in the salon or in company but on my own I am as dull as ditchwater and I don't like that. Hey presto, I am never on my own, not for long anyway.'

For Jung, solitude was a 'fount of healing'. Such a lofty attitude would seem relatively easy to adopt when you are a man with no housework waiting and the reputation of a genius. But even for us mere mortals, the image of solitude as a revitalising resource is within reach.

There *are* some life-enhancing discoveries to be made when you can face times alone with your own self, the most vital of which may be a deepening sense of inner reality and a lessening sense that reality, or your sense of gravity, is somewhere outside yourself.

Solitude is a state in which, as Winnicott wrote, it is possible to be 'calm, restful, relaxed and feeling one with people and things when no excitement is around'.

That lack of excitement or distraction is what Shelley can't tolerate. Coming to solitude step by step, Shelley could discover that it is a state in which it is possible to experience your potential wholeness rather than the aspects of yourself (or even of your adapted self) which seem to be demanded by social situations and other people's needs. Yet it is often avoided precisely because of unconscious fears that without other people and the distraction they bring — along with their demands — your shaky inner reality, your lack of wholeness, will be painfully revealed to you.

What Shelley dreads and avoids is not solitude; it is loneliness. Someone who is comfortable in their own company and can be alone without feeling unduly anxious, defensive or half-alive is experiencing solitude. The difference is vast between those two states.

If you can experience solitude rather than loneliness — at least some of the time — you have this capacity not because you possess a superior emotional backbone but because you have had satisfying connections with others.

You have experienced, to emphasise Winnicott's vital insight, '*being alone while someone else is present*'.

It's a nice irony, isn't it? You may be able to learn to endure loneliness through practice and acceptance; you may prefer the 'nothingness' of being alone to the dangers of being with other people. But solitude is likely to come *because you have been comfortably alone with someone else*.

For the infant this is a literal experience. The tiny child comes to know that he (or she) is alone in the presence of his mother who is, as Winnicott described it, 'reliably present even if represented for the moment by a cot or a pram or the general atmosphere of the immediate environment'.

In that atmosphere, the child can afford to forget about his mother because he feels secure enough to do so. And when he thinks again about mother, *there she is*. 'The baby gains proof,' explains psychoanalyst Harry Guntrip, 'that his trust is justified by remembering his mother again and finding that *she is still there*. Then in time he can tolerate her actual absence with no feeling of having lost her or of being alone in the world.'

The child can also be relaxed in her presence without fearing that her presence will dissolve into an intolerable absence.

When mother's presence is loving and secure enough, the child learns that he can extend this trust even when she is briefly absent. The child takes in an image of mother and *goes on having that internalised experience*, and the safe feelings that go along with it, when mother is temporarily not there.

So, when the child is alone, he is alone with Someone. This

Someone is not just his infant self but the Someone who is standing in for satisfactory experiences of connection: his internalised image of Mother.

In periods of solitude, you are benefiting from having been alone in the presence of Someone. Of Mother first, then later of other loved ones with whom you could be in a room without the 'excitement' of interacting and whose image you could carry comfortably as part of your inner reality, even in that person's absence. You are then enjoying — probably without thinking about it — your capacity to 'take someone in' and to 'have them' internally. You are enjoying your capacity to go on having good experiences of people even when you are not with them. This is not a matter of memory. It comes out of a rather different process — of which memory is a part — of 'taking in experiences': having them become part of you, and feeling that it is safe to do so.

However, as precious as those internalised experiences of connection are, and as vital as they are to your capacity to be comfortably alone with your own self, you are likely to go on wanting more.

You are likely to go on wanting connection itself.

Seeking distraction

A group of people stand together in a bar.

Or perhaps they are not a group at all but separate individuals. What are they looking for? Sex? Companionship? Contact? Stimulation? A chance to forget themselves? A chance to find themselves boosted by the interest of others?

Two women friends sit in a booth, watching the bar. One notices a man she finds attractive. His appearance exhibits enough signs which she associates with past pleasures and satisfactions, or perhaps with pleasures she would like to try.

'Is he with anyone?' she asks her friend.

Her friend shakes her head, although while they watch the man is talking — not to no one, but to someone who is nevertheless not anyone. He is another man, and this is a bar for heterosexual pickups. She is quite right therefore. In the terms of this bar, and for many situations outside this bar, he is not 'with anyone'.

The interested woman steps forward to buy drinks. She places herself opposite the man whose appearance she believes she has 'read' and liked, so that he might assess her and respond.

Perhaps he does respond. Would you like him to? I wonder why. Because if this woman is foolish, courageous or desperate enough to take him home, have sex with him, he might — despite the signs of good humour, casual wealth, disdain for money, or whatever it is that fits her model of Pleasant or Sexy Man — be violent. He might have AIDS or herpes. He might be pompous and self-absorbed.

Would you prefer her to take those risks rather than facing that other risk: of being alone? Worse yet, of being lonely?

But let's not take her side only. Perhaps she was responding to a gullibility which might allow her to get him to take her on somewhere much more agreeable and expensive than this bar. And to pay for it. Or perhaps she is desperate for money and thinks she can go to his house, jerk him off, pick his pockets and leave.

Then again, they might discover that despite their separate presence in a pickup bar, they have never done this kind of thing before, will never do this kind of thing again, and are mutually committed to family values.

Is *this* the outcome you would prefer? Do you wonder why?

Could it be that despite your awareness of the perils of loss of self in the quicksands of 'we-self', in your heart you think this outcome — coupledom — will save them both from loneliness?

Or perhaps you are questioning why these people cannot stay at home and take a look in their mirror if they need to find affirmation? After all, can the approval of a stranger have any real value? If they need stimulation, why can't they explore their own thoughts and memories? Do they not have old friends who could embrace them with affection?

Why would loneliness be a worse option than going home with and perhaps to bed with a stranger?

Biology might provide as many answers as psychology. You may well be driven out of gene memory to seek a mate. And this 'seeking a mate' cannot be a reproduction imperative only, for those of us who seek a mate with whom we cannot reproduce — because we are of the same gender — probably hunt with just as much intensity. Perhaps even more so, as it can seem vital to have a mate who shares your idea of what is normal, when the majority chooses something different.

There is more to it than sexual coupling.

Standing at the bar, looking around, feeling lonely or randy, who stops to consider Erich Fromm's notion that 'Intense sexual desire... can be caused not by physiological but by psychic needs'?

The real nugget may be the power so many of us unconsciously long to hand over to somebody else: the power to tell me *who I am* and to confirm that *I am real and alive*.

To be distracted from your own self-doubts by the admiration of a stranger is, surely, peculiar, yet peculiarly seductive in a way many people would never want to resist. To expect someone else's thoughts to be more stimulating and more welcome than yours is so 'ordinary' it may not even be a matter for conscious choice.

Yet 'getting it together' with someone else is no more of a challenge than 'getting it together' with your own self. Not to wallow in egocentricity, but to be able to trust and enjoy who you are, to be able to take yourself for granted and so be open to others.

The paradox is worth repeating.

I cannot be 'together' with you unless I have some sense of my own separateness and autonomy. I can't be my own self with you if I am bound to you in dependency. When our togetherness enhances my life but my life does not depend on it — I can be together with you *and still be myself*.

With some sense of your own separateness and autonomy you can go on being yourself, and make satisfying and varied connections with other people, whether or not you have a special someone in your life. This is because you know that your liveliness — your sense of being alive — comes from within. It is enriched by connections with people outside yourself, but does not depend on them.

In solitude you are aware of being alive and having needs, and of being able to meet some of those needs without turning to others. In solitude you do not feel empty. In solitude you do not fear death by emotional starvation.

11

Solitude or loneliness?

Proximity to others — or lack of it — does not of itself determine whether you feel lonely (uncomfortably alone without someone) or whether you are experiencing solitude (reasonably comfortable with your own self). That may be a difficult concept to grasp. It may also provoke uncomfortable feelings of uncertainty for you: how do I know if I am in good contact with my own self? Is 'good contact with my own self' something I can achieve through my own efforts? And if not, what can I do about it?

Being in good contact — with your self in solitude and with others in intimacy — is not a matter of striving (as for slimmer hips) but comes out of increased knowledge and, with that, self-acceptance and self-encouragement.

This goes along with a willingness to be open to how you as well as others are *in reality*, rather than in dreamland at the end of your particular rainbow. Maybe it takes a shift in consciousness from the kinds of encounter in which *what you are not* and *what is not happening* dominate, to the kind of encounter in which *who you are* and *what is* can be experienced with reasonable satisfaction.

'I have always felt pretty good about myself,' Joseph told me, 'and was astonished to discover that Ma Li did not. I adored her from the moment we met. But a few months into our marriage I found myself coming up against her self-denigration. She would compare herself unfavourably to Anglo women and would often make remarks to suggest that I would probably be better off with such a woman. As I admired her so much it took me months to take her seriously and to realise that there was a mass of pain behind her illusions that I would be better off with any wife but herself.'

Talking with Joseph a year later he said, 'It still isn't easy. I don't love Ma Li any less, however. I am trying to take it as a compliment that she feels safe enough to express her anxieties to me. She couldn't do that with her own family. I am hoping that if I can stay steady she will grasp how much I love her, and that my love means something. But that won't happen overnight.'

Sharing your thoughts and feelings openly with others; becoming familiar with the desires and conflicts which drive you to behave as you do; being prepared to listen with acceptance to what other people are attempting to express about the reality of their lives: this is all part of getting more in touch with your own self and becoming more aware of other people's separate reality.

Such open self-and-other encounters are part of daily life for many people in ways which were unthinkable even a generation ago when, as my comments about Murray Bowen have already noted, the pressure was immense to keep hidden even from close family or friends your anxieties or pain or questions about life's meaning. This, too, is part of the legacy of the liberation movements of the 1960s; it is nothing less than a triumph.

A moving demonstration of how recent and profound this change has been — of self-knowledge and expression of emotions — emerged almost as a sideline during a stimulating evening I spent with Alice. She and I had a conversation which although intense and wide-ranging was experienced by both of us as normal. It was just the kind of conversation her parents (and most people's parents) could never have had, revealing as it did family 'secrets' to an 'outsider'.

What talking with Alice also revealed was that just as important as keeping household events a secret from the outside world, was the dictum that there should be no secrets within the household, nor much privacy or solitude either.

Alice is a Canadian academic, a woman with a strikingly original worldview who, nevertheless, acknowledges a good deal of personal pain. She was the second of two children in her family. Her brother was ten years old when she was born to elderly parents.

Alice's description of her father's emotional neediness provides a telling example of how easy it is to feel dramatically out of touch with your own feelings and therefore to feel unconsciously alone, even in the midst of family life. (I stress *unconsciously* because had you asked this man if he felt alone he would probably have told you — truthfully — that he did not, because he lived with a devoted wife and loving children. However, let's look at his behaviour, as it is remembered and reported by Alice.)

'At eight I was coming out of thinking that my father was the most important thing in our household, and the person I liked best to be with. One Saturday morning when I was about six I remember saying to him, very confidentially, "Daddy, I like you better than Mommy," and I remember him having a very mixed response. What he said was, "That's an awful thing to say and you mustn't say it because Mommy is worthy of your love and should have it." But there was also a split second of gratification before he said this and I know that feeling began to change fairly soon afterward. Within a year I began to see my mother more clearly and get a fuller idea of who and what she was.

'In my family I became increasingly aware that solitude was something which it was very difficult to get. My mother couldn't get any of it at all for herself because my father was so terrified of letting her out of his sight. If she was in the kitchen doing something and he was watching television he would endlessly be saying, "Clare, Clare, come and watch this." He was terrified of being by himself and had a high level of free-floating anxiety. She coped with it in the sense that she gave in to it. I resented bitterly for her the fact that she didn't get solitude, that even if they were in the same room he couldn't bear her to be reading a book. He couldn't bear her eyes to be off him.

'Solitude had a very negative meaning for my father. Implicitly by his action, but never explicitly by his words, what was wrong with a marriage that a wife might want to sit in the same room with her husband and read a book?'

Not taking mother in

I cannot presume to analyse Alice's father's inner state from such distance in time and place. However, I can speculate that his need for such constant and explicit reassurance came from his lack of capacity to 'take the experience of Clare' into himself and to have that even when she was not with him. What he seemed also to lack was any certainty that without Clare's love and attentiveness he could go on being someone. With Clare's eyes 'off him' would he be real, even for himself?

'Taking in' the experience of someone is a capacity that stretches back to infancy and those long-repressed images and experiences of feeling 'safe' or 'not safe' with your primary caretaker, and 'safe' or 'not-safe' in the way she was able to be present, as well as in the way she handled her absences.

If, as an infant, Alice's father had felt safe enough with his mother (or primary caretaker) to be able gradually to learn to 'take her in', her absences — provided they were brief, and the substitute care was adequate — need not have been distressing for him. But if her absences were prolonged, if her substitute carer was inadequate, or if she was not able to be emotionally attentive in the ways that he needed it even when she was physically present, then he might have missed out on those vital early experiences necessary to build trust and thus a sense of self, and necessary to believe that it is possible to go on 'having' someone even in their absence.

Of course, factors other than his mother's parenting would also have affected him. The steadiness or lack of steadiness of his father's presence would have touched both his mother and him. His own emotional constitution would play a part. ('Nervy', 'difficult' babies are born as well as made.) Later experiences would leave their mark too. Perhaps he was badly knocked about emotionally during the Second World War, as were many of the fathers of my contemporaries. There are certainly no pat analyses to fit everyone. But it seems useful to acknowledge that the lack of capacity to be alone in a comfortable and rewarding way is not someone's *fault*. It is far more likely that it is a haunting replay of a childhood which was, for reasons lost to the conscious mind, less than ideally safe.

It is also worth emphasising that no one would choose to be an inadequate parent. That too is a haunting replay: too little self leading to too little awareness of others, even of your own infant children.

Alexandra is a landscape painter living in the South of England, a courageous woman who has managed with years of effort to overcome a family pattern of emotional blindness and inadvertent neglect. This has allowed her to become wise and generous not only to herself, but also to the mother who was far from ideal.

Alexandra knows that when she was a baby her mother 'chose' to leave her right at the bottom of the family's large garden where her crying wouldn't disturb anyone. The pain of this knowledge is not lessened but is made more bearable by also knowing the circumstances of her birth.

'About two years ago my mother became very angry with me. It was one day when I was visiting her. I think that in some way I was threatening her sense of our fusion. Anyhow, she became so angry that she embarked on the story of my birth. It was the first time she had told it to me and as she told it I understood that of my mother's hatred for me, this was the deepest part (I don't mean that she doesn't have other feelings), and that nothing she could ever say to me would be worse than this. It may sound awful but it was terribly real and so ultimately freeing. She said that the pain of my birth was the worst thing she had ever experienced and that even now she remembered it as vividly as when it was happening. (In fact, she had a quick labour with me.) I caused such intense pain in the process of my birth that she was convinced I was going to kill her. She said to the doctor that she felt she was going to die, over and over. He said that people did not die in childbirth these days, but that made no impression on her.

'Then, somehow, she got the idea she could prevent me being born. Mum said, "I thought to myself, no, this child has a right to live. I must allow her to be born." So I was born amidst her fear and anger. Well, when I came out I looked at her, and Mum said that with that look she felt I could see right through her, and that I saw into her soul, and that nothing escaped me. I seemed to be detached, observing, and seeing. (Which seems to be the source of some of her paranoia about me.) I suppose she felt I could see her anger.

'Then she felt obliged to breastfeed me for three weeks. This was an experience she detested as it made her feel like a cow (she has a cow phobia, is terrified of their vacuity, their passivity). In addition she felt I was attacking her and damaging her as I fed. I caused her considerable pain when feeding. So she stopped.'

Three weeks later, this mother whose experiences and fantasies told her that her infant daughter could see 'into her soul', began to leave that tiny child at the bottom of the garden where no one could be disturbed by her crying. No one, that is, but the infant herself.

Feeling 'at one' with yourself

That image of the crying child at the bottom of the garden disturbs me deeply. It works on my own worst fears of abandonment and despair, fears which are real in all of us, even when we are well-protected infants; fears that are only partially and impermanently contained as we reach adulthood.

This may add to your understanding of why solitude/solitariness/aloneness/loneliness are often lumped together and given an extremely bad press, with many people believing that being in the company of almost anyone is preferable to being in no company at all. Yet that bad press takes no account of the potential richness of solitude and also ignores the reality of many people's lives.

Up to a quarter of the population in Western countries lives alone. They would seem to be the people most likely to be hard up against the questions which aloneness can raise, but it is worth repeating: it is neither the presence nor the absence of others which of itself dictates whether you are experiencing solitude or enduring loneliness.

Rafe explains this. 'In my family of first-generation migrants I never stopped hearing "Italian this" and "Italian that" as though I had to live my life not only by my own large family's rules but on behalf of every Italian ever born. It was an expression of their grief and ambivalence that they had ever left Italy that they had to recreate their ideal of Italy in our own home. I always felt different to the rest of them and uncomfortable about this and guilty even, with no possible way of expressing it. I almost always felt shut out from the others of them and was often truly lonely.'

When you feel relatively 'at one' with yourself you are most likely to be able to welcome and take up solitude: feeling, to quote Winnicott, *calm, restful, relaxed and one with people and things when no excitement is around* — whether or not you are actually alone. During times when you are experiencing yourself as fragmented or incomplete, or 'invisible' to those around you, and when that feeling is accompanied by self-doubt, then you are more likely to experience being alone not as solitude but as loneliness — when what you *don't have* dominates your thinking and feeling.

Feeling not-whole usually expresses itself in a wish to bring something into your life from the outside which will, in your fantasy, fill you up and make you feel whole on the inside. We are all vulnerable to this. Our fantasies may vary but the desire — to increase your sense of wholeness — stems from the same 'not-whole' source within. Maybe in your case your longing is for a partner, a more loving partner, a better job, a job at all, a baby, another baby, a house, a change of town, a change of appearance.

A loving partner, a decent job, children if you want them, reasonable housing: these are legitimate needs, but it is possible to have all those needs met and still to feel empty, incomplete, unsatisfied, not-whole. And why? Because of those same problems of 'taking in', which can extend beyond taking in good experiences of people to 'taking in' good experiences of any kind.

To take in what you have in your life you need to have some sense of inner legitimacy (I have a right to good experiences; I can trust them; I can own them). This is not the same as a narcissistic greediness (give me more; charm me more; cajole me more) when what is 'given' is falling into a bottomless pit.

A sense of inner legitimacy (thank you for your love; I am worthy of love) goes along with a reasonable feeling of self-acceptance, and a reasonable steadiness in your sense of self (I am someone; I am someone who is lovable; I can accept your love without feeling threatened or overwhelmed by it).

This sense of steadiness within may never be part of a person's experience, or it can be part of someone's usual experience but vulnerable to disruption when something or someone outside yourself disturbs your internal balance.

I remember a couple of years ago talking to Hanna who had been suffering as a consequence of feeling desperately in love with Matt, a man in his late forties who is a compulsive womaniser and who sets women up in complex triangles with himself at the apex.

Hanna was suffering not only because of the inevitable failure of this relationship but also because she could see how ruthless Matt's behaviour was (and probably is). This did not diminish her passionate desire for him or her lingering fantasy that, despite the evidence, his rhetoric might turn out to be true and they could live happily ever after.

Hanna had for some time been seeing a Jungian therapist who was suggesting (in an unpushy Jungian kind of way!) that Hanna needed to look inside herself, to identify what the qualities were which this man was stirring up so deeply, qualities which perhaps she needed to develop in herself. The therapist's phrase was, 'It is not the husband you are missing but some part of yourself which you are not in touch with.'

I was so struck by this thought that I wrote it down in my note book, querying to myself: *Can Hanna make this shift in emphasis from 'outside' to 'inside'? Could anyone do so by an act of will or consciousness?*

I still don't know the answer, but I do know that when you are convinced that something or someone major needs to come into your life so that you can be happy you are expressing a painful sense of not-wholeness, feeding that devouring myth that your Ultimate Rescuer is someone or something other than your own self.

A friendly hand, the 'right person' at the 'right time', a sense of being understood: these are all immensely enhancing experiences for your sense of self, but they do not negate the need each of us has to find our solid ground within, and then to reach out and to be reached toward.

Needing solitude

Claudine is an accomplished playwright now in her forties. She has discovered what she elegantly describes as her 'feelings of safeness' through solitude, through 'learning to pay attention to myself as I would to a friend' and 'coming to trust that I can deal with most of what comes up in my life, and knowing that I can withstand'.

One of a large family, Claudine picked up a high level of anxiety from her mother and, as oldest daughter, felt this very much as an implicit demand, although it was not until she was twenty-five and a mother herself that she could acknowledge her resentment that her mother needed her to be more of a parent than a child, and that her father's absence to pursue his work helped create this need in her mother.

Claudine's early memories of solitude are comfortable, coming out of a feeling, bound to her culture and class (wealthy middle America), that in her family there was an expectation that family members would be 'self-contained'. Reading, being alone in one's bedroom, were encouraged activities.

As a mid-life adult, Claudine chooses to be alone at least fifty per cent of the time. She sees her woman lover and her friends regularly and with pleasure, but now that her son has grown, she lives alone.

It is not possible to draw any simple equations between childhood messages about solitude and adult experiences of being alone. Some of the people I talked to who expressed most enthusiasm for being alone in adulthood had learned to use solitude as children; others remembered that getting time alone was almost impossible, and perhaps not even desired. Each and every outcome turned up in my interviews.

What we can wonder about, however, is whether someone who was sensitive, as Claudine was (and this is certainly more characteristic of women than of men), to her mother's moods and especially to her unspoken demands, will find solitude more of a respite, or perhaps even a more needed respite, than someone who is not 'tuned in' to explicit or unconscious demands from the people around them.

Certainly Claudine's perception of solitude is markedly different from that of Denis, a businessman of much the same age. With considerable frankness he told me, 'You know, I hate to be alone at home because it's a stark reminder to me that Brenda does as much caretaking of me as she does of our boys, despite a career that's every bit as demanding as mine.'

If solitude is your chance to take care of yourself, and offers respite from caring for others, your craving for it will be very different from the person who can remain relatively unaware of others' needs, and relatively unabashed about asking for or even demanding that his own physical and emotional needs be noticed, prioritised — and met.

Solitude can be an emotional life-saver. I know that is the case for me and given a choice between an eternity in which no solitude was possible and an eternity in which solitude only was available, I would be very hard put not to choose solitude: the chance to go back into myself to renew myself; the chance to check out what I am feeling and thinking; the chance to drift and dream and think at my own pace; the chance to cease to be attentive to the needs, demands or simply the presence of other people. It is in times of solitude that I feel restored to myself. I really could not do without it.

Solitude can also play a vital part in fuelling someone's work life. The examples I know best are of people who work, as I do, 'from the inside' as painters, writers, musicians, or in some medium that requires you to respond not only to what is going on around you but to your inner impressions of those external events.

In times of solitude, and especially in that lovely state which can variously be described as reverie, day-dreaming, tuning out — or tuning in — images can reach you from your own unconscious, unimpeded by the usual restrictive patterns of rational thinking.

Marcel Proust believed (or anyway wrote) that 'Ideas are like goddesses who appear only to the solitary mortal.' I would disagree. Ideas can also 'appear' in the most hectic situations and often do. It is what one does with those ideas that may demand some solitude and inward reflection.

Sebastian now works in the film industry in Southern California, but grew up in Australia. Solitude is very much part of his professional life. His childhood pictures of solitude come out of memories of a very closed-in but unintimate family, and also from a sense of himself as an outcast in male society. 'I was Catholic among Anglicans, then an intellectual in a non-intellectual country town. And I was brought up in a society not of women and men, but of me and my parents.'

In the absence of any person to turn to, he developed an intense need to read and, eventually, to write.

Now in his late forties, Sebastian sees himself as restless, competitive, controlling. (He is also capable of being extremely charming and kind. But that is not part of his self-image.)

He says of solitude, 'It's a creative thing. There is no such thing as "dead time" when you're by yourself. You're actually doing something creative, something important. There's real peace in the genuine sense of the word. I'm not restful by nature, but I am most restful and rested then.'

When Sebastian was in his mid-twenties his first marriage broke up. He stopped having recurring nightmares, and also stopped dreaming. For him, some of the functions of dreaming have been taken over by solitude. 'When I'm alone my imagination works and things happen and my mind turns over. I am sure for people who dream the dream fulfils the function of allowing them to shake out the costumes, and dress up in them, and race around. Being alone inside my head allows me to do that.'

Not everyone will recognise that image — *being alone inside my head*. For many people solitude is a time to *be in your head* with thoughts and memories and plans which concern other people, or perhaps with music or reading which can be enjoyed without interruption. There is no right way; when you are lucky, there is *your* way.

Maude also feels passionately about solitude:

'My most stimulating time is when I am alone. I feel best about myself when I am alone. When other people are there, they want things so much that I never have a chance to want anything. Being alone saves me from people, from petitioners. I am alone whenever I can be but it's almost never possible. What I like is to be alone every day, and to be with people every evening. I am not happy alone in the dark. It seems a time for conviviality, around the light — whatever there is of it.'

Maude became familiar with this idea of solitude as a child. 'Solitude was the state we lived in. There was very little being together. My father had his political cause, my mother had her pals; they each had their writing. I was left for the servants. I have letters in which we seem to be overflowing with tremendous affection yet we would get together and be as stiff as boards.'

A similar childhood with 'very little being together' might have produced a bottomless need for reassurance or a debilitating fear of closeness. However, and this is significant, what Maude did have was someone who loved her unconditionally.

For Maude, this is her father. 'It's beyond love. I adore him. He loves me unconditionally. I have had that. Everyone has to have that. I don't think it matters who it is from. Maybe that is why I have love, because I had it. I can do no wrong for him. He will go to such pains to understand why I have done wrong — but it isn't wrong anyway because I have done it.'

This adoration 'beyond love' may be part of why Maude seems to have a strong sense of self, and part of why she looks back and finds it hard to remember times when she seriously lost her emotional balance.

'If I look back for moments which gave me that feeling of the rug having been pulled from under my feet, I suppose I think of romances that went wrong. But it was only temporary. I often come across old bits of diary where I have written, "The bottom's fallen out, I am plummeting through a void, and he has done this to me and he has done that" and at this point I can't remember who the fuck he was, and that really is devastating when you realise how absurd some of these things have been.

'On the whole for the last ten years I have been feeling very good about my life because I am living so much more in the present. I am not looking at what is happening. I am just doing it. It was a trick of focus, and I had to remember it for quite a long time: *Be here now*. It's a way of clicking into the present.'

Not solitude but the absence of intimacy

In almost every encounter I had while writing this book, I was poignantly reminded that being alone can be experienced not as solitude but as the absence of any potential intimate (connecting) contact. Claudine again: 'When I was younger what frightened me most when I was alone was the feeling that *this is it*, I'll always be alone. I'm reminded of that in dreams sometimes, when I am alone not by choice, and that can bring back a terror of abandonment which I remember well.'

And from Rafe: 'I hate to be alone in company, like at a party or a concert. Seeing everyone else there with someone makes me feel like there's really something wrong with me. If I'm on my own and alone at least I don't need to face what other people are thinking about me. Nor my envy of them either, I guess.'

In loneliness you are usually painfully aware of what you do not have: the prince or princess who still has no name, the prince or princess who has long since turned into a miserable toad.

In loneliness you are haunted by the absence of love. Absence of love can literally kill human infants. It seems extremely hard for human adults to bear also, especially when that absence feels unremitting, and beyond your control.

Loneliness is one of the great dreads of our time. Most of us have experienced it in our own lives, and most of us fear it. It is surely not by chance that the worst punishment likely to be given to a prisoner is solitary confinement, although whether this is, in fact, a nightmare beyond imagining or something which can be tolerated depends not on the crime but on the sense of inner empowerment of the unfortunate prisoner.

'Naughty' children are often sent outside the classroom or to a corner to stand alone. Being alone is not something people seek for their children. Nor is it something children seek for themselves, at least, not most of the time, although the capacity to play alone and bring to one's environment a sense of creative play emanating from within does indicate psychological good health in a child. But this goes along with the desire and need for relationships.

'A baby's primary need is not to gratify oral sexual drives but *to seek relationship*,' said psychoanalyst W.R.D. Fairbairn. His conviction precedes most convincingly the quote from Erich Fromm given earlier: 'Intense sexual desire ... can be caused not by physiological but by psychic needs.'

That push, that drive towards loving connection is with you through most of your life. Being alone for protracted or involuntary periods is likely to be tolerable only for someone of relative maturity, whose sense of self is reasonably reliable — someone who can comfortably hold onto feelings of connection, *even when there is no one else there*.

Those people who cannot endure being alone, who cannot, as one man put it, 'be in a house by myself for longer than fifteen minutes', lack that vital capacity to hold onto the presence of others. Lacking that capacity, they need constant reassurance or, failing that, distraction. Yet because those experiences (of reassurance, of distraction) cannot comfortably be 'taken in', such people continue to feel empty and compelled to look for or even demand 'more', without awareness that more — from the outside — can never be sufficient.

There can scarcely be a human being alive, at least in Western countries, who did not experience loneliness during the first eighteen months of life, that period of life when the foundations are laid for a person's capacity to love and trust.

No matter how devoted the mother is she must sometimes make her baby wait, even if it is simply while she undoes her clothes and sits down before she can put the screaming, angry baby to her breast. And sometimes the wait must be much longer. For the infant, without any conception of time, and living absolutely in the present, the feeling is not one of 'hang in there, mother is coming' but rather 'She is not here, I am alone.' Worse yet, 'She is not here, "I" am not here.' Of course, the infant does not *think* this. She or he *feels* it so completely that the feeling is who that baby briefly is. He *is* the feeling of abandonment; he *is* the feeling of being without. Nothing else exists. Certainly no future exists in which mother will come back and things will be all right. That kind of forward-thinking is not available to the infant until later and it will always be vulnerable in times of stress, even in adulthood.

When the mother holds the baby in her arms, and metaphorically 'holds' the anxiety in such a way as to reduce it or take it entirely away, the baby senses that he is returned to himself. Through her literal holding of her infant the mother is also unconsciously telling him that he is not just his anxiety, that he is, in her experience of him, a whole person.

Mother has come. With her comes his sense of self.

In loneliness the adult re-experiences those infantile panics. These are not word-memories which can be dealt with rationally. They are re-enactments from pre-verbal life when each experience was felt intensely throughout the entire being of the small human. (Watch a tiny body move with rage or joy, every fibre of its being fully engaged.) The re-enactment means that for the adult — as was true for the child — the loneliness of the actual moment springs into a future so boundless as to feel infinite, defying rationality and eliciting despair.

The re-enactment can also trigger in you, the adult, fear tha̶
not only has the other gone — or never come — but also your
sense of self. ('I have no reason to go on living.') With this comes
the crisis that the point to living lies outside your self, and can
only be given back by that other person — just as the infant's
incipient sense of self is 'given back' when his mother returns to
hold him and emotionally restore him.

Tangling thought with feeling

Catherine is a therapist, mother and writer. She is a warm
woman, exceptionally generous with her wisdom, who gives
every appearance of having her emotional life in the kind of
order some of us only dream about. A few years ago, in her late
thirties, she began a new relationship. Her lover is a charming
South American, a free-lance graphic artist. Aldo lives for the
moment. It is something which Catherine loves about him and
very much part of why she was attracted to him. He is also
irresponsible, even by Catherine's easy-going standards. An
arrangement to meet a friend can disappear into thin air if he is
doing a job, or even if he is having fun.

Aldo and Catherine had been friends for years before they
became lovers. She knew these 'flaws' were the flip side of his
creativity and playfulness. But once they became sexually
involved, she lost her perspective on this part of Aldo's life.

When she is expecting Aldo and he fails to turn up, Catherine's mind does not rush to reassure her that this is typical Aldo
behaviour. Instead she is flooded with *feelings*: of abandonment,
fear, anxiety. 'He is not coming, he is not coming back. He
doesn't love me. He has never loved me. No one has ever loved
me.' These are the kind of mad 'thoughts' which grip sane
Catherine and provoke her to despair. And when Aldo does
eventually and inevitably return, she has to deal with the anger
which just as inevitably follows her experience of terror and self-
abasement. And even in her anger she is subject to that entanglement of thought and feeling which means that she is functioning
least effectively for her emotional well-being.

This degree of aloneness or loneliness is not the same as
missing someone. Missing someone can be rather cosy and

...nce in their return. Deep loneliness comes out
...tual person who has gone forever, or from the
...g a kind of contact, a level of communication,
...perhaps never has been available, or which has
been available but now seems out of reach.

That despair — that what you want is out of reach — brings
with it feelings of powerlessness, unworthiness and insufficiency. It might also bring with it feelings of envy: that others can
have what you cannot. With those feelings of envy might come
rage: how is it others have what you do not? Why should they
have what you do not? *What is wrong with me?*

Again the same point arises: the infant gradually recognises
that mother matters to him, and that he 'has her' even when she
is not actually with him. Just as important as the knowledge that
he has his internalised image of mother even when her physical
presence is absent, is the gradual awareness in the child that he is
wanted as well as wanting. That just as mother matters to him,
he also matters to her.

When you feel terribly lonely, that dread is frequently part of it
(*I don't matter.*). Perhaps the dread is: I don't matter to my
special someone or, I don't matter to anyone. It is tempting to go
further: I do not matter even to myself.

It is generally poor comfort to acknowledge that people can be
lonely in large crowds, busy marriages, at a boardroom meeting
or on a bed during group sex. The fantasy persists: I will not be
lonely when... I would not be lonely if...

Catherine knows intellectually that she reacts as she does to
Aldo's behaviour because as a child her vulnerability to stress was
pushed to the limits. Her mother had a serious illness and
literally was not there for her little daughter. *But her intellectual
'knowing' does not save her feelings from running riot.*

There will be people who have been through similar experiences who do not go into abandonment panic as adults. Perhaps
they have an emotional make-up which inclines them to greater
equilibrium. Perhaps when they were children there were
mother-substitutes who could recognise their needs and meet
them. Perhaps, as Catherine herself suggested, 'Some people are
not cursed with so much imagination that every situation is a
potential disaster.'

Fear of death

Analyst Melanie Klein considered the fear of death (the fear of no longer *being*) as part of the infant's earliest experience. This is the fear of 'nothingness', against which humankind has throughout history woven stories to promise 'somethingness'. Heaven, reincarnation, the sphere beyond: they may exist (and I hope something does) or they may exist only as creative defences against that awful possibility: that one day I will not be here, nor anywhere else.

But, in the meantime, let me know *through my body* that I am alive, because it is certainly my body which will be unequivocally dead.

And how best to feel through my body that I am alive? Through sex, or through the promise of sex: the most powerful reminder of my own physicality.

Among that group of people pictured earlier standing at the bar, you may be able to see yourself. Each of you has your own reason for being there which might include the need:
- to be distracted from problems or self-doubt
- to be admired
- to avoid your own thoughts or feelings
- to be stimulated by someone else's thoughts or feelings
- for external direction
- for contact.

This last reason is probably central. Drinks are cheaper at home. The air at home is cleaner. The chairs are usually more comfortable. What is missing at home? Distraction, the promise of adventure (turning the old you into a new you), and *contact*.

'Being in contact with others' does not necessarily mean communicating well, being understood, or feeling that a positive connection exists. Your way of being in contact may be extremely uncomfortable. It may humiliate you. But even uncomfortable contact confirms that you are alive. And for many people that reassurance *from without* is vital.

People who are literally dead cannot remain in contact with you, and your contact with them is decidedly unilateral. You can shout. They will not shout back. You can mourn. They do not mourn with you. You can hold onto your sadness as an attachment, but this brings little comfort to you and presumably none at all to the dead one.

But what does this have to do with solitude (the experience of good contact with your self)? Not much. But with solitariness, with aloneness, with loneliness, death has a very close relationship indeed.

The 'helplessness' as well as the 'being without' feelings of solitariness take you closer than you may want to go to a conscious acknowledgement that you will die. And that *you will die alone*, no matter how crowded the room in which you die, and no matter how caring the people who have gathered to say farewell.

The little trust we have in our own selves is frequently propped up with the myth that someone else will save us. (I cannot be the hero in my own life, but I can make a hero welcome.) But in solitariness you experience your own lack of heroism, and the stark absence of the hero without. *No one is coming to save me.* And, from death, I cannot save myself.

I am not suggesting that the people gathered in any one of millions of bars tonight or any other night are consciously choosing to curtail unsettling thoughts about their inevitable death. We also have perfectly valid needs for companionship, warmth, distraction, sex. What I am suggesting is that for millions of us individually, and for our society collectively, death is simply not on the agenda of life. Death is something that happens to other people: poor buggers.

Death is the ultimate lonely experience and the absolute rebuff to our childish beliefs that someone 'out there' will save us.

For most people the associations between death and solitariness remain largely unconscious and therefore easy to deny although not so easy to defend against. Such defences might be recognised as a whirl of activity which makes solitude unlikely and introspection 'impossible', or perhaps as depression, a partial death that is better than a total death. What is often more readily conscious is the fear that solitude (alone with your self) can too easily become solitariness: the feeling that you are alone without Someone, or without some vital source of nourishment that lies outside yourself.

But suppose that you resist the need — as you experience it — to empty a bottle or to roll in the hay as a defence against your death anxiety? What then?

Existential psychotherapy, which regards the big questions of life's meaning as central to human concerns, would suggest that by accepting your fear of death — perhaps by accepting that you will die and that nothing can change that — *you can live your life more fully.*

'The horror of death,' said Norman Brown, 'is the horror of dying with unlived lives in our bodies.'

It may also be the horror of living the life of an adapted self driven by other people's perceptions of what matters, rather than the inner-directed life of someone making an attempt to be true to their own self. Terminally ill patients give testimony to that, making sharp decisions when it comes to those final months or weeks. Yet those of us who are dying more slowly are oddly deaf to the message.

What is the message?

You will frame it in your own way. It may be discovering, as Diogenes did, that you can throw away your tin cup and drink as well with the cup your own hands make.

It may be discovering that waiting for what you most desire is blinding you to what you actually have.

It may be discovering that living for tomorrow adds up to living for an illusion because all you have is 'now', a 'now' in which you can choose to be more or less alive.

The everyday fear of loneliness

Coming to terms with your own mortality; becoming familiar with your own inner world; lessening your grip on fantasies that other people should or will provide meaning to your life: it may be possible to go some way toward doing all those things and still to slide into periods of awful, aching loneliness.

'You are not alone with a Strand', the makers of that cigarette promised, cynically exploiting the equations of aloneness with loneliness and company with consolation.

The fear of loneliness is very real and the murky ground across which solitude slides into loneliness is part of why solitude is often seen as second best to almost any situation which contains the promise of intimacy. Just like that smoky, over-priced bar.

For Jetske the negative side of being alone is 'a feeling of falling slowly into depressive-like moods that I can't pull myself out of.'

Jetske's experiences echo those of Alice. 'I feel freer in solitude. There is nothing one can't say, feel or express, but because of that it is quite easy for solitude to tip over into loneliness because there are no answering needs to be met. Reciprocity is not a possibility. There is no constraint on what level of negative emotions you might feel. I am aware how unexpectedly solitude can shade into loneliness, and no matter how well you think you know your patterns, you can suddenly find yourself on the brink.'

At the core of loneliness often lies a fear of abandonment, usually experienced as a fear that the loneliness — the feeling of *not being wanted by someone*, of not being recognised, or understood, or sought after, or appreciated — will go on forever. No rescuer will come. You will always be Kai, wretchedly polishing floors for the Wicked Snow Queen. You will always be Rapunzel, comb in hand.

And behind the fear of abandonment is something else: a lack of trust in your own self. (Do I exist in any meaningful way? Does my existence matter?)

If you knew for sure that you would have only eight hours of loneliness to bear, or even eight hundred in a lifetime, it could be much easier to sustain than the dread that loneliness may be the tenor of your entire life. At least, until someone comes to save you. And if you are already locked in with someone and still feel lonely, that can be experienced as most terrible of all because then the illusion is gone that further ahead you might be rescued or saved.

For I may leave you, perhaps everyone may leave you, yet if you could trust your own self you would know that even then you are with someone, *you are with your own self*. Not only that, you have all your experiences of connection — and these cannot be taken from you. They are part of who you are.

I am aware this is a mighty hard lesson to take up, especially when you are struggling with feelings of emptiness or even despair. On the other hand, it is also hard to live without self-knowledge and without self-love.

If you pity yourself, if you regard yourself as unlovable, if your pity and lack of self-love keep you glued to yourself and unaware of others, then can you be surprised when others also regard you with pity, lack of love, contempt, or boredom? You have directed them towards those attitudes.

You have the choice to direct them differently.

Caring for yourself

As an infant, your *mattering* to your primary caretaker was literally a question of survival. As an adult in a state of relatively good mental health, it is possible to choose to learn — albeit with great difficulty — that you can be your own primary caretaker.

Indeed, the genuine experience of *not being lonely* can only come through acceptance of the limitations of what others can supply, and through renewed attempts to understand that whether or not mother or your beloved comes in answer to your shrieks, your safety does not, as Gail Sheehy expressed it, 'reside in anyone else'.

As long as you are alive you may actually or potentially be physically alone, but you are alone with your own body, and alone with your own rich — and richly populated — inner world.

Everything in our culture pulls against that insight. The persistent myth of the 'other half' outside yourself warns you of your individual insufficiency. There are few cultural imperatives to suggest how you might develop your self so that when you communicate with others there is someone there, inside you, whom you are in good contact with and who is free enough from self-doubt and self-absorption.

'I am so lonely,' cries Jacqui, a woman with many friends and without a lover. And perhaps when Jacqui finds a lover she will be less lonely, at least for some time and, who knows, maybe forever. It *is* more fun to do things with a loving companion. It *is* good to have someone pleasant to come home to. Most human beings do welcome the warmth of another body in their bed: your need for the touch of human skin is very real. But when Jacqui 'finds' this longed-for lover she might also find herself confusingly enmeshed, 'lost' in the relationship, disappointed, or even plain bored.

She could improve her chances for contentment by exploring, as Hanna also did, what this lover/husband is expected to rescue her *from*: is it lack of purpose, lack of meaning, fear of meaninglessness, fear of nothingness?

But that asks a lot of her. Traditionally women have defined themselves and have been defined through their relationships, especially through their marriage relationship to a man. Jacqui, like most other woman, will have internalised few images of emotional autonomy to validate or inspire her.

And while men may seek validation beyond the garden gate, they too are capable of feeling lost when they are without a major relationship. Taking care of themselves emotionally, taking care of other men who are distressed or uncertain: these are not capacities which come easily to most men. They are rarely talked about; there are few models and many prohibitions, yet for men just as much as for women, self-nourishment and the capacity to nourish others are the best possible — the only possible — bulwarks against aloneness.

12

Locked into yourself

Many people fear loneliness and will do virtually anything to avoid it.

There are other people who use aloneness as protection against the prospect of pain or disappointment. They may even be alone because companionship is something they feel unentitled to have. Such knowledge is potentially disturbing, and the conscious mind will fight against knowing it. What is much more likely to be conscious — and perceivable — is an attitude of withdrawal, of indifference to other people, or disdain.

Gregory revealed this in our talks together. A handsome man in his mid-thirties, he is a stockbroker in a big international firm. Unusually perhaps for the conservative man he seemed to be, Gregory has been in psychotherapy for years and with little prompting told me what his therapist thought of him in a way which was curiously unsettling. He might have been describing a character in a novel or play, and at that not one he knew well. But he certainly did know that too much company, or the 'wrong' company, brought about in him a compelling desire to flee to the safety of his own relatively solitary life.

He has enough friends, he said, and organises his social life around activities which have a clear structure. He closely monitors how much of himself he reveals to people. Even with his therapist, he offered with some pride, he sometimes withholds information, and although she knows that he does it and they have discussed it, he continues to do so and could not imagine a time, or a change within himself, which would mean he would not take pleasure in those evasions.

While I was talking to Gregory I sensed that he was very caught up in what was going on in his own mind. He listened politely to me, but without the active curiosity that demonstrates an expectation that someone else might have something to say which you would like to hear. What was going on in his own head was virtually overwhelming.

I would suggest that for Gregory the issue of trust is profoundly 'unsettled'. He could not trust what might become of his own self if 'people' were to get too close to him. Every aspect of his life is designed to keep people away, or under strict controls.

In the early couple dance between self and other, set to take place between infant Gregory and Gregory's mother, we can conjecture that Mother had largely sat the dance out — unavailable either physically or emotionally, or unable to respond to the child in the way he needed it — and Gregory-self had to dance on his own. Not much fun for a little boy, nor for the man he eventually became. Yet he functions within parameters that would be called normal and, as he is a handsome man who earns a big salary, he would probably be regarded as a success.

Is Gregory lonely? Can he experience solitude?

He believes that he chooses to be alone and takes pride in his self-sufficiency. I would speculate that when he is with others they do not impinge greatly upon him. 'I find I can readily hold people at arm's length,' he confided.

He does not regard himself as lonely, but lacking trust in one's self and in others is not a good starting point for making sustaining connections.

Has he embraced *solitude*, with all that implies of taking aboard one's own self, one's own inner reality?

That was virtually an impossible question to ask, or to ask in a way which would be intelligible, because a person who has no genuine feeling of connection to others has little feeling of connection to himself. Gregory is at 'arm's length' from others, and seemed no less separate from himself, despite the all-consuming interest he took in his own thoughts, ideas and plans.

The Gregory who is alone when he is with others (relatively

locked into his own head), is probably also 'alone' when he is physically alone. The key element to this somewhat bizarre concept is the bridge-building which connects a person's outer and inner worlds, creating a capacity to 'take in others' and have those internal experiences, even when the real-life others are not with you. Such a capacity did not seem part of Gregory's life.

Someone who has that positive experience of self 'holds' the resonances of being with others and 'holds' expectations of being with others again in ways which are relatively unproblematic.

So, as we have repeatedly seen, 'good' experiences of solitude follow good experiences of being with other people. In this context 'good' means experiences which have been taken in as 'good', held onto as good, and which are not turned around and made into 'bad' experiences as an especially painful kind of defence against being hurt (or hurt again).

This rather nasty trick of turning good experiences into bad ones can happen to the best of us. Almost everyone must be familiar with the scenario in which you inexplicably ruin a perfectly nice evening. Something 'good' has happened, and you turn it into something 'bad' — or anyway, something less perfect. This may go on inside your head only, or you may drag others in and ruin their pleasure for them.

'Guess what, I got my promotion!'

'What do you mean "guess what"? It will be heaps more work and the money won't be worth it.'

This does not mean you lack the capacity to take in good experiences. Nor does it mean you lack a sense of entitlement to good experiences. It may simply mean that you are sometimes bad-tempered, you are certainly capable of feeling envy, and you are also only partially aware of those inner conflicts which can result in your wanting many things at once.

'Guess what, I got my promotion!'

'Good for you!' *Will this mean less time for me?*

'When you are used to living with someone else,' Virginia told me, 'it's only too easy to blame them for everything that is going wrong whether this is fair or not. I think Jim and I are really into that, and I am aware that on those rare occasions when I have had time to myself and can think over things, I get a very different perspective on them. When I am alone it is sometimes easier for me to see both sides of the story. When I am with Jim I often have the feeling of needing to defend myself and therefore taking a more extreme position than really makes sense. When things are boiling between us the only thing that saves me from explosion is getting off on my own and thinking things out.'

Knowing what you think; understanding how conflicted and inconsistent your thoughts can be; assessing other people's thoughts without feeling the need to respond immediately nor to defend your own position: these are also opportunities offered by time spent in solitude.

Aspects of yourself

In *The Analytic Experience*, Neville Symington claims that 'Man [*sic*] wants to feel that he is a unity. He strives for it and usually consciously vigorously defends the notion that he is. He likes to feel of a piece.'

And how does he achieve this illusion, that he is of a piece?

Symington again: 'Either he clings to a unified system outside himself or he tries to unite something inside himself. In the first case the disunity within remains, but he protects himself from nameless dread by hanging on to a religion, a political ideology, a cultural value system, or national, tribal or familial traditions. This method can work well in a traditional society or one with a single value system, but given the pluralistic value system of the modern large conurbation it does not work as well, or it is more likely to fail.'

What then? Symington continues, 'The other way is for man to go into himself and forge his many different complexes into a cohesive whole.'

Symington is borrowing the term 'complexes' from Jung who meant something like psychic personalities, or bits of the psyche which, according to Jung, 'have a tendency to move by themselves, to live their own life apart from our intentions'.

When you can 'take a break' from your illusion of unity, and recognise that you are not only capable of a fairly vast repertoire of behaviours, but that you sometimes display marked contradictions, you can learn something enormously useful. It is this.

When you experience something 'out there' as a conflict which really stirs you up, or when someone 'out there' is behaving in a way which tears at your emotional defences, it is likely that you have projected outward what is actually a conflict within your own self — between your psychic 'bits'.

If Symington is right, and if we are reluctant to face up to the absence of unity in ourselves, then we would prefer to see the conflicts as being outside ourselves, rather than as standing in for conflicts within ourselves.

Some years ago I worked with a woman whom I came almost to hate, and as I was in a position of some power over her, I made her at least as miserable as I was making myself. What stirred me up so much? I can't know exactly, for undoubtedly part of that knowledge is unconscious. But my conscious mind seized on justifications like: she is intolerably untidy; she doesn't take enough care with her work; she is asking for help and not giving it; she is emotionally eruptive; she is unreliable.

Summing that up, I might suggest that it was my experience of her lack of 'control' or 'order' which drove me to behave crazily. Is that because I am so in control, and so orderly that I cannot tolerate those who are not? No. It is because that *part of myself* which wants to run riot, which wants to subvert the 'quality' of my work, is so feared and repressed, that when it was 'tickled' by someone else *apparently* acting in that way, I could find no useful way to cope.

What's more, and this will come as no surprise either, this same woman could have been experienced by someone else simply as a talented young woman, unused to office life, who needed practical help to bring out her best in a work situation. But that sensible solution was lost to me as I drowned in my own emotional reactions, made extra strong because they honed in so directly on territory within myself (loss of order, control, excellence) that I especially feared.

It is worth examining from time to time the 'characters' who inhabit your mind when you are alone. Why are you wasting so much time thinking about a boss you claim is a fool? The woman whose beauty is a reminder to you of your own loss of looks: must she be your constant companion? The man your lover is now with, can he really be such a monster?

The one-dimensional players in your inner dramas have lodged themselves within your psyche because in their one-dimensionality (all good, all bad, all lucky, all loathsome) they rather usefully represent 'bits' of your self. Of course they are real people too, and of course it is perfectly reasonable to give a great deal of thought to the person with whom your erstwhile beloved is surf-riding in Hawaii. But when a 'great deal of thought' translates into obsessive thinking, and when it is the people you envy or loathe who accompany you in times of solitude, it is worth some self-questioning about whether they represent parts of yourself which need some airing.

I could, for example, have acknowledged at the time I was turning my workmate into a monster in my mind, that I was tired of being so tightly in control (always a big illusion) and that I wanted the chance to make mistakes without hating myself and fearing that any mistake would override in people's minds everything of value I might ever have achieved. Instead, I pushed that aspect of myself — that lack of trust in myself — further into the shadows, and railed fruitlessly against its 'personification' outside myself.

More conscious knowledge — gained in part through experience, and also through the good luck of his temperament — is demonstrated by Ned.

Ned is a medical doctor. He has four children, a partner who is a successful theatre director, and the kind of lifestyle adored by advertisers. It was easy to get him to talk about intimacy, but it was remarkable how much more alive and fluent this charming, gregarious man became when we began to focus on solitude:

'I simply couldn't function without it. If I were not alone some of the time, with that luxurious comfort that I'm not going to be interrupted, then I know I couldn't bear to be with my patients or even with my family and friends, and I see myself as a pretty easy-going kind of bloke. Always have been, but I've always made ways to be alone too.

'As a kid I used to fish, out on my boat. It was just a little dinghy, but for me it was perfection. I loved that drifting around, not really thinking, not really doing much. I never analysed it then, but I would say now that I was enjoying the luxury of just being, rather than doing.

'There were years when I lost track of that altogether. Even times spent back in my old haunts were more like "doing" times. But now I am slowly moving back towards the possibility of "being" again, without doing. It is different now, of course, because there are my internal monitors asking me: am I in the present, drifting as I intend? And as long as I am asking that question I am not entirely in the moment. But I reckon that wanting to be is a good start, and feeling that I am entitled just to *be*, and that I don't have to act out the role of Dr Important twenty-four hours a day.

'It's not that I feel like I'm Ned Unimportant when I am on my own and drifting. But what I'm trying to get at is that "out here", in the world of relationships, we're racing through a series of value judgements so automatic they are largely unconscious, yet they inevitably affect our conscious behaviour. "In there", if I can make that kind of distinction, I am just myself, not a role, not even particularly a man. I don't mean that I am not a man, but that is unimportant enough to cease being a salient factor. It is not one of the measurements.

'I use the solitude in other ways too, especially when I want to quietly discover what my views are on something that matters to me, not my views in reaction to other people, rather my un-reactive views. And I use the time to make contact with God, or my idea of God, a sense I have there is some purpose, and if I am ever going to know more about that purpose, then it is quiet and solitude that will help me find it. Generally, though, I just hang out. The boy fisher is alive and well!'

Ned Unimportant, Dr Important, the boy fisher: these are all names which Ned has chosen to describe different aspects of his identity. None of them is his self but it is helpful to imagine that his self reaches out through these aspects to make contact with others, to express Ned, in more or less rewarding ways.

Ned's discovery is simple: that when he gives himself enough time to get into good contact with himself, he can stay in good contact with others. When he is not in good contact with himself, he is short-tempered, resentful, even judgemental.

This is because solitude — his way of being alone and in good contact with himself — allows him to have good contact with others. And being in good contact with others, being fed internally by others, allows him to be alone without feeling lonely.

Alone — and safe

The capacity to be alone without drowning in loneliness mirrors the capacity to be with others safely, and vice versa.

But what of the person who can easily be alone, perhaps even 'too easily', not just for the pleasures of solitude and self-knowledge, but in order to *avoid* contact with others which may be, in so many differing ways, unbearably uncomfortable?

Reviewing *The Drama of the Gifted Child*, Anthony Storr usefully summarised one of Alice Miller's insights: 'It is just those children who begin life as oversensitive to what others are feeling who later find difficulty in forming close and fulfilling relationships. As adults, they either withdraw into an ivory tower of apparently superior solitude or else form partial relationships in which their partners feel a lack of commitment and both are aware that something important is missing.'

Storr's remarks are not gender specific. But among those people I talked to it was women who spoke passionately about how quickly they feel impinged upon and therefore how potentially exhausting contact with others could be, *especially when it is open-ended*. The irony is, of course, that such people, 'sensitive to what others are feeling', often draw to themselves the very people who most quickly exhaust them. (Those 'exhausters' are likely to be needy, talkative, self-absorbed and unselfconsciously intrusive.)

Constance is possibly the most gifted listener I have met and is aware of the irony of being 'a good listener' and of being potentially exhausted by it. She went further. 'I can often not bear to go out and be among people because of my dread of being impinged upon. So, whether or not I am actually impinged on is beside the point. The dread is in itself exhausting.'

She spends a good deal of time alone, although she says of it, 'I see my desperate need to be alone as quite neurotic. When it seems to me to be absolutely vital to be alone, it doesn't necessarily mean I am alone in the sense of solitude, or even in the sense of not being lonely, *but I am responding to a feeling that my affective space, my internal space, has shrunk as a result of responding to other people*. So, my way of not feeling bombarded is to create physical space which will compensate for my not being able to create or sustain that space internally.

'I feel very easily invaded by people who talk *at* you. I feel it more often with men, but certainly there are women too who can go on and on about themselves and who think that you can and will want to listen. They are people who appear to feel very full of themselves and tell you more about themselves than you want to know. I would benefit from having a bit more of that capacity. It would mean being able to make myself more important in a rather trivial way.

'What I experience instead is a feeling that they are taking up the psychic space between me and them. As they get larger, I shrink. And what I need to do is to take up some of that space myself. It feels like this is a much more existential issue than whether I feel I am important or not, or whether people know I am important. Or not. It really does feel like a question at the level of: do I exist at all, as the other person goes on talking and talking?'

I think it is worth interrupting Constance because that last question, 'Do I exist at all?' is an intriguing one that pertains not only to the talking/listening relationship, but also to other kinds of verbal and physical communication (including sex).

My own experience as a 'good listener' is that with the needy, compulsive talker I, the listener, do not exist. At least, I do not exist *in the talker's mind* as a whole person. I exist as a function — in this case as an Ear — as something the talker *needs* without specific individuality except as a better or worse listener. Their pauses are my cues.

Of course I do go on existing for myself, but my existence in the context of the communication is fragile. That can be tiring, time-wasting and, over a long period, potentially damaging to my sense of self.

To return to Constance: are there any interactions that do not exhaust her? Are there times when it feels safe to let down her boundaries? Her reply was confident and immediate.

'When it feels as though I am having a real exchange or when I am excited by what the other person is saying, for some reason or other. And also when I feel that I am getting something from their interest in me.'

This need to withdraw to take care of your own self — to protect your boundaries, to regain inner space and use it to recuperate — is something vital to my own well-being.

It stems from a childhood where a premature (fake and

unreliable) independence was needed from me after my mother became ill when I was six and died when I was eight. Being alone was the only way I could survive my profound feelings of aloneness and, paradoxically, was the only way in which I could fuel the lively, engaged self I presented to the world.

Feeling lonely behind an animated, cheerful face; feeling lonely *because* that animated, cheerful face was only partly *who I am*, are themes I have been forced (by depression and feelings of unreality) to look at repeatedly.

During my adult life there have been two periods when this familiar inner sense of bleak aloneness was matched by dramatic external circumstances. That combination, or its psychic effects, seemed to threaten my 'animated, cheerful' aspects altogether.

The first came when I was twenty and wanted to leave New Zealand and travel alone. But because I lacked any resource but the imagination to envisage myself travelling alone, and the will to buy tickets etc, what actually happened was that I almost entirely lost contact with my capacity to be alone. Being alone did not nourish me; it told me I was unloved, frightened and lonely. *It told me that I did not matter*. I had to attach myself to people, often men, in situations of instant fake intimacy to get an instant fake sense of mattering.

Six months after this frenetic, isolating period of travel I got married to someone whose prime qualification as a husband was that he needed me. I mattered. That was another lesson in loneliness, in two people's loneliness, which came to an end a year or so later.

In my mid-thirties, and after rewarding years of professional work — work with which I could identify and through which I could feel I was being *myself* — I had a different experience of loneliness. Again, I could not locate a place inside myself which felt nourishing, or familiar. This followed the birth of my son, and continued after the birth of my daughter, a year later.

I can now see that through the processes called maternal identification, a healthy part of mothering, I picked up on the fears of abandonment which all infants have, but that because of my own history (my fears that I had abandoned my mother by not saving her from dying; my unreachable anger that by dying she had abandoned me) they attached to my own fears, and felt terrifyingly out of control. I was afraid that if I was away from the baby — first him, then her — for any time, something dreadful would happen which would involve either the baby or me being left alone for ever. And whoever was left alone would be no better off than the one who was dead. This made it almost impossible for me to drive the car, for example, 'in case something happened'. I remember wanting to have my hair cut and being torn with indecision whether to risk my life/my child's life for so trivial an event.

From inside my psychic world, it felt as though no one was there to experience that danger with me (which involved appreciating the preciousness of the children), or to understand what I was experiencing. Part of that, seen with hindsight, was a repetition of loss: both the loss of my mother, and the loss of any understanding as to what that meant to me. Those old losses were reactivated by the new loss and plain sadness of being a mother who had herself been too briefly mothered (albeit so well that along with being anxious and bereft I was also healthily and joyfully concerned with the babies). Yet the lesson was there: attachment was dangerous; passionate attachment more dangerous still.

The internal demand I responded to was one of concentration. If I were to withdraw my concentration/attention from the babies, day or night, they or I might die.

What I lost, therefore, was the chance ever to sleep deeply. Sleeping deeply, I might miss the moment at which not a loud cry but a small whimper would tell me that my infant needed me. This was, need I say it, exhausting in the extreme. What I also lost, and this felt catastrophic, was the choice to go into myself, in order to take care of myself.

This capacity was something that had saved me in every crisis I had ever faced. Now going into myself equalled withdrawing from the children. But without being able to take care of myself, I lost the 'lively, engaged self' who had so effectively hidden my feelings of morbidity and dread. I was mother not only to a chicken, but also to an egg.

The children's father was with me, but he was not with me in that experience. He did not, from my perspective anyway, see himself as responsible for the emotional well-being of the babies.

I saw that as my responsibility, and he colluded with my need to do so. His sense of the world had not transformed virtually overnight. In large parts of his life he could present himself and 'act' — perhaps even feel — much as before.

Maybe those shake-ups to my equilibrium would have been less monumental had we not moved to a new country while I was pregnant (my fault! my fault!), or had I had intimate friends nearby, or had I had more continuity with my pre-maternal life; if I had not also had feeding problems, one premature baby, two children born one year apart, two volatile children who slept only in short snatches, and so on and on. But those kinds of 'if onlys' *add* to the experience of loneliness, and add to the tendency to self-blame or even self-hatred which so many lonely people feel.

My feelings of loneliness were experienced with children and with a partner. The emotions aroused will be recognised by others in what might look like very different situations: the person who is without a partner and would like to have one, the person who feels he or she cannot make friends, the separated or bereaved person, the 'foreigner' in a strange country. What they, what *we* have in common is a sense that we are lonely, and *alone in the experience*.

The relief many people express when they go into therapy and feel, perhaps for the first time, 'understood', tells you most poignantly how difficult it is in ordinary daily life to express deep feelings of distress or uncertainty, and know that these feelings can be acknowledged and will not be worsened by banal assurances that there are plenty of other people worse off, that it will all come out in the wash or even right in the end.

The shock of feeling so tossed out of myself and so alone in that experience — even while passionately wanting, loving and enjoying the children — has been the most demanding experience of my adult life. Much more demanding than setting up and running a publishing house, because the demands were internal, solitary, 'shameful', and did not stop for weekends. It also deeply jolted my somewhat smug confidence that I relished solitude and could 'handle' loneliness. Some handle!

Choosing solitude

Being alone may come as a relief after being with people, and with the expectation of being with people again; or it may feel like a pain-filled state of aloneness, apartness, disconnection. Within any situation of being alone, you may feel lonely (anxious, sad, frightened, abandoned) or you may experience solitude (confidence that you have and can use inner resources).

The difference is usefully expressed by Nadia, a teacher who is the daughter of Holocaust survivors.

'For me it is quite clear that I am "choosing" solitude when it is solitude that I am having, and "resisting" loneliness when it is loneliness I am somehow threatened with. I think "threatened" is the word I want. And a lot of that is to do with choice. Those times when I know I can break the solitude, or if I am really enjoying having it and getting something out of it, then it certainly is solitude I'm experiencing.

'When I feel trapped into it then it's quite another feeling altogether and it takes a conscious effort to get into the solitude mode, if I can put it that way, rather than feeling negatively connected to what I don't have. The example in my mind being the lover, or friend, who hasn't given me what I expected to get. But when I put it like that I feel clear that the opportunity for either experience always exists. It is I who don't always feel sufficiently up to exercise a choice, despite knowing that it is *choice* that gives me solitude, and restores that belief that I certainly need of having power over my own life.'

Nadia is demonstrating the responses of a true self, if you take as a definition for that Harry Guntrip's description of such a self as being 'creative and able to contribute what is fresh and new to the environment'. What seems equally important is that Nadia is able to *take from the environment* a perception which is new and fresh, even when the environment stays the same.

Like Nadia, Alexandra needs to feel that she can choose to be alone in a positive way. Her associations with solitude are more familiar and in some ways less challenging than those with intimacy.

Alexandra said, 'The way that I would talk about it is that I always felt alone. It has been one of the most dominating feelings of my life, being on the outside, being alone. It relates to both solitude and loneliness in my life as an adult. I see it as having two faces: a sort of necessary silence in which I can create. But I also see it in the way that I have continued it in my adult life as a very defensive and unchanging stance.

'I actually think that until comparatively recently I didn't know how to use it constructively because on the one hand solitude had such familiar overtones, but on the other hand, such terribly painful overtones. It's actually only through doing meditation, *learning to shake hands with the silence*, to make friends with the silence, that I have realised how valuable it actually is to be able to be on my own.

'There are certain things I think you can only achieve in silence, silence within yourself, and silence around you. Solitude has strong overtones of silence.'

The gradual processes of coming to understand what solitude can mean to her have been part of Alexandra's explorations of her early life and the experiences of intimacy and of solitude which shaped her childhood. Alexandra believes that for her mother, she, Alexandra, had very little separate existence. 'I thought I only existed inside my mother's mind, that I was actually some kind of thought in her mind. She experienced every move, every gesture on my part as a demand because of her own feelings of insecurity and insufficiency about meeting those demands.

'If I touched her, she would freeze. She would experience it as an intrusion and something to be protected against. I touched her very little, but then, you see, I hated her touching me. I hated it. When she had to touch me she was bathing me or putting plaster on my toe, something she was very ill at ease with, so she often hurt. I can remember my younger brother and I screaming if we had to have plaster taken off. She would have to get my father. It was the same when she washed our hair. We knew she would get soap in our eyes. She had this great physical tension about touching us. So this feeling, that any movement towards another person is first of all not something they are going to welcome, and secondly, that it will be seen as a demand, runs very deep.

'I would describe myself as a person who was forced into a very premature sense of independence and disconnection, and there-fore that I never had a really positive sense of the rewards of independence. My mother is not inhibited, but she is very estranged from herself. *Having little connection to her own self, it follows that she could have little connection to me.*

'I would say that from about six weeks old I was in an enforced situation of solitude, or solitariness, which was terrifying. [It was from this age that Alexandra was left alone to cry at the bottom of the garden.]

'In infancy the baby comes to experience himself through a sense of connection. I believe that a sense of disconnection gives a very artificial sense of self. If some part of your experience of yourself, as an infant in the beginning, is through another person's experience of you — let's say, your mother's experience of you — and if she is absent physically or in other ways, you can experience that as a sort of existential death. Then you can only really get to know yourself in other ways.'

Alexandra was badly hurt. As a highly sensitive young woman in her twenties she withdrew from the pain of her childhood into alcohol abuse, and then was confronted with a life-threatening cancer. Despite those harsh experiences, and in part through those harsh experiences, she has succeeded in getting to know herself: through her painting, through an active spiritual life, and through many years of psychoanalysis. She is convinced that, 'Your sense of power cannot be dependent on how other people behave. That isn't power. It has to be something else which is entirely within yourself. When I am at a really low ebb the only way I can cope with it is to say, This is the *way* I am experiencing this. This is not how it is.

'That's where you don't have to be at the mercy of your past. You may not be able to avoid going through moments of pain, but you don't have to stay in them. I am thinking about that injunction from Krishnamurti: *Do it now*. Change now. This instant. When you are in your worst state of feeling abandoned, or of *total* estrangement, and you say to yourself, I am *now* going to experience connection, do it *now*, you then get that sense of heaven and hell being within our experience of everything around us.'

It is not chance that both Nadia and Alexandra emphasise choice. Nor is it chance that having survived difficult experiences, and worked with them, they are internally rich enough to reach out to others with humour and compassion.

American feminist poet Adrienne Rich wrote in 'Dream of a Common Language':

Only she who says
She did not choose, is the loser in the end.

It is a sentiment I feel like cheering.

Nadia and Alexandra each feels she has emerged from a long struggle to have the right to that 'choice' and each knows how vulnerable she remains. Alexandra expressed this in a way to which I could certainly respond.

'The step of being able to carry your own sense of self, no matter what the situation, is a step which has to be taken. That is the big challenge. I am not sure that it is something I've achieved in a genuine way. I know I have achieved it in artificial ways, but there is a lot of difference in how I experience myself, how strong my identity is, according to who I am with. The step of carrying this sense of my self in whatever situation, is something I am only beginning to achieve.'

13

Knowing less, learning more

From *The Art of Intimacy* comes the refreshing suggestion to approach others in a state of 'not knowing' them. When you 'know' someone, the authors say, you have already shut your eyes to that person's constant processes of change. You are rooting them not in the past, but — and this is even more limiting — in your past perceptions of their past!

It may be that the only person you can know subjectively (from the inside) is your own self. If that is so, then you can be truly intimate only with your own self, even if most of what you learn comes from interaction with others.

It is worth bringing those two ideas together: the idea of learning more by knowing less, and the idea that solitude offers an opportunity to know yourself without the interference of others' preconceived ideas, judgements and needs.

In solitude, you are alone with your memory, your imagination, your self-created portraits of others, as well as with your anticipatory ideas and feelings about how you and others will act, react, behave, feel. Letting go of some of those 'anticipations' can be an exhilarating way in which to be physically alone, or in a space of aloneness.

It can be an exhilarating way to learn that you are alive within; to learn *who I am*.

Maybe you are someone you can trust. Maybe you are someone you can trust *and like*.

Surviving the boredom of your own company, reaching through the boredom to discover that you are alone with feelings that both connect you with others and 'describe' your individuality: these are some of the rewards of solitude.

Knowing yourself/remaining open to know yourself; feeling entitled to 'personal space'/feeling some freedom within it; acknowledging the bridges that link your inner and outer experiences: these are more of the possibilities solitude offers, along with the chance to relish the paradox, that when you are most in touch with yourself *you are least conscious of yourself*.

A useful analogy comes from intimacy. Often when lovers are courting, they feel impelled to be fairly constantly 'in touch', often emphasised by physical touching. A couple of years later, if their relationship survives and grows, they can be just as comfortable in a room together, largely ignoring each other, while still aware of the other's presence. They are, in fact, re-enacting that early vital experience: being alone in someone else's presence.

Someone who has a similar confidence in his or her own inner reality, and who trusts that he or she goes on existing whether or not anyone else is present, does not need to be constantly checking on their sense of self.

He or she is 'calm, restful, relaxed and feeling one with people and things when no excitement is around'.

Alice brings Winnicott's thought to life.

'The moments when I feel most what I would call myself are those moments when I am actually with something which is comforting me, having to be taken for granted. Standing in the garden for fifteen to twenty minutes, looking and enjoying and thinking, it's happened again. It's spring. *Feeling myself because I don't need to feel myself at all.* Because spring will happen, whether I am here or not. It makes no demands on me. It is there. And every year it happens and if it doesn't, it is because everything has stopped.'

PART FOUR

Intimacy: Knowing the other

'If I can't make a success out of the
relationship with people I supposedly love,
then everything else is bullshit.'

John Lennon

14

Intimacy: Knowing the other

Intimacy is not a matter of extending your self-absorption to include someone else. Much more than that, it is a matter of tuning into someone else's reality, and risking *being changed by that experience.*

It may be that the very idea of talking about intimacy in the profoundly unintimate world of late twentieth-century 'civilisa-tion' is a ludicrous proposition. Even the barest definition of intimacy involves the idea of someone other than yourself. But can we seriously take on the idea of the other — the idea that other human existence is as valid and as real as our own — when the cry to 'get ahead' dominates in the developed world, and lack of clean water, fuel and food affects the daily life of billions in the third world?

How can we attempt to think about intimacy when the very word is mocked by the banal, saccharine or even pornographic imitations of intimacy that permeate every aspect of our public culture?

Yet we can. Not least because most of us persist in our habits of optimism. The longing, the need, the desire for intimacy remains as much a part of life as it ever did. It is tempting to say *even more so* if you experience yourself as lacking the feeling that you 'belong', or lacking the feeling that you much want to belong in a society where so much emotional intercourse, never mind sexual intercourse, is coloured by infantile narcissism: *Are you useful? Let me suck at you. And then move on.*

It may not, however, be a case of 'even more so'.

It is not difficult to imagine that human beings have always wanted to love and to be loved; to accept and to be accepted; to feel close and welcomed; to feel valued themselves and proud of those they can also value. Most people want this and many people have it, more or less satisfactorily. But the experience of intimacy is not evenly spread across nations, cultures or within families. Nor is the capacity for intimacy always stable or even reliable within your own experience of self.

Caroline and Robert are two people whose lives crossed when they took part in workshops on intimacy. Individual as each of them is, they are also typical of people I have worked with and talked to on the subject of intimacy. Each is socially adept, has a good job (Caroline works in the area of computer training; Robert is a television cameraman), each has family connections which are reasonably pleasurable and yet, when it comes to intimacy, they have grave self-doubts.

'I really don't even know what I'm wanting from intimacy,' Robert told me early on, 'and it could be that I am fantasising that something is missing instead of being satisfied with what I do have. But sometimes this feeling that something is missing is so overwhelming it convinces me that I should do something. The trouble is, I don't know what to do! It's like punching at a hole and nothing bounces back. There is often a moment at the beginning of a new relationship when I feel sure that this time things will go well, but then quite quickly whatever it is that I want, or whatever it is that would satisfy me, seems to be missing.'

Caroline's complaints are no less painful.

'I believe that I know what intimacy could be like. Sharing and caring are very much part of it. I've had that. Trusting too, and feeling that I can really be myself. My problem seems to be that I don't know how to keep intimacy going. When I have a boyfriend I often feel like he is spoiling things — usually by invading my privacy in some way or other. When I don't have such a relationship I'm obsessed with wanting intimacy and that makes me act in ways that aren't really me. I mean ways that are pushy and awkward and I feel ashamed that people will see how weak and desperate I am. It just doesn't seem possible for me to strike the right kind of balance either inside myself or between myself and the people I want to be intimate with. It's worst with men I'm open to having sex with, much worse than in my non-sexual friendships where I feel that less is asked of me and that I do have some of the answers.'

I met Ruben on a plane, but he too was eager to talk about intimacy.

'I play tricks with myself and make do with situations which are not really intimate any longer — which are truly horrible sometimes — because I am so afraid of getting left. The thought of getting left and having nobody at all freaks me out. *I can't stand grieving for someone who isn't there, and feeling connected to someone who's not with me any longer and is probably not giving me a second thought.* I'm feeling pretty strung out even talking about this. Ridiculous, isn't it?'

How you define or value intimacy, how you experience your own self in times of intimacy or in your desiring of intimacy, is a product of many factors. These may arguably come out of your constitution (tense, easy going, reflective, extrovert and so on). They are also shaped by your earliest experiences as an infant in a safe or not-safe world, as well as by your experiences of the larger world of family, school and community of which you become increasingly aware as you grow.

It may also depend on how individuality — that ideology so prized in the West — was interpreted in your communities of home and school. The competitive attitude which underpins 'getting ahead' makes it difficult to stay in touch with other people's reality and to care about that. A competitive attitude tends to narrow achievement along fairly predictable lines, often over-valuing intellectual or sporting achievements at the cost of the more creative, flexible, intuitive aspects of self which may be just what are most needed when it comes to self-awareness and self-and-other intimacy.

Luck plays its part too. You may have a genuine interest in other people that encourages them to feel open and trusting with you. Maybe you live in a city or town where you can readily meet enough people to feel that you are making choices in your friendships. Perhaps you have the money, ambition or imagination to get yourself into situations where being with other people is enlivening. Those factors are important and can substantially affect whether you feel you are living the life you want. But what matters most in the way you experience others is *the way in which you experience your own self*.

'Self-esteem,' psychotherapist Neville Symington claims, 'is directly correlated with a capacity to love.'

I prefer the word self-acceptance to self-esteem, but the message is much the same. Until you are at home in your inner world, and can accept and trust your own self, it is difficult if not impossible to know, love and trust someone else except in fairly limited and self-seeking ways.

When you don't have that vital sense of self, you are in danger of experiencing other people as 'self-objects', that is, as people who are more or less useful to you but who have little separate existence or validity in their own right. Experiencing people in this way — reducing them to their functions and valuing them according to how well they carry out those functions — is largely what happens in the everyday life of work and casual social contacts. But in intimacy you are likely to want something different, something more.

You are likely to want the feeling that each person knows how the other one feels, *and that he or she cares about that* and can act on that caring, even when it may not be in their immediate self-interest to do so.

You are likely to want the feeling that what is actually happening and who is actually present *matters*, and is not overshadowed by what is not happening and who is not present.

Out with the toad, in with the prince

If the intimacy ideals you cherish are not being met (as is true for most of us at least some of the time), then only limited change can be achieved by turfing out the old toad and wheeling in the new prince or princess. Substantial change needs to begin (and probably end) *with your own self*.

This is a liberating thought.

You cannot bring other people to heel, or even into your life if that is not where they want to be. But you can, *through changes of attitude*, increase the feeling of freedom you have in regard to your own life. (I have problems, *but I am not my problems*.)

You can, with effort, *accept what you cannot change*. Accepting what you cannot change, you will lose the tension involved in maintaining your fight against fate, the universe or your own self. If you are alone, for example, yet would like to be married, chastising yourself for your failure to find a spouse will add to your anguish, not diminish it. It will also keep your thoughts fixed on what you do not have, which is guaranteed to narrow your horizons.

Accepting that you are not married does not mean resignation, nor passivity, nor a sense of helplessness, nor even approval of not-being-married. It is, rather, what psychosynthesis calls 'collaborating with the inevitable', a process which, when you can allow it to work for you, frees both your mind and your emotions to an awareness of what is (which may include some aspects of life which are positive), rather than what is not. This will increase the flexibility with which you approach others and allow others to approach you because you will be open to how other people are *in the present*, rather than how they exist in your pre-judgements of them.

Robert, for example, may well be holding an ideal of intimacy in his mind which could be fulfilled only by an angel. Perhaps he wants his special someone to make up for the self-knowledge he has been reluctant to acquire. Accepting his own inconsistencies, and understanding how these relate to the tugs of war taking place within his own psyche, could help Robert to take on a flesh-and-blood relationship with another human being with more confidence, and perhaps even with greater good humour. Or he may come to realise that what he wants is not a special someone, but the chance to have a number of close relationships which leave him free to find out more about what he wants from life, and what life wants from him.

Caroline's need for closeness and her acute anxiety about being invaded reflect a common pattern among women. Her desire to be close to someone else seems entirely 'natural', even admirable, but maybe it comes along with a tendency to overload that relationship with meaning at the cost of her other non-sexual relationships. It may also be that her feeling of being invaded comes from a relative incapacity to know her own mind: which includes the privilege of saying no without feeling guilty. The pattern of being overwhelmed and then having to physically leave or unconsciously poison the relationship *in order to get a little space* is also a common one, with women and men. But that pattern is no less individually painful for its frequency.

Ruben can be seen, from the outside anyway, to be suffering from the *Can I really matter to anyone?* syndrome. This is also antagonistic to feelings of self-acceptance because along with anxiety about whether you matter to other people as much as they matter to you comes a barrage of self-denigration which can even persuade you that you barely matter to yourself, the very self with whom you must 'shake hands in a spirit of compassion and acceptance' as Nadia expressed it, before you can shake hands with others in much the same generous, tolerant mode.

The temptation will return repeatedly to believe that improvements to your life can best come from the outside and, more poignantly, that intimacy is something that can be brought into your life only by other people. The hidden agenda of that tempting thought is that other people, or that special someone, has more power over your life than you have. This is not so. Rewarding contact with others — 'a haven in a heartless world' as Christopher Lasch described it — is something that most of us want. It is what Caroline and Robert and Ruben want. It is what I want. But it is not something that you can 'make happen'. *It is something other people can only enhance.* Joy, compassion, trust, empathy, security, love: these feelings arise from a reasonable feeling of safety within — and then radiate out to others.

So, with or without satisfying others in your life, you can discover:

- what needs you are loading onto your actual intimate relationships, or perhaps onto the idealised relationship which exists in your mind
- the reasons why intimacy may seem dangerous or threatening to you, even while you want it
- the 'demands' you are putting on intimacy — which may be out of human proportion.

15

Intimacy — an experience of transcendence?

Alexandra shared with me a wonderful description of the possibilities of intimacy and it was this, when I began to think about the joys of intimacy, that returned to me with tremendous power.

'I was on holiday in Yorkshire, driving in the countryside and suddenly in the middle of a conversation I realised that I was speaking to my companion in a way I had never spoken to anyone before and that I had a completely intact sense of myself, and a very connected but distinct experience of the other person. And I felt in a state of great connection with myself, and with him. One thing facilitated the other.'

- You develop the capacity to be alone when you feel safe in the company of someone else (usually your mother).
- You develop the capacity to feel safe with someone else, and to be your own self in someone else's presence, when you also have the capacity to be alone without undue anxiety.
- Through good contact with someone else, you come increasingly to know yourself.

Even the idea of intimacy can be associated with a level of excitement and 'aliveness' which is hard to locate in the general round of paid work and domestic chores. It may be your means to try to transcend limitations of nationality, class, social custom or even time and place ('Nothing much mattered but the room where we both were. I felt transported into another world.').

Through intimacy, you may want to transcend your gender also ('I felt like we came together not as man and woman, but as two beings who can truly accept one another.').

Transcendence *can* be part of intimacy, and not only when intimacy includes the hormonal rushes that accompany sex. But delicious or even addictive as that kind of transcendence can be, transcendence of any kind tends to be temporary. In the experience of intimacy you are usually stuck with who you are! And 'who you are' is in part signalled by your body.

Your first physical contacts with your mother after birth involved, if you were lucky, the touch of skin against skin, an experience that tells you that you are the same, and also different. That you are as one, but that you are not one.

Your body continues to matter. You touch, speak, stare, pause, lean forward, lean back, look ahead, look away, *all with your gendered body*. This is true whether the person with whom you are being/feeling/acting out intimacy is of the same or other gender as yourself, and whether the relationship extends to sexual contact. And how could it be otherwise? In this life, at least, it is difficult to leave your body behind.

Alive in your body

The ease with which you are at home in your body can colour how you accept the physicality of other human beings. It is, of course, possible to be easy-going with your body and still to be shut off from your feelings or so lost in your own feelings that other people's feelings scarcely matter. But it is also limiting to be locked into patterns of anxiety which limit your aliveness to your head only.

Wilhelm Reich, the original body therapist, had many ideas which remain debatable, but he was certainly convincing in his introduction of the notion that the infant child 'armours' himself against emotional pain, and against the pain of not being able to *express* emotions, through a tensing against that pain which blocks the body increasingly until sometimes — perhaps often — less pain is felt, but what is also suppressed is the possibility for spontaneity and appropriate feeling through the body.

Alexander Lowen and David Boadella are two therapists who have taken Reich's ideas forward. Both suggest that until some of this armouring is relieved, probably through bio-energetic massage and exercises and gradually increasing physical release of emotion, or perhaps through the practice of yoga or other physically expressive movements, change within the psyche leading to self-knowledge and self-acceptance is limited and unlikely to endure. I think that they and other body therapists are probably right. Certainly the experience of a deep massage or of certain yoga positions have most unexpectedly aroused knowledge of painfully withheld feeling in me.

Reich saw the ability to enjoy the pleasurable release of an orgasm fully throughout the body (and not in the genitals or pelvic area only) as 'an important sign of the health of the organism, indicating that energy is moving freely around the body'. He saw sex as a key outlet for the release and regulation of the high energy level of a healthy person. He also noted that the person who is capable of experiencing sexual satisfaction does not need to be obsessive about sex, turning the 'loving embrace' into a 'pornographic act'.

Pain that is 'armoured against' in the crucial pre-verbal period is most likely to manifest in sexual problems. These may be any one of a variety of problems which come out of difficulties with actually feeling emotions, or perhaps allowing others to feel or express emotions in your presence.

Sex which is cut off from the emotions; sex which cuts one aspect of a person off from their wholeness — as in fetishes; sex where there is a lot of emotion but a disappointing lack of expression in the body: these 'opposite' situations point to blocks in the ideal flow of energy between mind, emotions and body — and thence from self to other.

Defences which may have been helpful to the infant or child, or which may even have allowed the child to survive, can lead to patterns which in adulthood are very far from helpful. These patterns you may recognise in yourself, or in the people with whom you are intimate. Lowen categorises these patterns of defence as character formations. Boadella warns against this, correctly I think, suggesting that if you see the defence as 'character', you risk losing the subtlety of what the defence is expressing about your (in)capacity to be close to others in times of intimacy.

There are five patterns, *which should certainly be read as pointers only, and not as statements of fact.*

- *Schizoid pattern*: 'If I don't hold everything in, it will fall apart.' 'My life is at risk.' A person showing this pattern may feel lots of tension in the back of the neck and retraction in their eyes. Fear will be a dominant emotion. From anxiety during birth?
- *Oral pattern*: Fear of abandonment expresses itself in a need to hold on, wanting to take something, and feeling unsupported. A tendency to helplessness. Much sadness, and grief for the lack of someone who should be there. Difficulties may be felt with the intake of breath. Related to breast anxiety?
- *Psychopathic pattern*: The winner who must stay on top. He (or she) makes other people need him, rather than admitting his own needs, as a defence against vulnerability. May be adept at 'walking over' other people's feelings. Top part of the body is often heavy. Possibly little feeling in the arms. Walking too early? (Please note that if you recognise your boss, your father or your husband, this does not mean he is psychopathic! That is a different and tragic state of being profoundly out of touch with the world of feeling.)
- *Masochistic pattern*: Easily feels invaded. Swallows back his or her protest. Compensation for suppressed anger is to take on other people's burdens. Anger held in the guts, buttocks and compressed in the trunk. Invasions of privacy during toilet training?
- *Rigid pattern*: Holding back against feeling, especially against feelings of love. *Combining sexuality and love is very difficult.* Stiffening of the pelvis and the lower back. Oedipal anxieties? Anxieties about masturbation?

You are more likely to recognise in yourself a combination of these patterns than one only. It is also worth repeating that these patterns are merely pointers or 'maps'; they are not facts. Realising that you are prone to masochistic patterns, or to what the neo-Reichians call psychopathic patterns, does not condemn you to a lifetime of feeling easily invaded, nor to a life in which you must dominate others through fear of your own weakness.

Recognising yourself in any clinical or pseudo-clinical description is useful only when you take it as a guide toward action, if you believe that action is needed; toward appropriate help, if you feel that help is called for; or toward acceptance, if self-knowledge feels like all that is needed.

An awareness of the vital links between body, mind and emotions is always helpful and perhaps especially for those people whose addiction to rationality pushes them to the 'reasonable' conclusion that intimacy problems, like any other difficulty, can be solved by good sense or intellectual endeavour. This is unlikely to be so. Good sense and intellectual endeavour can certainly be your allies; but when distress has been 'recorded' in one aspect of your being, your emotions and your physical body will also be crying out for understanding and for attention.

The physical ease you feel with another person may assure you that you know someone intimately. Perhaps it is possible to say that when your own and the other person's boundaries are down, and each of you is comfortable with this — perhaps taking it so entirely for granted that no conscious awareness is needed — then you are sharing an experience of intimacy, or at least the experience of 'being yourself' in the presence of someone else.

Gestures of bodily intimacy can and do mean different things to different people, of course, depending on their upbringing, their culture and their personal sense of inhibition or lack of inhibition as well as their individual sense of 'what matters' when it comes to revealing *who I am*. In a Western context it is safe to generalise that when you feel free to bath in front of someone else, perhaps go to the lavatory and continue to talk, when you can eat with that person on a cluttered table while also reading your book or the newspaper, when you can offer them the butter still in its wrapper, when you can grunt or mutter by way of greeting or farewell, when you can shave or pluck out hairs on your chin in their presence, when you can tolerate their smells, finish their sentences for them, or enjoy the sounds of them pottering around in a space near you but not with you, you are probably experiencing some degree of intimacy.

This may not be ideal intimacy. It may, indeed, be not much more than familiarity or proximity, for it is possible to feel uninhibited with someone physically, yet shut off or even misunderstood emotionally or spiritually. Sharing an external space by no means automatically leads to or sustains sharing of internal spaces.

It is also possible to have an experience of sustaining intimate contact with someone — a friend, a therapist, a colleague — yet be appalled at the inappropriateness of over-familiarity, at the very idea of undressing, burping or going to the lavatory in their presence.

What I want to emphasise is that you will bring meanings of your own to this complex business of letting down boundaries. Familiarity may be part of intimacy; it can also preclude it. In the everydayness of shared bathrooms and smells, grunts, bottom scratching and half-completed thoughts, the desire to be open psychologically and spiritually can wither and die, often without anyone witnessing its departure.

Good at intimacy

Because you make intimate contact through and with your body — even if you limit this to your head, mouth, eyes, speech — you can be unusually aware of your sexuality when you are desiring intimacy. With this often comes a sense of uncertainty about what is acceptable to someone whose otherness seems exaggerated by their gender difference from your own.

For many of us there is a temptation to fall back on gender stereotypes when thinking about intimacy. Oddly — or is it oddly? — these can seem more generally true than false.

For some people — more men than women — adult intimacy is strongly associated with activity: intimacy equals, for many men, having sex. Sebastian said directly what other men expressed rather more obliquely. 'I would find it difficult to be intimate with a woman without being sexual. I do have acquaintances who are women but with whom I have had no sexual relationship. But those with whom I have had sex are in the majority.'

For other people — now women predominate — intimacy may be less a state of doing than of *being*. Being intimate is frequently described by women as feeling bound through tenderness to someone else, with feelings of sharing, openness, trust. While this may come along with sexual closeness, it need not always do so. Indeed, many women speak most confidently about intimacy when they talk of their children and their women friends.

However, while women find talking about, facilitating and sustaining intimacy in general easier than men do, 'being good at intimacy', or experiencing intimacy as a possibility for you, is no more a prerogative of one gender than it is of a nationality or an economic group. In fact, in this market-driven world in which we live, I enjoy knowing that the experience of intimacy is not for sale.

The aura of intimacy is associated with goods and products, but the rich cannot order intimacy into their lives; nor do they have fewer intimacy problems than the rest of us. On the contrary. Gaining serious wealth usually requires a degree of self-interest which cuts out awareness of others to a fairly alarming degree. The evidence for that is all around us.

There are all kinds of people — poor, rich, old, young, women, men, gay, heterosexual — for whom intimacy 'works', by which I mean, their intimacy needs are met in ways which suit them. Equally, there are all kinds of people for whom intimacy exists only as an idea. There are others (perhaps many others) for whom even the idea of intimacy is anathema. Speak to them of intimacy and they hear demands they must resist and, above all, loss of freedom. And why would this be so? The shortest answer is not that those people are hard-hearted, though individually they might be! It is far more likely that the boundaries which need to exist between self and other are weak or even non-existent so that they too easily feel trespassed upon, invaded, pushed around: although none of that knowledge may be conscious.

Some people believe intimacy is a part of life best taken for granted; there are others who believe intimacy is worth 'working at' and who invest time and money doing just that. Some adults want their entire lives to be suffused with intimacy; others believe that intimacy has long-term effects yet occurs only fleetingly, when two people, or perhaps a gathering of people, are most 'themselves'.

Such moments — when two or more people are 'most themselves' — cannot happen when one person is assessing another for their usefulness, nor judging whether this is someone to envy or to despise.

It is not possible to be intimate *without also relinquishing the desire to control or to be controlled*. Yet issues of control and of power dominate our inner and outer lives and have been internalised by every one of us in a configuration which is very much at the heart of our individuality.

There are people, perhaps many people, so needy of believing that they are in control that this issue — control — will always remain more important to them than the desire for connection. Or they may choose to make what passes for connection only with people to whom they unquestionably feel superior. The businessman unburdening himself to the whore with the heart of gold is probably the prime stereotype for this kind of dynamic.

In intimacy you risk being *who you are*, and risk facing who the other person is *in their entirety* — not just in those parts which are socially acceptable or 'useful' to you.

The following statements about intimacy emphasise this. They also reveal how difficult it is to define intimacy, because even in talking about intimacy, and hearing what that talk reveals about your inner self and your private neediness, considerable vulnerability — and courage — are required.

- 'In times of intimacy there is the smallest possible wedge between my feelings and my expression of those feelings to someone else.'
- 'Being really myself in the presence of another; allowing someone else to be true to who they are in my presence. No one in control and no one struggling for control.'
- 'Unconditional love — or as near to it as you can get. Acceptance, closeness, trust, no masks — surely that's what intimacy is.'

Those happen to be among the descriptions of intimacy that ring true to me, but finding yourself out of sympathy with them does not mean that you are someone who has no idea or experience of what intimacy is.

What intimacy might be

Intimacy can and probably does wear many faces.

When we discuss intimacy at a theoretical or anecdotal level, it is fascinating to explore those differences. However, if you and I were to do that strange human thing — fall in love — and then looked to each other to have our intimacy needs met, we might find ourselves saddened, angry and then perhaps self-pitying and accusatory because our hero or heroine frustrates our intimacy ideals.

This may mean only that you have one cluster of needs that you attach to the idea of intimacy while in my worldview 'being intimate' may mean something else. Such difference should not matter, but often it will matter a great deal, not least because unless I am unusually flexible I won't recognise your 'intimacy' as intimacy unless it coincides to some extent with my version of what 'intimacy' is. So, if your idea of intimacy includes taking it for granted that we understand one another, while mine includes self-revealing conversations as we walk hand in hand by the ocean, then getting together might lead us both to feeling cheated, misunderstood and decidedly 'unintimate'.

Or perhaps it is in bed that difference will show up most. That is certainly the case with Virginia and Jim. Jim wants sex to be exciting. He wants variety and enthusiasm and believes he needs to be able to lose himself if sex is to 'work' for him. Moreover, if it is not 'exciting enough', then he often loses his erection and becomes anxious about ejaculating.

At the end of a day of paid work and childcare, Virginia rarely feels exciting. Exhausted would be more like it. Her anger with Jim about the unresolved emotional issues between them also boils away, preventing her from wanting to make the kind of effort which Jim apparently feels he needs. Virginia says that her ideal sexual encounter would be consoling, affectionate, good-humoured, and if this occasionally developed into spontaneous excitement, she would be delighted. But to be required to be exciting is more than she can face last thing at night.

Jim and Virginia each feels entitled to have their needs met, but their needs do not coincide. Their reading of intimacy, of all that precedes and follows sexual intercourse as well as sex itself, is so radically different that each might as well be — perhaps is — speaking a different language.

A couple of years ago I was at a workshop on bereavement counselling run by Mal McKissock, well known for his outstanding work with bereaved people. He was explaining — and it took our group some time to take this idea on board — that people have very different ways of expressing their grief.

Most of us would assume, I think, that grieving people weep a lot, feel terribly sad, lost, depressed, and have little interest in events other than their own loss. This portrait may fit many grieving people. There are others, however, whose grief may be no less powerful and no less keenly felt, who will express their grief through other emotions, for example, rage or lust. As Mal explained, that rage or lust is that particular person's way of expressing grief.

But it doesn't take a great deal of insight to imagine how threatened and potentially isolated two people could quickly come to feel who share a loss, but react to that loss quite differently. If the mother of a dead child, for example, is withdrawn and constantly weeping, she is unlikely to believe in or validate the grief of her husband who rages around the house bullying family members or is out all night fucking with strangers.

Our ways of being intimate can be as dramatically varied as those different ways of grieving.

It is difficult to allow yourself sufficient flexibility of mind to take this concept to heart — and then put it into practice. This would mean allowing someone else their way of being intimate, even when it fails to satisfy your ideals or needs. Or, more precisely, it would mean accepting that someone else *is being intimate* even when their behaviour does not add up to the intimacy recipe long ago writ large in your head.

As difficult as this idea is to grasp practically, it can also be liberating to realise that intimacy, or being intimate, is a fluid concept, and that in expressing my way of being intimate I am expressing something of my own individuality and my own learned expression of what 'intimacy' means. This may be different from your individual and cultural expression of intimacy — but *that difference need not be threatening*.

Let me turn this same thought around slightly: *The freer you are from expectations of what intimacy is, the more likely it is that you will be open to enjoy what intimacy can be.*

Adam demonstrated this point when he was talking about his ten-year marriage with Katy. 'When I first lived with Katy I would sometimes be moody and difficult or even critical. That was certainly part of what I assumed was possible within an intimate relationship. In my family people had felt very free to be unpleasant with each other or to ignore each other. But Katy was always pleasant, always tolerant. I have no explanation for it but that she is a very good person. And gradually that has affected me. I came to feel like such a heel for being unpleasant to someone who didn't complain but who more or less ignored it and kept on being generous to me. I learned from her that you don't have to behave like a shit just because you live with someone.'

16

Listening is essential to intimacy

The languages of touch, of gesture, of bodies meeting are very much associated with intimacy. But spoken language as well as silence can make or break intimate relationships also.

In the early days of a relationship which contains the promise of intimacy (and this may not be an explicitly sexual relationship) there is usually a strong impulse to tell. People heading into an intimate relationship often use language to emphasise similarity, contact and companionship. They may revert to a kind of baby-talk which reminds them, unconsciously, of times when they felt held by and safe with Mother. They may also comment on what a relief it is to be able to say whatever comes into their mind, and to feel listened to and accepted ('Madeline is the most wonderful listener. I would not have believed that I could speak that frankly to any woman.').

This sense of expansion and freedom often extends beyond talking to the lover or friend, to talking more freely to others ('I've never felt better. I've met this wonderful woman. She's clever, famous, kind, beautiful . . . magical . . .').

But — and it is a significant *but* — when the relationship has passed through the honeymoon phase it can sometimes be more difficult to tell 'all' or even very much at all to the person with whom you are supposedly intimate. Indeed, it can seem easier to confide in others, even strangers.

But why should 'telling' frequently become more difficult rather than easier?

And why should 'frankness' so often shift from being experienced as flattering to being experienced as threatening?

The answer to these conundrums lies much less in the other person than it does in the conflicts *which exist inside your own self* and are unknown to you even while you are acting them out: through your words; through your lack of words; through your body's openness; through your body closing down.

The conflicts I am talking about circulate around needs most of us have to be close, while also fearing that closeness could lead us into powerlessness, dependency and even helplessness.

It is worth repeating that this is because your first experiences of closeness, as an infant with your mother, were experiences which were, if you were lucky, warm and rewarding. Nevertheless, you also experienced how needy you were of mother, and how intolerable it was for you to know that your needs existed *inside* yourself and that the person who could meet your needs was *outside* yourself — more to the point, was *outside your control* — and that often you had to wait for those needs to be met, and occasionally you had to wait forever.

As you grew up, if you continued to be lucky, you learned to tolerate those frustrations and to discover that some of the needs which mother/other had been meeting — or failing to meet — could be met by you or *various and less crucial others*.

This change in conscious knowledge is essential to maturity but, alas, it doesn't permeate every part of your being! There remains within you a bell warning you that opening up is synonymous with vulnerability or even with loss of self. How this is experienced is very much a matter of individual temperament and experience, but it is certainly central to many people's ambivalent feelings about intimacy and intimate relationships.

So, too, is the more easily observed phenomenon of wanting two or more conflicting things at once.

I want to be loved; I want to be free.

I want you to be happy; I want to do what pleases myself.

I want security; I want variety.

As greedy (or needy) as most of us are, and as unwilling to order our priorities and compromise as many of us remain, these conflicting desires can lead us to extremes of behaviour which can be intensely damaging of our self-acceptance, and very painful.

Many of the paradoxes which veil our understanding of intimacy and of solitude can be glimpsed through language. What you say, the words and tone and manner you use to describe someone — or your relationship — show this. But language has other lessons too: through its flow or its ebb, its presence or absence, and through the non-verbal language of the body (I lean forward; I turn away). Language can be an instrument of intimacy — revealing who you are to someone else, revealing who someone else is to you. It can also be a powerful means to avoid intimacy, or to push intimacy away when closeness threatens to become dangerous to your sense of self. 'I can't stand this person.' *I can't stand the emotions this person stirs up in me.*

When you can't stand the emotions that someone else stirs up in you — and these may vary from fear of closeness to fear of loss; from ambivalence about the relationship to uncertainty about your role within the relationship — then the bitterness and pain which follow a fight may be easier to bear than the more appropriate feelings of sadness or uncertainty which might dominate if you allowed yourself to acknowledge those emotions. The noise, the drama, the tension, the immediacy, the familiarity of fighting can be a powerful distraction from the much harder tasks of attempting to understand your own inner conflicts, as well as those conflicts that inevitably exist between two people, each of whom wants their needs met, each of whom wants to be accepted in all their bizarre entirety. Anger, even violence, can be a welcome distraction from uncertainty and vulnerability.

Sounds crazy? It may well be, but it is precisely in relationships of intimacy that your craziness (and mine) will be hardest to conceal.

Under the steamroller of words, intimacy can readily be crushed. Virginia is talking again about her vexed relationship with Jim.

'I will need to get something off my chest, like I might want to moan about the children or in some way just get him to acknowledge me, or that I need some encouragement or even some affection which is not sexual, but what I get back from Jim is a kind of universal and derogatory statement about my entire being. He'll say things like "You never do anything but complain." "You are never grateful, are you?" "Nothing is ever enough for you, is it?"

'Instead of a pat I get a kick in the guts. Does this mean then that I should not complain about anything ever? Yet who else should I let off steam with? That seems a minimum you can ask for in an intimate relationship. But with Jim I am always punished for it.'

The capacity to listen to what another person is saying, to take in both their words and also the meanings which lie behind the words, is crucial to intimacy. It is a skill which is at the heart of acknowledging that what is going on in someone else's inner world *matters*.

This skill is something many people never learn:

• While someone is talking, they are thinking only of their response.
• When someone is describing something joyful or painful it is eliciting only a memory of the time when...
• A cry for help is heard as something to be defended against, through cliché, sentimentality, or attack.

Part of the problem is self-absorption. *I can't leave myself behind in order to listen to you.*

Part of the problem may be resentment, or the envy which often lies behind resentment. *Why should I listen to you? Who has ever listened to me?*

Part of the problem may also be a simple lack of awareness that listening matters, or a lack of practice in listening *with an open mind and without interruptions.*

The capacity to listen is an indicator of the development of a safe sense of self. From that safety, taking in someone else's otherness becomes possible: through talking, through listening, even through shared silence.

It needs also to be remembered that speech is only a partially adequate tool to communicate internal phenomena such as feeling. I may, for example, tell you that I am sad, and badly want you to understand me. But your experience of 'sad' may be different from mine and therefore your understanding of what I mean by 'sad' may also be different. When I say *I am sad* I may mean grieving-needing-relief-sad, while when you say *I am sad* you may mean helpless-hopeless-leave-me-alone-sad. And such differences and potential misunderstandings can apply to any feeling state.

Virginia, for example, may want to convey to Jim, 'Please acknowledge, even briefly, that I have had a hard day but that nevertheless I am managing.'

And Jim may want to convey in return, 'Don't tell me how hard your day is because it makes me think you expect me to do something about it and I can't. Therefore what I feel is inadequate about myself and furious with you.'

But what comes out of their mouths is quite different from their intentions, and is rapidly poisoning their relationship.

I want to throw in another reminder about language — unspoken language this time — which is that often in long-term relationships there is a real pressure to *know without being told*, and a real likelihood of some kind of punishment if this knowing is not acknowledged and acted upon.

This is, as you will recall from reading about Margaretta and Tomas, a powerful relic from infancy when the mother's absorption in her child allowed her, if things were going well, to tune into her baby's needs and to understand and meet those needs, without a formal exchange of words. Even when things were not going well, and the mother either could not or would not allow herself to tune into what her baby was expressing, the need was there, and was inextricably associated with the first self-and-other dyad.

So, in your longing for and in your experience of intimacy it is helpful to understand that tensions can and do exist between:

- your conscious and unconscious desires
- your 'meanings' and someone else's 'meanings'
- 'understanding already' and 'needing to find out'
- feeling accepted for who you are and feeling judged for what you are not.

Such internal and internal/external tensions are usually painfully close to the surface of what is happening between people who are — or are struggling to be — intimate. Is it any wonder then that many of us harbour a flourishing suspicion that intimacy is something that most other people manage very much better than we do?

17

Not only a self, but also an other

Before your first year of life was over you began to under-stand that you are a self. You also began to discover that you are an other.

This is not always quite the same person! How you experience yourself can vary considerably from the way other people ex-perience you. And a third dimension is added with your percep-tions or fantasies of how other people are perceiving you — which will depend on your moment-by-moment levels of *self*-acceptance.

Part of knowing that you are on 'solid ground within' comes from feeling confident about your self-perceptions, while remaining open to what you can learn about yourself through social and sexual interactions: when you are, or are perceived as, the other.

Two people who want to be close are likely to be unusually aware of how they are being seen and judged — or how they imagine they are being seen and judged. Most of us are at our best in the first rush of a new relationship. Our glow comes in part through simple happiness, but also because we tend to like the way that we are being seen: as delightful, charming, understand-ing and so on. (Our real selves, at last!)

But this is yet something else that does not stay fixed. The open sharing which characterises the early period of an intense friendship or sexual relationship can come to feel like more of a demand on your otherness than you want to meet.

The demand may even be that your 'otherness' should in some mysterious way make up for my insufficiency of 'selfness'. This may be expressed very much between the lines. The person who is making the demand may not even be conscious of doing so.

'You're never home any more.'

You no longer make me feel important to you. I need to feel important.

'Why can't you ask for a pay rise? You don't care about our family.'

I feel insecure. I want you and your money to take better care of me.

'Sex with you is really boring.'

I am afraid to feel sexual with someone I really like.

The situation is further complicated because you experience intimacy and solitude — as you experience everything else that happens in your inner world — 'on the move'. The 'you' created by the people for whom you are an other, will wax and wane in part as a consequence of your behaviour, reactions, feelings and so on, but also as a consequence of their own fund of self-acceptance waxing and waning.

The heightened language of romantic love/lust makes this most obvious ('Joe is the most wonderful man I have ever met. He is everything I have ever wanted. Everyone who meets him adores him' to 'What a complete and utter shit Joe is. I don't know how I can be expected to put up with him. No wonder he doesn't have a single friend.').

Has Joe changed? Probably not. What have changed are his lover's perceptions of him — which come out of her fantasies (this is how Joe should be) and the clash of her own desires (I want Joe to be devoted to me; I want Joe to be independent. I want to be with Joe; I want to be free of Joe).

When you sense that a demand is being made of you, or that a demand is being made of your otherness, *but you do not know what that demand is*, you may feel anxious or irritated ('If I hear another word about Joe's years in foster homes I think I'll go crazy. I know it was awful for him, but surely he can put it behind him? I know I would.').

Joe may indeed be demanding that his lover make up to him

for those awful years in foster homes. That is how Carol, his lover, interprets his constant re-telling of the same story.

His need, however, might be different. It could be more modest ('I want you to acknowledge what I went through, and then I can stop going on about it.'). Or it could be monumental ('The world has treated me badly and you alone can set me to rights.').

The problem with emotional demands, and especially those which cannot be explicitly stated, is that it is often difficult to name them, even to know that they are there except as feelings of anxiety or anger or depression. Little wonder then that many of us resort to wholesale blaming and to total rejection ('Piss off Joe, I can't stand you any more.').

This pattern will already be familiar to you. It emerges when two people are muddled about where one ends and the other begins — or what is being expressed and on whose behalf — and therefore feel they have no choice but to cut free.

There is another choice, which is for two selves to live alongside each other, rather than in and through each other; but that is rarely easy to achieve.

At a conscious level, most adults know other people will not meet all their needs and that it is inappropriate to rage and howl when they fail to do so. But we are not only rational, conscious beings. We are also unreasonable, changeable, in part unknowable, even to ourselves. Emotions can erupt; needs can run riot and refuse utterly to be corralled by reason. And this is most likely to happen when you are at home, most fully 'yourself' and least circumscribed by your adapted self behaviour of work and social relationships.

Listen as I did to Miranda, a competent senior social worker in her mid thirties.

'I knew that phoning Geoff back was the worst possible thing I could do. But I couldn't help myself. I really wanted to make contact with him. Even hearing him shout at me was better than absolutely nothing.

'And then, when he did finally come home, I knew that it would be best if I kept quiet and just let him relax a bit, but as soon as I heard the key I found myself like a screaming mad-woman going on and on and on as he walked through the house to the back door, and then he turned on me.'

The dangers of intimacy

Coming to a mutual understanding of what intimacy means to people in a long-term relationship must precede each person getting their needs met. Part of that mutual understanding is accepting the limitations of what someone else can do for you, and what you should do for someone else. This does not imply a limit to loving. It does suggest taking someone seriously enough to believe that he or she is better off standing on his or her own emotional feet, even while being loved.

It also means discovering when intimacy feels dangerous for either person — which may be acted out as restlessness or boredom or a desire to shut off or turn away.

Maintaining a balance which suits both people between 'getting too close' and 'too far away' is something over which you will have little rational control because those very perceptions *too close* or *too far away* are deeply subjective, arising as they do from unconscious fears and pressures.

'The person one turns to,' said Fairbairn, 'becomes the person one must get away from.'

How this happens varies between people.

Some couples, as you have seen, have disruptive or even terminal arguments in order to push each other away, preferring to feel angry rather than needy ('I can't wait to get Henry out of the house. His limp devotion drives me mad.').

Within other couples one partner may have an affair so that the new third person will take the heat off the couple — and whatever it is that they don't want to face ('We spent all our time fighting about Mimi and never looking at what was going on between ourselves.').

Someone else may take on a job which takes most waking hours. Men tend to find this a familiar solution to their intimacy anxieties.

An unconscious solution can also be found through being intolerably unpleasant — or critical — in order to drive the other person away because you literally cannot bear the love or hate or rage or envy that their closeness stirs up in you.

The dynamic in all these scenarios is that the very closeness which seems to be what both people want is also dangerous for at least one of them.

The unconscious dangers vary according to individual make-up and experience, but include these themes:
- fear of loss of self
- fear of loss of the other
- fear that deep caring leads to too much vulnerability
- fear that deep caring will give the other person intolerable power to make you unhappy
- fear that deep caring will seriously curtail your freedom.

I feel a good deal of empathy with people in this particular emotional boat. My constitution inclines me to a fairly high degree of anxiety, and I hate not to feel free (I am a Gemini!). Moreover, the early death of my mother led me to experience the world as an unpredictable and frightening place. Without over-emphasising a cause-and-effect relationship, for these outcomes are always more complex than our rational minds can encompass, it would seem to me that this combination has made me excessively cautious about emotional commitment. A state of partial withdrawal seems natural and easy to me, a state which pushes me toward solitude and is also fuelled by my capacity for solitude.

And what is the risk for me?

Some utterly tenacious part of myself has linked together love and danger, and I can't seem to separate those twinned associations.

Thirty years after my mother died, with a therapist whom I deeply respected and with whom I felt safe, I returned to that time of my mother's death and saw myself as a tiny, ugly, rat-like creature, hiding under a kitchen table in the basement of a huge house out of which there was no escape, for the house itself floated on sea and was far, far away from any land. In my grief I was like a piece of debris, of rubbish almost. That was what my loss had reduced me to. Without my mother I was lost in the vastness of a dark, doorless house which was my grief.

Seeing this shamed, rat-like thing, crouched under a surreally huge kitchen table, appalled me. Yet I recognised her, for she was me, or part of me. I had to accept that and attempt to feel compassion and love for her as well as repulsion.

Small wonder then that the risk of abandoning myself to a full-hearted relationship, braiding together love, trust and vulnerability, has seemed so difficult, although of course it has taken me many years to discover this and to ease up somewhat on blaming myself for not being what other people thought I 'should'.

But even the danger that I am musing upon is complex. It is most obviously a danger that I will love someone wholeheartedly and risk losing 'what matters most' should I lose him or her. Yet I love my children with all my heart. That has been the great discovery of my own maternity: that I can love with all my heart and, indeed, could not love them any other way (although they also exhaust me and see me at my worst, as well as my best).

So what other danger can there be? I suspect it is the danger of taking on what I unconsciously perceive as responsibility for someone else — worse yet, responsibility for their happiness — and being unable to cope with this demand as I experience it, which may of course not be a demand at all except in my inner world.

You cannot make other people happy. If who you are increases someone else's happiness, that is a joy for you both. But it is impossible to accept the burden of someone else's happiness (or their unhappiness) without coming to resent it, and risking losing respect for the selfhood of that person.

I have often wondered if for me, and for many other people too, intimacy might exist as a state, rather like nirvana, which can be only occasionally tasted. Psychoanalyst Charlotte Wolff may reassure others who share those feelings:

'It is a banality to mention that any true and complete intimacy between people is always temporary, and sometimes only momentary.

'How could it be otherwise? Human emotions and impulses are ambivalent and vacillating, and if we were to express the whole range of them we should devour ourselves and others.'

Could it also be that it is precisely those people who are capable of very deep feeling, *and who are vulnerable to being stirred up by deep feeling in others*, who may have most difficulty in balancing their needs for and actual experience of intimacy, and who may sometimes recoil from their own intensity, thus bringing about in their partners the feeling Anthony Storr defined as a 'lack of commitment' and an 'awareness that something important is missing'.

For along with concern that what I felt was never 'enough', I have throughout my adult life found it extremely difficult to judge what was being asked of me in even a quasi-intimate situation. (Am I an adequate 'other'?)

I can feel very quickly overwhelmed or invaded by other people. This may be quite out of proportion to what they are actually asking of me. But experiencing their demands crowding in on me will fairly quickly send me into a panic of defensiveness. Then I feel I have no choice but to turn away, if only to regain some inner (breathing) space for myself. In such a dilemma, when I am experiencing the other person's needs as potentially overwhelming, it is difficult for me to get a grip on what the person's needs are in their own perception of them. It is also virtually impossible for me to keep hold of any sense of what my own needs might be — except my need to withdraw in order to recover, and my guilt about doing so.

There is another side to this dynamic. Feminist therapists and writers Luise Eichenbaum and Susie Orbach have explored this in their work. They suggest that when someone has had to suppress their emotional needs, perhaps since infancy or childhood, fear builds up in them that were those needs ever to begin to be expressed, then they would turn out to be outrageous in scope or even insatiable.

It is, as you can see, a mirroring image: I can't do or feel enough for this person. And deep down and much harder to contact is the belief: this person could not possibly do or feel enough for me: *better to shut off and not to risk it.*

What I am talking about here has nothing to do with rationality. Rationally I know full well that I do not have to take care of someone else's needs to the extent of keeping that person happy or even alive. Rationally I am appalled even by the idea that I might have emotional needs too great for someone else to meet. Indeed, so buried are those needs I can know that they exist only theoretically, and much more easily as they apply to people other than myself.

The irony of these dilemmas is not lost on me!

After all, am I not the person who has studied psychoanalytic and existential literature for years; who has had therapy for years; who has spent a decade of intensive work preparing myself to write and then actually writing this book? Am I not the person who knows that 'my safety lies in my own self' and that when I believe the care of someone else is in my hands I am infantilising that person or even dishonouring them?

Yes, I am that person. But, once again, I am talking about eruptions from the past which tremble in the present, fears arising from within which have no name but which have tremendous impact on our daily lives.

This strange and most uncomfortable mix of grandiosity and helplessness is not mine alone. In my case it is exacerbated by the combination of having been passionately in love with my mother, then failing to save her from death and myself from grief. More generally, and in my case also, it comes out of an insecurity about psychological boundaries: *where you end and I begin*. It also exists in many people whose emotional antennae seem permanently fixed in an 'up and ready' position, and not at all in people who are free of worrying about the inner lives and needs of others.

Alexandra believes that an easy-going robustness of attitude towards intimacy is largely the prerogative of men. She envies, she claims, 'their expression of intimacy which has some extremely negative aspects but is also in some ways healthier or anyway more self-protective'.

In reflecting on her own life, and how she might like to change it, Alexandra said, 'Probably the way I would like to be able to express myself in intimate relationships would be to be able to move more easily in and out of a relating state instead of feeling taken over and having to push the entire edifice — or person — away in order to regain my boundaries and my sense of who I am.'

Having intact psychological boundaries, which may lead to a 'robustness of attitude towards intimacy' that Alexandra envies, is not a male privilege only. And it does have an ugly side when what 'I' want dominates, to the exclusion of other people's rights or needs. Nevertheless, that image evoked by Alexandra of being able to 'move more easily in and out of a relating state' glows attractively to me.

Succeeding at intimacy

While writing this book I could not fail to notice that when I told people what I was working on, almost without exception they showed more curiosity about my work on intimacy than they did in my work on solitude. Is this because intimacy is much more visible in the public domain of conversation and shared revelations as well as in the fantasies and myths of films, novels and advertising slogans? Is it because 'succeeding at intimacy' — which in conventional terms usually means getting into a relationship and staying there — is praised and rewarded while 'succeeding at solitude' hardly ranks as a challenge in most people's minds.

Or is it that people suspect that accepting your own limitations and gaining a reasonable sense of autonomy and self-awareness, is a private matter, while getting along with someone else is self-evidently a more complicated affair?

Perhaps intimacy excites and daunts people because of its associations with sexuality and because there is always at least one judge — the other person — standing in for a society which seems, superficially yet powerfully, to 'value' intimacy and to divide the world into those who have intimacy, or the outward signs of it, and those who don't. (Consider how cruelly the lonely and the 'undesirable' are shunned in favour of those who are 'sought after'.)

Of course, the weighing up of one state — intimacy or solitude — as more or less difficult than the other, or more or less rewarding, is a pointless task. *This is because you bring to intimate relationships the same self you are in touch with — or not — when you are alone.*

When you can:
- trust yourself
- in general like yourself
- trust in your own existence
- trust that someone else has an existence separate from yours
- trust that others' separate existence is as valid as your own
- trust that your existence does not depend on their continuing existence

then you are likely to be able to experience a closeness to someone else, a sense of sharing, understanding, acceptance, interest and trust which may add up to what most of us could call intimacy.

Notwithstanding this deceptively placid list, it is entirely possible to be fleetingly intimate in ways which do not involve taking an interest in someone else's history and in their future. As a mother I can exchange a glance or a few words with another mother — especially at times of stress in a public place — which is intensely but fleetingly intimate. In a single look a woman can say to me, 'I know how hard it is and I really feel for you' or 'Yes, but it is worthwhile, isn't it?' and I am certainly cheered by that flash in at least as much measure as I am infuriated when a glance of contempt reaches me that I can't silence my infant children, or otherwise prevent them from allowing their feelings to intrude into a public (i.e. adult male) space.

Those whose sexual lives have not been entirely monogamous might also have experienced intense sexual intimacy, a literal laying open of the body, with someone with whom little other intimacy exists, or will exist.

What the body is 'telling' under such circumstances can be highly revealing, although more often to you than to the other person involved! And that is perhaps a clue to the intimacy I am talking about here. While in no way discounting those momentary enhancing connections, I want to continue to explore intimacy which embraces the idea of the other, intimacy which is not an intense moment of self-discovery *in the company of someone else* (as in the fleeting sexual encounter), but is a self-and-other discovery.

18

Discovering the other

Y̶ou are a different 'other' for each person you come into contact with, depending on how they need to 'read' or experience you. And, of course, each person you meet is an other for you in a way which comes very much out of your reading of who that person is, as well as what could be called facts about the person. This self-and-other dance continues ceaselessly:

- You are a self and an other.
- Your 'others' are in part your own creations.
- This in turn affects and shapes your experiences of self.
- Your levels of self-awareness and self-acceptance largely shape how you perceive others.

I have been using the word *other* as though it were self-explanatory, yet who the other is must always be something of a mystery. It is a mystery at an immediate level in the sense that no person is entirely knowable. That's not only because you are in a constant process of change but because you are affected by what is going on in the unconscious part of your mind, as well as by what you can more readily identify and attempt to control.

The other is also a mystery in ways which echo the mysteries of the self. You could ask — the Eastern mystics ask this most persistently — is there any such thing as an other?

'Who is there?' God asks of the person knocking on the door.
'It is I.'

'Go away!' God replies.
And when the person returns and again knocks, God asks,
'Who is there?'
'It is Thou.'
'Enter,' God replies.

Is the other anything more than an idea which has specific cultural and social functions coming out of our need to see ourselves as separate, distinct, individual?

That is a valid question.

However, it does not easily take you closer to understanding your relationships with other people at the level at which you experience them: as people with whom you want to be more or less 'in touch'.

So, I am assuming that at an experiential level — how we experience ourselves and other people — there is someone who can be called me, and there is someone who is not-me who can be called other, or you.

What is most interesting about this idea of the other is that who or what the other may be, as I have said, somewhat a matter of subjective experience that depends only in part on the information the other person makes available to me. It also depends on who I want or who I unconsciously need that person to be.

> *With my thoughts I make the world.*
> *With my Self I make the Other.*

You see a photograph of a violent rapist in the newspaper — you gaze at him with loathing. You meet the woman who has broken the heart of your best friend — you can tell at once that she is a bitch. Your spouse was beaten by her parents as a child — you can scarcely bring yourself to be civil to them. Someone saves the life of your child — your home and heart are ever afterward open to this person.

To the flow of recognition between my 'I' and your 'you' I bring my desires, my prejudices, and the force of my needs — conscious and unconscious — to the 'evidence' before me. In doing this, I create my own version of you. What this adds up to is that you are a somewhat different other for each person with whom you have contact.

I find this thought intriguing and also something of a relief!

And it seems to be true even within the most unequivocally intimate relationships such as parents and children have. Ask two or three siblings to describe their parents and you will hear two or three different versions, each one of which is 'true'. That is, it is true of that person's experience.

Ask each parent to describe their child and, again, two children are likely to emerge from the narrative except when the parents have done a great deal of cross-telling, merging their experiences into one spoken version. This does not, however, necessarily mean that their feelings coincide so tightly. Rather, it may indicate that those two adults cannot easily tolerate difference and have unconsciously agreed to meld their interpretations, thus minimising their anxieties.

My version — the true version

It is an exceptionally useful piece of information for me to know that I am creating my own version of you. However (and alas), even when I know this, and even when I accept that my creation of you is somewhat different from anyone else's creation and experience of you, *I am still likely to behave as though there was only one version of you* — mine. Worse yet, I am more than likely to carry on as though my version of you contains some essential truth and is the *correct* version, more correct even than your own.

How rarely do you hear someone say 'I *experience* my husband as a pig' and how frequently do you hear an absolute statement instead ('My husband *is* a pig.' 'My daughter is impossible.' 'My boss is a bully.' 'My wife is self-pitying.').

The very human addendum to that is if you think your husband is a pig you will want others to agree. In fact, you are likely to think rather piggish thoughts about me should I disagree! What's more, in your heart of hearts you will probably want your husband also to agree. If he were not such a pig he *would accept that what you see is who he is*, however different his internal experiences of himself might be. It sounds outrageous, I know, but this is how almost all of us function, even when we 'know better' and are aware of what we are doing.

Similarly, if you think your new lover, Angelo, is the sweetest man who has ever been in your life and your bed, you will want me to see this right away also! You want your version of your lover to be *who Angelo is* (in order that your self-created Angelo can be confirmed).

And when this doesn't happen? When your dearest friend confides in you that your Monsieur Piggy is *her* best lover ever, and that your Angelo is a two-timing tart, how should you take this?

Do you cast her out, telling her that she is wicked as well as wrong? Does your self-created view of the other collapse — Piggy is now seen as not so bad, Angelo as superficial and cheap? Does your sense of self collapse, throwing into disarray your trust in your own judgement?

It should not be difficult to accept the idea that someone else is, *in your experience of them*, in part your self-creation.

But it is difficult and sometimes impossible. Impossible because accepting the idea that you are in part creating your 'other' forces you to take on board a high degree of self-responsibility. Few of us will do that.

It is also difficult because you are blessed with the power of fantasy (out of your own wishes, needs, desires you can create a more wonderful or more terrible other, whatever the 'evidence' before you). And you are also cursed with a drive to control those around you.

And why should you want to do this?

The short and now familiar answer is in order to minimise your fears of helplessness, those same fears which go back in an unbroken line to infancy when mother (your first and most important other) was all-powerful, and when you really were utterly dependent on her capacity to *give herself over to your needs* so that within your infant universe the world felt safe.

Reality has changed. You no longer need someone else to give you that level of total attention in order to survive. But parts of you don't know that. When people refuse to act in ways which you think best (for yourself, if not for them!), you may well go into panic mode.

It can be profoundly disturbing, as any parent of a wilful teenager will testify, to have significant others who refuse to allow you even a remnant of the illusion that you have some control over their lives and destiny.

The reasons seem relatively simple.

The world is a frightening place. What you cannot control, what you cannot predict, can seem unendurably threatening. This very human fear has been exploited since political leaders first took to standing on rocks; it is the fear which right-wing certainty exploits with its spurious promises of order predictability, control.

Within more liberal traditions lip service is given to the idea that other people should be as free — free to be themselves — as you are. Yet at a level just below our rational exterior, our good manners and our well-meaning liberalism is a pretty fierce desire that it is *our needs which will be ascendant*. And all this in order to stem the anxiety which accompanies the transmutation of those precious notions — difference, change, freedom — from theory into practice.

Sucking someone in

Again, we need to consider the value of cultivating a steady sense of self.

Writing in the mid-1980s on 'The Myth of Endless Love', Dennis Altman said, 'Feminists were right in stressing the need to love oneself before one could love someone else. I don't mean by this the "looking after number one" ideology which has had such a vogue on American best-seller lists, but rather what Greg Millen, writer of the film, The Clinic, had in mind when he said: "A relationship doesn't work until you accept that it may break up tomorrow, and if it does you'll be all right."'

This does not imply a pseudo-tough stance of fake invulnerability. It does not exclude the possibility of feeling sad, mourning, grieving, raging if the relationship comes to an end. But it does exclude the possibility of feeling that without You, *I* will no longer exist.

The crucial question is not: am I with Someone, but rather, am I Someone?

The needier you are and the less you trust that someone is at home in your own inner world, the more likely it is you will need to keep people out — or suck people in.

'Sucking in' is not intimacy. It is using someone as a 'self-object' to fill up your emotional holes in an attempt to make up for the nourishing and nurturing that probably did not take place at the appropriate time, or in the way that you needed it. 'Suckers' of this kind may not be nasty vampires; indeed they can be charming and persuasive, exuding an aura of intimacy which is easy to mistake for the real thing — at least until you get up close.

Lucy Goodison is a fine writer and thinker on psychological and spiritual matters. She suggests that many people who are strongly charismatic are concealing a neurotic drive for intimacy impelled by an inability to 'contain' or bear aloneness. The need they radiate is itself seductive, giving people the feeling that 'there is a place for me here'. There is also an apparent openness characteristic of such people, a broadly embracing charm which will almost certainly effectively mask feelings of emptiness, again, feelings which are so feared they cannot be consciously recognised and must be avoided by 'sucking in' so that others may 'fill them up'.

This term *sucking in* is doubly defining, for such people are likely to have emotional handicaps which began during their 'sucking era' in early infancy when the infant's need is paramount to be 'held' both physically and emotionally (held and acknowledged as a whole person).

The compulsive womaniser whose most satisfying feeling is one of conquest as yet another woman passes through his bed may come into this category. And part of his power surely comes from the potent mix of sexual energy and neediness which he both consciously and unconsciously displays.

The seductive, promiscuous woman who charms lovers into her bed but gets no sustaining pleasure from sex may also be revealing this painful inner emptiness which urges her toward new sensation to avoid intolerable self-knowledge, or consciousness of lack of self.

Men who use physical violence against women, in Goodison's view, similarly lack the 'ego boundaries' to contain their emotional vulnerability. They suck someone in, and invade her. Goodison names this invasion as the ultimate violence. The woman who is sucked in becomes, in the man's emotional framework, part of the man, and therefore vulnerable to being kicked out, kicked on, or plain kicked. Sucking in and kicking out are two halves of this neurotic picture. The kicking out may not

be physical violence. It can be emotional violence, or neglect.
Karin May: *She is taken up, she is put down/and what is she to do/but think of it as put-down?/Should she be put out?/Whatever did the girl expect?*

This kind of emptiness/openness is a psychic pain which is ungendered, although the effects of it will differ according to gender.

If a woman experiences herself as having no internal boundaries so that when she 'sucks in' she feels invaded, she will also have to be violent or, more usually, numb. But when she is violent, her violence is often acted out against her own self rather than against the man who 'carries' the threat of submersion.

19

When intimacy has a chance

Oscar and Jude are in their early twenties. They are successful and happy in their work. Their social life is hectic. They are as optimistic as young cynics can be, and they have each other. Are they happy together?

They have a wonderful sex life. Each of them is keen to mention this and to talk at length about it. But happiness ... they hesitate.

Jude says, 'I never know what Oscar is doing. It makes me frantic, he's so casual. Even now that we're living together I never have the sense that I can pin him down. I know he thinks I'm a nag, but I feel frightened sometimes and it drives me crazy.'

Oscar says, 'I adore Jude. She's a great girl, gorgeous, you can see that, but she wants to know where I am all the time. If I'm not at her side she's phoning and checking up on me. I have no chance any more to spend time with other people because she causes these huge scenes and it's just not worth it. Basically, she doesn't let me out except with her and to work. Last week, for instance, I know she did agree that I could see some guys from college but when I got home she threw this huge scene and stone cold denied she'd said I could go.'

Has either Oscar or Jude left home?

The breakdown of intimacy — when intimacy has existed — can frequently be traced to two linked factors:

- a refusal on the part of the other to accept or collude with your need to control them
- the breakdown of your illusion of who the other is.

When the other is no longer behaving like the other you have created (out of your needs and desires) this may be impossibly hard for you to bear.

You may feel cheated. You may also feel a tremendous loss. What you have lost are your hopes that you have found an other who suits you — or who you believe suits you. More crucially, you have lost that lovely illusion that if you could have your ideal other you would have something else as well: a sense of order and control in your life and some protection against chaos.

It is an illusion which many of us cherish. It is an illusion which is extremely difficult to give up.

When intimacy 'succeeds' — and by this I mean when trust, mutual responsibility and pleasure continue to exist beyond the romantic phases of illusion — it is because you are able to cope with the differences between your ideal other and the person who is gradually revealed to you with all the surprises, disappointments, human faults and failings that each of us has in varying measures.

In other words, when you can accept that the other is not an extension of your needs, desires and wishes but is nevertheless someone you can enjoy, trust and appreciate, then intimacy has some chance.

Is that difficult to imagine?

To return to Jude and Oscar, Jude would, in an ideal world, accept that Oscar's idea of togetherness is not the same as her own. She would see that keeping his moves secret is part of who Oscar is, and that being with other people sometimes, without her, is part of what Oscar wants. This may not be how she wants Oscar to be. But Jude cannot by wishing it transform Oscar into that ideal person, nor even pursue her attempts to do so without great cost (to herself, to Oscar, and eventually to the relationship).

Oscar might, again in an ideal world, find out that although he believes he wants Jude to be more self-sufficient ('freer'), in fact there is some part of him which is reassured by the attention he is getting when she phones, screams, throws scenes.

It is possible to speculate that although Oscar is complaining, he is also colluding with this push-me-pull-you aspect of their relationship and is unconsciously encouraging Jude to behave in a possessive and unrewarding way. With some help he could think about the ideal Jude he wants, the Jude he is actually experiencing, and attempt to understand what he is getting out of that rather dramatic difference between those two Judes. Having done that, he may be able to let Jude be genuinely rather than theoretically 'free' to express her own self within their self-and-other relationship.

It would also seem that if each person felt more reassured about the other one, the temperature of their relationship could come down to a level where discussion and negotiation could take place. But what must precede a comfortable self-and-other relationship is a reasonably good sense of self within each of the two people, and at least some sense that their safety resides within their own selves, and has not been leased out to the other person.

Between people who have little sense of separate self, and who are in a self-and-other muddle, there is very little *relating* going on. There is a great deal of demanding — but much of it remains unheard and unanswered.

While both Oscar and Jude feel needy and unfulfilled, it is difficult for either to step back and appreciate the other person's point of view, or even to acknowledge that the other person has a valid point of view. In this current scenario, each is making a great deal of noise about what 'I want', but gives little evidence of steady contact with their own individual sense of self or a willingness to take on the other person's wholeness.

Does this mean that Jude and Oscar's relationship is not intimate?

No and yes. Their relationship appears to tie them up intimately, and they see themselves as mutually dependent. But it does not appear to be a relationship between two whole selves. Rather, it is a relationship in which each person's functions — or lack of functioning — dominates.

Each is overwhelmed by what she or he wants. Those 'wants' feel paramount. Neither is able to discover how this coincides with what the other person wants.

Where these wants coincide — around sex — their relationship is 'blissful'. When these wants are less obviously in harmony

— around the issues of time together and time apart — their relationship ceases to be much of a relationship and is instead a battle for self-supremacy.

No *intimacy without isolation*

Satisfying experiences of intimacy depend on an awareness that isolation is as much a part of the human condition as closeness is. Indeed, without some acceptance of that 'essential aloneness' which is part of the human condition, the experience of closeness is often difficult.

Coming home from talking to Jude and Oscar I found myself looking again at my notes from the interview I had done with Rebecca. Sitting on the floor in her Soho flat, reflecting on her present life and happiness, Rebecca had stressed to me how important meeting her current partner had been in helping her to discover new and freer attitudes.

'You have to find somebody who doesn't want to control you and who wants you to be yourself, and who actually likes what you are and not what they want you to be.

'But I couldn't get used to it. It took ages. I was still thinking along the same lines for ages... but it was amazing to meet someone who wasn't possessive about you but watched you with enjoyment when you were being yourself! That was really incredible. And I am only really beginning to enjoy that.

'My previous boyfriends had been musicians and very selfish really, and wanted me to be part of their world. And made it very attractive. Not unattractive men at all, and very stimulating. But not like him. Just wanting to possess me and put me in their world. Not wanting to see me from a distance. And although there are problems about distance and distant relationships there are also good things — which I have discovered.'

Two halves longing to become one whole is still the myth of which some romances are made, but in general people are more aware that where there is a loss of self within a relationship, there is also more likely to be an impoverished or endangered relationship.

Yet many relationships depend for daily ease and survival on one person's capacity to be flexible: to be able to give rather than take; to be able to accept rather than demand; to be able to hold back rather than rush forward; to change when change is needed.

It is no coincidence that in heterosexual relationships it is far more likely to be the woman whose sense of self is less 'ego-bound' and more adaptable. It is also no coincidence that it is likely to be the woman who is in much greater danger of allowing her sense of her own unique self to slide or be submerged into a 'we-self' which largely serves the needs of the male partner.

This comes about for many reasons:

- The woman is likely to have been socialised into emphasising an awareness of others rather than self-awareness (believing that self-awareness may be synonymous with selfishness).
- The woman may be more flexible than her male partner.
- Her sense of self may be less burdened by her sense of how the world judges her.
- Her self-worth may depend on her capacity to make life pleasant and agreeable for others.

But all this preparedness to be accommodating does not mean that she is freed from the costs of losing herself within the relationship; on the contrary. And she may additionally pay a price for her male partner's inability to get in touch with his inner world of feeling and attunement with others, especially if his instrumental, rational mode pushes him to despise what may be her more intuitive, inclusive way of being.

One self accommodating the other

In gay and lesbian relationships there is also likely to be one person who 'gives in' rather more than the other one, whether consciously or voluntarily. Meeting two men at a theatre festival gave me an example of this.

Larry is a gay actor–director with a large following worldwide. He and Jack have been together for five years. Jack was an athletics teacher and a good one, but Larry hated to travel alone, Jack hated to see Larry go off alone, and so Jack has given up his career to be full-time partner to Larry.

So far, so good. Yet talking to these two men it is possible to notice the same patterns of 'we-dom' which some heterosexual couples display.

'We're taking a year off this year,' Jack said. 'We have had such marvellous invitations and anyway after putting on the same kinds of shows several times over, we need a change. This year will give us space to think about that.'

Does Jack write the shows with Larry?

Well, no, he does not. But his self-identity is now caught up with Larry's. While they still 'totally adore each other' this might be fine. But when one or other needs to breathe a little more independently, this could feel like a devastating blow to the other one, and like a huge disruption within their we-locked relationship.

Nora and Hilary were a couple I knew over several years. They had independent careers and also a tiny farm where they errati- cally tended sheep, raised chickens, and did a fine Vita/Virginia imitation in their large and rambling garden.

They were, understandably, proud of their relationship which they displayed through their possessions, their livestock and plants, and the charming way in which each 'presented' the other.

Whether they were alone or together their conversations were scattered with references to the abilities of the other one. Each shone for and through her lover.

'How clever she is/*how clever I am.*'

'How successful she is/*how successful I am.*'

'How lovable she is/*how lovable I am.*'

There is nothing wrong with taking pleasure in the person you love, but there was an intermingling of selves which did seem even at the time, among the chickens and the roses, to be somewhat fudging of the boundaries between two separate selves.

In the end Nora and Hilary did not live happily ever after — at least, not with each other. They had a messy parting which, almost inevitably, involved someone else. (I say 'almost inevi- tably' because the person who is so heavily invested in a we-self relationship is unlikely to be able to make the break alone, if indeed a break is needed.)

Several years later each woman has a tale to tell of pain, unresolved sadness, anger and recrimination — one which almost mirrors that of her former partner. Each feels she has been hurt, cheated, misunderstood.

Nora and Hilary now share a sense of disillusionment which probably has very similar proportions to the idealisation which once they found so buoyant.

Same-gender relationships can bring to each partner a level of understanding which heterosexuals may long for and envy. But same-gender relationships by no means automatically solve the dangers inherent when too many needs are piled onto one sexually intimate relationship, or when the self-and-other dance is performed cheek to cheek, for then individual, personal power is inevitably eroded, along with a vital sense of separate self.

It is impossible — and useless — to say with any certainty whether Nora and Hilary's relationship might have been saved if the two women could have experienced each other within their relationship as two separate people instead of what became an overwhelming we-self which required a dramatic break to shake it. This resulted in the loss of a relationship which had many positive aspects.

I am not, however, talking about conscious choice here. I am talking about two women who felt themselves to be swept into a relationship (on that vigorous high tide called lust), who thought themselves enormously 'lucky' then just as dramatically 'unlucky', and who did not know how to ask themselves whether things could be a little different between them.

Like most of us, Nora and Hilary found themselves and their own relationship tremendously absorbing, yet not an arena where conscious choice should be exercised:

Are things going the way we both want them?

Are things going the way that suits us *individually*?

Could they be different?

How could we make them different?

Where do we find room to negotiate?

Can you survive it if I say what I mean?

A couple of years from now each woman may well be able to see how she and her lover got into that self-and-other muddle, but without the distance that hindsight gives, it can be only too easy to be lost in emotion, and lost to thought.

When feeling and thinking are muddled functions it is very difficult, as you have seen within this book, to:

• sort out past from present
• distinguish between self and other

- avoid thinking in black and white terms ('She's wrong.' 'I'm right.').

The lucky person who has a sense of him or herself as a separate self, who is enjoying intimacy with another separate self, has a fair chance of being able to allow for differences without feeling threatened.

Acceptance of difference, and of the inevitability of change, can be experienced as lack of interest or care. And perhaps sometimes that is precisely what it is. Yet it need not be. A conscious willingness to accommodate difference can reflect a genuine interest in the other person's growth and well-being. It can also reflect a deep recognition that while your friend or your partner is fully alive and open to change *you will be the beneficiary*. For there can be few situations more stifling than those where someone clings to the raft of the past, and attempts to hold you there with them.

Boundaries are good for intimacy

Being intimate means, I think, being true to yourself in the presence of someone else and accepting the other person being their own self in your presence.

Being intimate does not mean:
- behaving as though you were one person
- dictating how the other person should behave
- expecting the other person to take care of your needs
- denigrating the other person because you believe they have no choice but to take it.

That kind of pseudo-intimacy is often horribly damaging, not least because it erodes the sense of personal power which is crucial to a comfortable relationship with others, and with yourself.

In psuedo-intimacy several things are likely to happen:
- your sense of I diminishes rather than grows
- you feel increasingly dependent upon 'your other half'
- your sense of *who is in charge of your life* becomes muddled
- your sense of the larger world shrinks.

'Hand in hand,' says Jungian analyst Robert Stein, 'with the need to be coupled goes the need to be uncoupled, always there as soon as the coupling instinct moves us toward another person. Seen from this perspective, the freedom the soul needs is to be able to experience being simultaneously coupled and uncoupled.'

When two people are together, enjoying their 'separateness' as well as their 'togetherness', enjoying relationships with a diversity of people other than their sexual partner, this is a very different experience from that where sameness of feeling, expression and purpose is worshipped — whatever the cost.

A quote from Claudine is useful here. She is speaking as the veteran of a marriage and of several long-term relationships with women.

'For me intimacy involves letting down the boundaries of my personality which separate me from other people. But I see this as a temporary merging, possible only because it is temporary and not permanent.

'I would guess that in most permanent merging one person is actually in control, even if the other person is colluding with that. To me you don't have intimacy if one person is in control. Part of intimacy for me is the relinquishing of control on both people's parts.'

What struck me when thinking about this was Claudine's affirmation that *it is possible to choose to let down your boundaries only when you have a reasonably safe sense of self.*

Boundaries are, like self and other, concepts only and subject to many interpretations of meaning. Yet, still like the concepts of self and other, they are rarely neutral in your actual experience. Most of us know whether or not we have a sense of 'boundary' in our relationships with other people:

- Your boundaries allow you to sense where you end and where I begin.
- Your boundaries allow you to feel for me when I hurt, to share my hurt, but to know that it is my hurt — and not yours.
- Your boundaries allow you to understand that when I am angry it is not necessarily because of something you have done, and to know that when I am depressed it is not necessarily your responsibility to 'cheer me up'.
- Your boundaries allow you to know that when you are angry or depressed or anxious that it is not my fault, and that the effects of your anger or depression or anxiety should not be laid at my feet or poured over my head.

In other words, if you and I are in a relationship together we can, with our boundaries in place, feel a great deal for each other, while also acknowledging that neither one of us is responsible for the emotional happiness or distress of the other.

This does not mean that I cannot make you unhappy, or that you cannot brighten my day immeasurably. Of course that can happen. Two or more people who relate closely to each other will have continuous and often dramatic effects on each other's feelings: *and part of intimacy is being aware of and respectful of that*.

What is not intimacy is the feeling that my happiness is dependent on you; or that because we live side by side you have the right to make me unhappy.

This quote from poet Rainer Maria Rilke says it most beautifully:

We need, in love, to practise only this:
letting each other go. For holding on
comes easily; we do not need to learn it.

We do not need to learn *holding on* because that is what we learned in our families of origin — either because we had it, or we needed it and felt our longing for it. Families are prime sites for self-and-other muddles and the fear that intimacy leads to a loss of self, which so many people correctly associate with family life, often keeps people fearful of intimacy, sometimes for a lifetime.

20

Unconscious limitations on intimacy

If a relationship is to allow each person to grow individually, it is vital to acknowledge that each person is individual and separate, and is deserving of respect and 'space' *even when they are not fitting in with your idea of how things should be*.

This life-saving slip of information, however, will not automatically save you from continuing to muddle up:

- self with other
- past with present
- thinking with feeling.

Nor will it automatically allow you to have your intimacy needs met within the relationships that presently exist in your life. It will not even necessarily help you to bring a new quality of intimacy into future relationships.

And why not?

Because of the push of your own history, those aspects of your life which are repressed and unconscious. In intimate relationships, when you are least hidden by the masks of everyday life and civility, your unconscious can push you very hard indeed, often without your understanding why, or what the consequences will be.

For some of those behaviours 'caused' by unconscious forces there are terms which gather under the heading *ego-defence mechanisms*. These terms should be used with caution, but they can help make sense of chaotic and unruly behaviour emerging from within yourself, and between yourself and other people.

Abraham and Daisy's story which follows most neatly illustrates what I mean. These are not, however, patterns which emerge between couples or in families only. These same behavioural 'mechanisms' — almost always demonstrating on the 'outside' some conflictual clash that is happening on the 'inside' — may be preventing you from being intimate in a sustaining way, *or from being intimate in any way at all*.

Abraham and Daisy are two pleasant, well-intentioned people who live together in a smart, sparsely furnished apartment in the heart of a major city.

Daisy is feeling irritable with Abraham. Her period is due and she hasn't found time to go swimming. The only thing that has cheered her up for ages is the persistent attention she is getting from Gary, one of the most highly regarded men in her office. She enjoys this, but feels guilty.

She and Abraham are committed to monogamy. It is not just the healthiest way, it is the only way for people like them (as she unselfconsciously thinks).

Abraham arrives home with spicy chicken from the local takeaway. Daisy greets him with a warm smile. She reads women's magazines which specialise in articles on how to get and keep a man. That matters to Daisy.

When they have sucked the last bones of the chicken and drunk the last drops of their additive-free apple cider, Abraham mentions, again, a colleague, Juliana. He waxes at some length about the great results Juliana is getting in her preparations for a recorder concert with her class of intellectually disabled kids.

An hour later Abraham is still defending himself against Daisy's accusations of actual or incipient infidelity. Along the way each has heard a number of other statements which have startled and hurt.

Daisy has become convinced that Abraham is sleeping around and probably not only with Juliana. She has also become convinced that Abraham no longer finds her desirable and wishes that he had never married her in the first place.

Abraham is mightily tempted to lash back at Daisy about the crap she leaves lying around, and how she never reads a decent book any more, only those absurd, expensive magazines. He longs to say that she is a lazy-minded, predictable slob and not the forthright woman of lively opinions he thought he had married. The kind of woman Juliana still is, although that comparison had never actually occurred to him as he is too busy not admitting to himself that in praising Juliana's teaching, he is setting aside his very real fears that when the next promotion comes up, smart Juliana will get it and not solid Abraham.

Instead of saying any of that, Abraham hears himself telling Daisy what he thinks about her father, that selfish shit who is still charging them as much as a bank would for the money he lent them when he could have given them the money, for God's sake.

Tossing aside the cider, Abraham stalks to the liquor cabinet to pour himself a hefty scotch.

The night is not over yet.

Daisy has *projected* onto Abraham her interest in getting sexually involved with someone else. She is behaving as though those sexual desires were his and not her own.

The more excited Daisy becomes about her imagined scenario of Juliana and Abraham having a wild time in bed, the more she is *denying* her own interest in Gary. This interest may be a barometer of the bumps appearing in her marriage, or perhaps it is an indicator that she had got used to the excitement of sex which went with less certain relationships than she now has with steady Abraham who in turn sees her, she believes, as domesticated Daisy. Add to that Gary's prestige in the office, which romping with him would allow her briefly to 'borrow', and fancying Gary becomes a fairly complex proposition.

Abraham, meanwhile, has *displaced* his sense of injustice about Daisy's accusations onto Daisy's father's tight-fistedness.

He has also unconsciously chosen to defend his ego and decrease his anxiety about Juliana by engaging in what is called a *reaction formation*. This means that how he is behaving does not reflect how he is feeling. (In some part of himself he would like to see Juliana trip over her pile of recorders and fall flat on her face while he strides forwards to collect the promotion. He agrees that it's high time women were promoted. But why doesn't his stomach feel better, and what about the pain in his neck?)

Just for now things seem clear to Abraham. After all, he had done nothing worse than come home with spicy chicken and the expectation of a pleasant if unremarkable evening with his wife. He would now like to let fly at Daisy. The more he looks at her and listens to her complaints the more clearly he realises that she is a shrew and the further he gets away from his *unconscious* anxiety, produced by her accusations about Juliana, that she will find out that his praise of Juliana masks his unacknowledged desire to see her fail, and his *conscious* anxiety that Daisy will discover that when they were engaged he fucked her delicious sister, Sally.

Abraham has all but repressed the memory. He was sorry and so was Sally. But when the topic of infidelity comes up he feels a sneaking suspicion that this is part of the price of manhood. His own father, Jake, was a womaniser and regards good, kind Abraham as a wimp. Abraham loathed his father's behaviour as a child and still does most of the time, but riled up as he is now, and full of righteous rage against Daisy's father, Abraham thinks more kindly of Jake.

Abraham is *identifying* with Jake, giving his sense of self-worth a little help which he certainly believes he needs in the face of Daisy's onslaught.

The night is still not over.

Seeing the scotch in Abraham's hand is just about the last straw for Daisy. (It won't be the last straw. After a couple of miserable days they will make up but the scars may take longer to fade.)

Daisy's own father was a drunk. He called himself a social drinker but surely most social drinkers don't end their day unconscious? Adult Daisy now has the power to despise all drinkers and the sight of Abraham with a bottle in his hand makes her literally weep with rage and despair. She is unable to remind herself that drunkenness is not one of Abraham's faults. Daisy is caught up in what is called a *transference* situation. She is reacting to Abraham as though his drinking were her father's constant drinking, producing in her the feelings of helplessness and acute anxiety she suffered as a child.

As a child Daisy had been forced to deal not only with the upset for herself and other family members about her father's drinking, but also with the loss of the father she would like to have had (cheerful, loving and, above all, sober), instead of the unreliable man who took the ideal father's place and who was powerfully evoked by the sight of Abraham nursing his scotch.

What each self wants and is struggling to express has been sacrificed during the course of this unhappy evening to those behaviours 'produced' by each person's ego-defence mechanisms *and the deep inner conflicts they seek to conceal.*

- There has been little awareness of self, and virtually no recognition of the legitimacy of the other.
- The present has been dominated by the past.
- In the turmoil of accusation and counter-accusation, thinking and feeling have become hopelessly muddled.

At the end of a long evening, Abraham and Daisy feel exhausted, cheated and distressed. Each is only too ready to blame the other for their frustration and pain. Neither is ready to look inward to explore what conflicts are raging inside their own self.

I want to be loved; I want to be free.

I want to be understood; I want to have my secrets.

I want you to be known to me; I want you to surprise me.

I want you to be my ideal person; I am struggling to accept who you really are.

Could things have gone differently between Daisy and Abraham? Would it have been possible for them to express what was actually on their minds and to find some balance between their internal needs and the needs of their relationship?

Over the chicken and between sips of cider their dialogue might have gone something like this:

Daisy: I want to let you know that Gary — you know, the guy in charge of our major section — apparently fancies me.

Abraham: Who can blame him? He's obviously got great taste. And what about you?

Daisy: Well, he certainly is charming, and he's really into poetry. That's something that surprised me. Yes, I guess I do feel attracted, and flattered too probably. He is the most talented man in our organisation.

Abraham: Do you want to spend some time with him?

Daisy: Yes, I do. How would you feel about that?

Abraham: I reckon I could cope. Things have been a bit quiet between the two of us lately. I guess both of us could benefit from some admiration. There's a music specialist who's been coming to school, a really lovely fellow. I might see if he and I can get together for a concert and a meal.

Daisy: Sounds good. What about the weekend after next? I could spend the day with Gary in the mountains.

Abraham: Maybe we should also plan something special for us — one of those weekend meditations perhaps? But as you have raised the topic of Gary I want to talk to you about Juliana. I have seniority over her but I am getting really concerned that she'll get Drummond's job when he retires, and not me.

Daisy: You keep talking, darling, and I'll give your neck a rub...

It's okay. I am joking! That kind of dialogue would rarely be possible between real people. This is because we are, in our experience of self, a mixture which ranges from greedy infant to wise old being, from coolly rational to wildly accusatory and over-reactive. *And in your experience of the other, and in the way you create the other, those varying senses of self are all reflected*:

• We want to be slaves and we want to be masters.
• We want to be free to express our deepest thoughts and feelings; we find it hard to receive the thoughts and feelings of others without judgement and reaction.
• We want love, and we don't want love to bind us.
• We want to be ourselves, and often we don't know who this person is — or might be.
• We want those with whom we are intimate also to be themselves — but not to behave in ways which don't suit us.

Are you laughing at this last point? I hope so, for it is part of the human condition to be greedy and unreasonable. And it is crucial to maturity to acknowledge that. But in living in a world with other equally greedy and unreasonable human beings you are best off when you can understand what *needs lie behind your cries of 'I want'*.

Understanding our motives

One of Freud's most crucial insights was also one of the simplest: that we are frequently unaware of our motives.

This was the case with Abraham and Daisy. It does not ask

much of us to recognise similar short-circuiting in our own lives. Without understanding our own motives we can get caught up in believing that everything uncomfortable which happens to us is someone else's fault and that everything would be all right if only the partner we are now with could get their act together and do what we want or, better yet, if the Ultimate Rescuer would come to save us. (Hurry up! Hurry up!)

Abraham and Daisy are in all of us. Inner conflict is likely to be battering at you a good deal of the time. Hate as well as love is always part of your deepest feelings, and hate as well as love is most likely to be expressed towards those with whom you are intimate and upon whom you most depend.

'He says that he loves me. He says that I am the most important person in the world. But I am the one he comes home and dumps on, not the men at work, not his parents, me, his wife. It's not fair.'

This aspect of our inner life is often one we shy away from. Our capacity to hate, to envy, to destroy is not something we can easily find ways to talk about. However, it is part of who we are, and it is part of *how* we are in situations of intimacy.

But that knowledge rarely fits with our self-image. We would prefer not to be found out. And when we are 'found out', when our explosions of contempt toward ourselves and others are witnessed by those with whom we are intimate, it takes considerable courage to try to find out what needs lie behind those outbursts. It also takes courage to avoid blaming others, and thereby denying the complex reality of our own self.

Few of us understand why we do things, how we feel about them, whether we could behave differently. Freud was right. Our motives remain a mystery to us, and most of us accept this, too, without serious question.

Of all our attempts to understand the world and how it works, we can be most obtuse about and most resistant to knowing about our own motives and how those motives affect our intimate relationships.

The accusations flow so easily ('It is selfish to be self-aware.' 'Therapy is only for the weak.' 'Navel-gazers are time-wasters.' 'Understanding yourself is an occupation for head-bangers.' 'How could you spend time on yourself when the revolution is waiting/the stock exchange is waiting/the television is waiting/ sex, drugs and dirty dancing are waiting?').

Such accusations deny feeling, and express a great fear of feeling, but they can be tremendously powerful, and murderous to intimacy.

Intimacy implies an understanding between two people that their inner worlds are at least somewhat knowable and do matter. When one person in an intimate relationship pulls down the blind on his or her own inner world, denying feeling, and denying interest in that inner life, then intimacy becomes extremely difficult to sustain.

When your partner is willing to treat you badly or shut you out he (or she) is unconsciously telling you how he feels about himself. *For you cannot feel more for another person than you are capable of feeling for yourself.*

If your partner can't look at his (or her) own behaviour with insight and compassion he will be hard pushed to show you any genuine compassion either. What you are more likely to get is sentimentality, anger or even contempt, the same contempt which he feels for himself. This is the dark face of intimacy: when the self-and-other relationship leads away from the feeling that both people matter, and towards a *mélange* of feeling in which distress, mistrust and self-and-other loathing dominate.

Re-making the past in the present

The best possible foundations for a strong sense of self — and for rewarding experiences of intimacy — are laid when the mother has the capacity to be fully present while the child needs that and gradually to separate as that becomes appropriate, and when the father is capable of being supportive of the mother during the intense stages of early mothering and even more fully 'present' himself as the child grows and develops.

These foundations may not have been laid down as you would have wished, and there is nothing that you can do to remake the past. *But there are ways in which the effects of the past can be remade in the present.*

A few months after my interview with Ned, he called to ask if I would be interested in talking to his half-brother, a man in his fifties who is an Anglican priest. I was intrigued, and within a few days had begun the first of several talks with William, a small, lively man whose enthusiasm for life was contagious.

William is convinced that it is possible to change the emotional course of one's life. He knows that it is a difficult and never-ending process, and he does believe that he has the help of God, a belief which is not available to everyone. He also believes that it is usually through adversity that one makes a leap forward in terms of self-and-other understanding. This became most clear when he talked about his wife Isabelle and their thirty-year marriage.

'My wife and I got married soon after I had made the decision to become a priest. I assumed she was making a decision not only to be a wife but to be a priest's wife. I expect I thought — though not consciously — that this was a pretty superior role for a woman. It declared her spiritual commitment in a very upfront way.

'Years went by and we had the children and the usual ups and downs of a busy parish life. Then my wife had a nervous breakdown. She was hospitalised. She was so depressed she literally could not function.

'Well, gradually she did get better and after considerable psychotherapy which she had by herself she made me go with her to marriage guidance sessions. We struck lucky with our counsellor and after some time I made some startling discoveries. Startling. They rocked me to my core, I can tell you.

'I realised that my wife is someone to whom I feel deeply attached, but she isn't me, she isn't our marriage, and I am not her.

'There's no way of saying that without sounding foolish. But it took that dreadful crisis of Isabelle's for me to begin to acknowledge rationally that she is a separate being from myself, and to move on from that acknowledgement to try to make the emotional and even practical changes which were necessary after such an insight.

'Because our work, our vocations as I saw it, were so intertwined, we had become rather more entangled than if our professional lives had been conventionally separate. Although I want to emphasise that that entanglement had suited me, or anyway it had been comfortable enough that I would never have dreamed of questioning it. For me there was nothing to question. But my wife was dying through this entanglement.

'I haven't found these discoveries easy. Putting change into effect has not been easy at all. But my wife has been marvellous. She has been determined that we should not slip back into our bad old ways.

'Formerly if she were to express thoughts or feelings which seemed foreign to me — and I suppose she rarely did that — I would have cut her off. There would have been no question of my trying to respond. I would call that laziness now. And underneath the laziness was fear, I am quite sure.

'Now, at least most of the time, I am learning that Isabelle does have thoughts and feelings that I can cope with and which interest me. More to the point, so do I. Had I not been forced to see us as two separate people we would never have reached this new level of closeness and interest in one another which is quite different from our prior symbiotic nesting. It feels, I must say, like a most undeserved blessing on all our lives.

'There has been another spin-off also. I've found new joy in my spiritual practices which had become somewhat mechanical as the years went by.

'It's ironical really, I had always known that we die and go alone into the presence of God but there I was wrapped into and around my wife! I was dependent on her and unaware that my dependence was killing her. I was under her nose. She was under my nose. And still her breakdown came as a total surprise. I find that thought most dreadfully shocking.

'Isabelle is an intelligent woman who has never been a doormat, but I had come to see her through and through as "my wife" or secondarily as "the children's mother", and almost never as Isabelle.'

The ironies are clear. While William and Isabelle were in a self-and-other muddle, neither person had much idea what was going on with the other one, and neither person had much idea of what was going on with their own self. This lead Isabelle to break down, and gave William no warning of that breakdown before it happened.

Liberated from their need to be united, each can now see the other as a separate being and through so doing can also expe-

242 Intimacy & Solitude

rience the uniqueness of their own self. This has dramatically changed their levels of self-trust and self-acceptance. Moreover, they can trust that their relationship is not endangered by those secret dreams, thoughts and longings which each of us has, and which too rampant 'togetherness' can so readily imperil.

Overloading intimate relationships

The brilliant, inspiring family therapist, Carl Whitaker, emphasises the paradox that intimacy is supported by less rather than more 'togetherness'. 'The family's capacity to be intimate and caring and their capacity to be separate and divergent increase in careful synchrony. People can't risk being close unless they have the ability to be separate — it's too frightening to be deeply involved if you aren't sure you can be separate and stand on your own.'

William's remarks show what Whitaker means. It was not until Isabelle's breakdown forced the break-up of their old enmeshed patterns that William and Isabelle could experience themselves as two people living closely together, each one of them with separate needs, desires, thoughts and feelings which will sometimes be congruent, and sometimes be at odds. Out of this separateness they have found a new closeness.

That may not always be the case. The step from being enmeshed to feeling separate may lead to ... not much more than feeling separate. That, too, can be liberating.

Tomas described such a situation a year or more after our first meetings.

'Both Margaretta and I have thought a great deal about the issue of separateness and especially on not feeling depressed and guilty if we are not making the other one happy. I think we have made unexpected progress. I find myself much more often surprised by her and of course that's a delight in a long-term relationship like ours. In fact, my awareness that she can surprise me — and maybe also that I can still surprise myself — is the new element I feel most optimistic about. Overall, I'd say I feel lighter and less burdened. But are we closer? No. I don't believe that was what we were after. Closeness was double-edged for us; it felt suffocating as well as wonderful. At this phase in our lives the separateness we have while still being together is pretty good. What does Margaretta think? You would have to ask her!'

Talking to Tomas, and later to Margaretta, about the changes in their long relationship, I was again reminded that it is also Carl Whitaker who makes it explicit that most of us bring too many needs to our intimate relationships.

'It is very difficult,' says Whitaker, 'to be both parent and lover to someone at the same time.' By this he means, being both caretaking parent of and lover to your adult partner. He goes on, 'Once you each become sure that you can handle life's basic stresses on your own, helping has a different meaning.'

When both people in a relationship are fairly secure in their sense of self they aren't likely, Whitaker believes, 'to ask really major help from each other. They accept life's pain, its aloneness and its stress as something they must handle themselves.'

Whitaker acknowledges that for most people 'life can be more pleasant if they share some of the stress with someone else but they don't usually try to escape the basic demands of living [self-awareness, self-responsibility] by *making that someone else feel responsible for them as people*'.

You may well pause as you read this, for we are all affected by the myths of intimacy, central to which is the mighty myth of the Ultimate Rescuer. (Someone can make me happier than I can make myself. Someone can bring more life to my life.)

Free to see this as a myth you can more readily locate the only Ultimate Rescuer you will ever meet: your own self. From that contact with your own self, and knowing that self-and-other encounters are, in part, what you make of them, you can shift your perspective on intimacy.

You can begin to see intimacy not as something which only others have, or as something which you could have in better versions 'if only', but as a theme tune which can, like love, play more or less loudly at different times in your life and in tones of infinite and subtle variation.

And when will this be most difficult to achieve? When envy taints your emotions, even your life.

Intimacy is, like all other aspects of your emotional life, vulnerable to envy: that awful, self-defeating feeling that other people have something which you want and cannot have, or that other people have it in more satisfying ways than you will ever experience.

Then the feeling arises: I want it for myself; I want to spoil it for those other people who have what I don't have; I want to destroy those people who could give me more intimacy but who are not doing so.

Those adults who were emotionally deprived or humiliated as children — humiliated in the sense of expressing needs which were mocked, misunderstood or ignored — will be deeply vulnerable to feelings of envy and to pervasive and recurring anxiety that intimacy is something which is beyond their reach or which they may not even be entitled to have.

In Ruben's pain-filled cry that he fears longing for someone who doesn't give him a second thought, you can hear plainly the echo of the small child whose mother does not come or the mother who is unable to respond to her child in the way that the child needs. Ruben is now a man, charming, competent, but bound by his anxieties to the past and, in the present, infinitely wary that what he is longing for is way out of line. '*I am feeling pretty terrible even talking about this,*' he said. '*Ridiculous, isn't it?*'

Translating your perception of intimacy from something which is happening between two people while you remain shut out, to something which is within you and which can embrace other people, will not be achieved by a simple act of will.

But a simple act of will — of good will — can begin the process.

I am willing to be open to intimate moments and encounters.

I am willing to forego my ideas of what intimacy could or should be.

I am willing to recognise the unexpected faces which intimacy may wear.

Difficult as the concept may be to grasp, knowing that you are not dependent on one crucial other to bring intimacy into your life can be a tremendous relief. It can diminish self-judgement and self-blame. It can allow life to be lived first-hand, rather than endured in a waiting pattern.

Perhaps it is only old age or even death which will tame entirely your longing for the perfect lover, the Ultimate Rescuer, the special someone. But, meanwhile, your existence need not be postponed. The world is filled with people, none of whom may be that special someone, but many of whom may share with you an enduring feeling that you matter, and that their being with you does, in some significant way, also matter.

This can allow a life not shadowed by myths and longing for what might never happen, but shaped instead by less ambitious *pleasure in what is*, however momentary that may be.

PART FIVE

Desire: The language of your inner space

'Our love and sex lives are only as mature as we are and not more so — therefore mistakes and betrayals must happen.'

Damaris Parker-Rhodes

21

The experience of being securely held in earliest childhood,
which gives the confidence to let go, will be put to the test
again and again, especially in periods of change and risk and
perhaps most vividly in sexual love; for when the sexual
encounter is complete, it is essentially an experience of letting
go and of trust.'

Lily Pincus, *Secrets in the Family*

Wanting intimacy, wanting solitude

You want emotional support, and your freedom.

You want relationships, and to retain your individuality.

You want to be able to be alone without feeling isolated or bereft.

You want to know that you are capable of devotion without losing your sense of self.

You want self-knowledge.

You want the freedom to know others without anxiety or pre-judgement.

You want to be able to acknowledge your own conflicts without projecting them outside yourself.

You want the freedom to be yourself, and enough freedom from anxiety and envy, depression or rage to be able to tolerate other people's efforts to express who they are.

You want your uniqueness to be known. You are aware that the differences between yourself and other human beings are probably very slight.

None of this is too much to ask.

All of this is worth desiring.

The problem, or part of the problem, is that so many of us succumb to the temptation to load all our desiring onto our sexually intimate relationships. This is the relationship that is required to make up for all the pain of the past as well as the pressures of the present; the relationship that is to decide whether the future is worth welcoming.

Taking off your clothes, you may also be eager to shed the inhibitions of your adapted self. Unclothed and perhaps unarmoured, your needs may tumble onto the lap of the person with whom you are being most 'yourself'.

Yet it could be that often, or even always, this is too much of a burden for a single relationship to carry, given that even the most intimate relationship is made up not of angels, but of two human beings with multiple blindspots.

Falling in love — again

Across a crowded room, John's blue eyes meet the soft brown eyes of Janet. They gaze at each other for somewhat longer than is normally considered good manners and a number of things begin to happen.

Their heartbeats quicken and their pulses begin to race. Janet's hands sweat; she has nowhere to wipe them. John feels hot under the collar and wants to cough. Their cheeks flush. Blue and brown eyes shine. Their awareness of the room around them and of the people in it fades; their awareness of each other becomes the temporary focus of their entire being. Janet and John walk towards each other. They have met before. Each was hoping that the other would be in this crowded room tonight. Each was hoping that the other would notice, would also care, would also want to walk out of the door and into the land of happy-ever-after, that Elysian field where you can experience yourself as the wonderful person you have always wanted to be, and now are — at least in the gaze of the person who desires you.

You can follow Janet and John to Janet's house and then upstairs to her bedroom. You can sit on a soft sofa in the corner of the bedroom while they undress, slowly. They are enjoying unwrapping each other with many kisses and caresses, sips of wine, nuzzles, a word or two here and there. Janet puts on some music and takes off her slip. She has varicose veins but seems unaware of them. John is down to his underpants now but he seems equally unabashed by the weight around his middle. They move to the bed.

If you were to talk to Janet and John a week or two later you might well find them still in a rosy glow of lust, greed — and idealisation.

John is desiring — not Janet who has chronic PMT and is wildly jealous, but the Ideal Janet, whom he has in part created. The Janet of the soft eyes, the Janet of the warm welcoming arms, the Janet who hears every word he says and who strokes his head as he speaks. The Janet he has been hoping for.

Janet is also desiring — not John who goes on drinking binges, not John who has left two wives and four children, but the Ideal John, whom she, in turn, has in part created. The John who sees her as beautiful, the John who finds her wildly sensual, the John who is certain she will get the promotion she deserves. The John she has been waiting for.

Each of them relishes the other, and also what the other one sees. Isn't that the person they have always wanted to be? Isn't that the person they really are, deep inside.

'I have never felt more myself,' says John. 'I love you.'

'I have never felt more myself,' says Janet. 'I love you.'

Janet and John believe what they are saying. They *feel* the truth of what they are saying. They touch, they make love, they lay themselves open. They feel caring and cared for.

When they forget, momentarily, about the other one they do so knowing that when they remember, *the other one will still be there*. It's been a long wait.

Janet and John are re-experiencing the stages of mother-infant love that led them toward the twinned capacities to enjoy intimacy and solitude.

- I am with Someone.
- I can afford to turn my attention away from that Someone, because when I return my attention he or she is still there.
- I am experiencing my Someone's presence through my body, as well as through my emotions and mind. I am being held, physically as well as emotionally.
- My Someone can go away and if she or he comes back soon enough I will still have my safe experiences.
- I can be alone, without feeling lonely, *because of my internalised experiences of closeness*.

Janet and John are re-creating that lovely time when they were adored, admired and accepted; when they were appropriately idealised by doting parents and when their internal battles, their differences of opinion with those around them, and their exercises of will, still lay ahead in an invisible and unimaginable future.

They are renewing a sense of possibility that tells them the physical and emotional contact they want is within reach and that *they can have it without conflict*. With this comes an almost irresistible sense of being thoroughly alive: not only in the eyes of someone else, but in their own eyes also.

A month later, a year later, the Idealised Janet will have disappeared. Will the everyday John then love the everyday Janet? Can the everyday John bear to know who the everyday Janet is?

Is the solitude John needs comfortably balanced now with his need for intimacy?

Idealised John will also be no more, but can Janet love the everyday John? Can Janet bear to know who the everyday John is?

Are Janet's intimacy needs being met, and also her need for solitude?

Your guess is as good as mine.

What you can know is that when you meet someone and fall in love or, anyway, into bed, several things happen:

• You fall in love with an idealised image of who that person is. This image is in part your own creation.

• You fall at least somewhat in love with an idealised image of yourself. This is how the other person reflects you back to yourself (and which is why you tend to prefer that person's company — at least until the gloss wears off).

Into those processes of idealisation you pour your longings that, somehow, this relationship will make up for the lack of intimacy which sour most function-driven, everyday contacts.

'Sex can give you such an exalted view of yourself,' said Theo. 'I really miss it when I don't have it.'

Less sex, more desire

This was to have been the section of *Intimacy and Solitude* primarily concerned with sex. And in many ways it is that. But as wonderful as sexual feelings or expression can sometimes be, it is also a treacherous area to write about.

That I had to write about it if I was writing a book about intimacy and solitude seemed to me self-evident, right up to the moment of writing. After all, I was aware that for many people, and especially for men, the idea of intimacy is virtually synonymous with sex. Moreover, the idea that the 'real you' can emerge through sexual contact, or that through sex you will find some essential part of yourself or someone else, is highly potent, seducing both sexes and making a life without sexual contact sometimes hard to bear.

I prepared myself to write about sexuality at least as well as for any other section in this book. I read widely, took copious notes, pulled my own varied experiences through the wringer of memory. I had some wonderful interview material. So what was the problem?

There are, I believe, a number of problems. One of them is the intense subjectivity of sexual feeling and expression, a subjectivity which echoes that of intimacy and strenuously defies the limits of language. ('How was that for you?' 'Great. Magical. Terrible. Awful.') Between the speaker and listener fall many shadows. *I speak. You listen.* This does not mean that either one of us is in any real way 'reached' through words intended to describe non-verbal experiences.

A sense of gratitude and affection for your body; experiencing your body from within as the vital physical manifestation of who you are; refusing to see your body only through the eyes of others (or as you imagine others are seeing it): these are all aspects of self-awareness, self-acceptance and self-responsibility which are as important as any emotional or intellectual or spiritual caretaking of your self can ever be.

Yet how the body is symbolised in your understanding of it, how sex is symbolised in your understanding of it, is inevitably a matter of intense subjectivity, shaped by your individual constitution and also by the attitudes of those who make up your world. Sex, making love, being sexually intimate: these concepts would have one set of meanings for the person saving herself for marriage and quite another set of meanings for the person deciding if there is time to visit a brothel between appointments.

What complicates these differences is that when it comes to your desiring and expression of your 'sexual self', your defences are likely to be on red alert. Your capacity to keep your thinking and feeling functions reasonably separate may be shaky. In this age of so-called frankness, most of us are actually rather coy when it comes to sex. Many of us have sexual secrets about which we feel uneasy or even ashamed. These make us unusually vulnerable to real or imagined misunderstandings, attack or potential ridicule.

Such defences can push us to create moral edifices or even entire worldviews out of subjective experiences, in effect denying other people the validity of sexual expression different from our own. And if my experiences or my views are different from yours, you may be strongly disinclined to accept those differences as part of my individual expression of self. You may judge me or even tell me that I am wrong.

Such defences can also push normally reasonable people to illogical conclusions.

Henry is a paediatrician who has been in analysis for some years and would seem to be in a privileged position when it comes to sorting out sexual wheat from chaff. Not so. Speaking of the eldest of his sons, Lucas, he told me how concerned he is that eight-year-old Lucas shows little interest in sex or in masturbation.

'I am afraid,' said Henry, 'that he may grow up to be homosexual.'

Quite how Henry has made the leap from assuming too little masturbation could lead to homosexuality I was unable to discover but what I think he was expressing was: this boy is not like me in one aspect of his sexual behaviour in the present. *Maybe he will grow up to be profoundly unlike me in his sexual choices in adulthood.* It is a prospect that Henry could not face with equanimity.

If two people who regularly have sex, sleep nights together, talk about their feelings and more or less enjoy each other can have widely different and sometimes mutually incomprehensible ideas about what sex means or signifies, then how easy can it be for me to write down words in one room, knowing that you will read my words in another room, and that somehow (but how?) our meanings will coincide enough to make this mutual enterprise — writing/reading — worthwhile?

Feeling perhaps over-sensitive to this question of subjectivity was making it difficult for me to write about sexuality. It was making it difficult for me even to think about it. I felt increasingly burdened, weighed down by the impossible.

And I also found myself rebelling against the idea of tidying sex into an orderly pile of ideas which are surely better lived than written down, or if written down are best expressed in more lyrical forms than this book allows: through poetry or fiction, or perhaps through dance and music only, artforms beyond words.

Sex poses other problems too. It would be possible to point out, and quite validly, how sex is not all that important; that sexual expression is possible to enjoy in many unexpected ways; that sex is one means among many to express yourself; that sex can well be lived without. All of which is true, but none of which will do more for you than curdle your blood if desire — for someone, for something, for the freedom to desire — is eating at your entrails.

It would also be possible to offer much good advice, some of which I do indeed have at my writing fingertips, and some of which may indeed turn out to allow you to live happily ever after, even if it has not done as much for me! But that kind of well-intentioned instructional book is not my kind of reading, nor my preferred kind of writing.

So then I had to ask myself: does that mean there is no possibility for me to write about sexual expressions of one's self either alone or with other people in a way which breaches potential differences of meanings and avoids the pitfalls of inane optimism or equally inane proscriptions.

I went on worrying. I also went on thinking — not so much about sex or the different ways people act out or inhibit their sexual expressions of self — but rather what sex allows, especially in the stages of anticipation which are dominated by thinking, dreaming, fantasising and discovering *what you yourself are wanting*. This 'wanting' may be for physical satisfaction only, but it is more likely also to include some yearning towards closeness, comfort, emotional tenderness and understanding, perhaps even transcendence, that sense of moving beyond the limits of your everyday self and into the realm where self and other meet and are enhanced or even changed by that meeting.

Yet how to retreat from that moment with grace and sense of self intact? For as much as connection is part of life, so too is the capacity to accept your isolation.

As I worried I also wondered why it had seemed so necessary during the planning stages of this book to leave this particular section until last. I remembered, with affection, that when my sister Geraldine and I were little girls with a great inclination towards private jokes and giggling, we would often save what we liked best on our plate until last so that we could savour the treat, and savour it with particular satisfaction if the other had already succumbed to greed and devoured her special morsel. We enjoyed eating what we had saved. Even more we enjoyed parading the fruits of our prior restraint.

Did I regard sex then as a treat, as something I have saved up to be the climax to this book? After all, sex *can* be a treat. The enthusiasm each new generation shows for sexual activity points to that. But sex can also be a disaster, an experience of panic, shame, degradation, and dehumanisation, or simply a matter of routine and boredom.

So sexuality was not to be this book's *grand finale*, complete with drums and flags. Much more modestly it was to be the final major topic for this book because it is in or through your sexuality that you can feel exquisitely connected — or unutterably alone.

Sex is one of the ways you can bring intimacy to solitude, loving yourself, feeling safe with your memories of being loved by others. Sex is one of the ways you can bring what you have learned through solitude (who I am; what I want) to your experiences of intimacy.

In other words, the experience of your own sexuality, and of sexual contact with others, can be among the best or the worst of human collisions. Sex is something that you do or avoid doing; that you fantasise about, that you dream about, that you attach beliefs to. Sex fuels the myth of the Great White Knight and often of the Ultimate Rescuer.

Yet sex can also be largely absent from a person's life — and that person may be not one whit the worse off.

Sexual contact: the ultimate revelation?

Saving sex for last, I did not want to give weight to the idea that solitude is an experience of not-having: of not-having sexual contact or potential sexual contact with another person. Nor did I want to imply that sex is the peak intimacy experience for which all other experiences of intimacy are some kind of tame rehearsal. I know that I have had sexual experiences in which there was virtually no moment of encounter and I have had many more moments of non-sexual sharing which were beautifully sustaining of my need for intimacy. Sex is just one of many ways to get close — and to push away.

But the idea persists: that sex will bring not simply warmth and excitement and closeness and joy (if you are lucky), but also a sense of specialness sorely lacking in everyday life. *I matter.*

Lucy Goodison has pointed out that 'it is precisely the enforced repression and privatisation of sexuality, in the context of the isolation experienced by twentieth-century individuals, which has given sex an artificial role as a kind of secret barometer of our true selves.'

The power given to sex can also be fiercely negative and it is often when people fear sex — or maybe fear the potential anarchy of sexual feelings — that they also give it most importance. Fundamentalists' obsessive loathing of gay people, their outraged decrying of recreational sex, and their attempts to deny women control over their own bodies, speak volumes about how self-defining they imagine sex to be.

In their sex-directed perceptions of homosexuals, homophobes likewise reduce gay men and lesbians to their sexual functions, losing sight of their humanity almost entirely. Audre Lord responds to this.

'Lesbianism is not simply a sexual preference . . . It is not who I sleep with that defines the quality of these acts, not what we do together, but what life statements am I led to make as the nature and effect of my erotic relationships percolate throughout my life and my being.'

When the bodily sensations of sex are experienced obsessively, or when the distractions of sex are used to mask feelings of emptiness or unreality, then sex can loom extremely large. But struggling with public transport, worrying about work, getting through the day, balancing the bills, wondering what to cook for dinner, sorting the washing, listening to and caring for the kids, cheering for your team, tuning in to a favourite television programme: these threads of daily life may be just as important to you as sex, and certainly more constant.

Yet in my daily life, even as I folded the washing/fed the pets/ cared for the kids, still I could not deny that the idea of sex occupies people a great deal. I could not deny that even a promise of sexual adventure in the air enlivens people considerably. I could not deny that sex makes quite sensible, considerate people behave in irrational and self-serving ways. I could not deny that sex can bring people unusually close together, at least momentarily. I would not want to deny that sex can be a moment in which the concepts of *self* and *other* are experienced as wonderfully meaningless.

Sex can allow someone to experience to the full that she or he has a body, and is living in that body.

Sex can also be dull, painful, alienating, brutal, deathly.

Round these thoughts went, and as they rolled, not only was I feeling increasingly crushed, I was also experiencing my own sexual history as increasingly unreal.

Intimacy. Sex. Solitude. Sex with this person. At that time. What did any of it mean or matter? What exactly is it that one is left with? Or should the question be: what sense of self is one left with?

Looking for I don't quite know what, I opened Stuart Schneiderman's short, interesting book about Jacques Lacan and found these lines (and much else besides): 'That the ability to copulate is not clinically a meaningful indicator of much of anything has not shaken people's belief that if they can fuck they are fine: they are judged healthy, with all that implies about the fulfilment of life.'

And I understood, then, that in thinking about sexuality and its relationship to the larger picture of intimacy, solitude and self, that what emerges as most interesting are not the functional aspects of sexuality (*I fuck therefore I'm fine*), but rather what sexuality in its broadest meanings stands for: what sexuality hints at about how a person experiences him or herself; what sexuality expresses about how a person engages or does not engage with the world of others.

Or, to put it very simply, what matters most in the context of this section of *Intimacy and Solitude* is not sex, but desire.

22

Desiring who, desiring what?

Sexual desire can be a chance to leave the limits of your own self behind. It can also, like any other expression of intimacy, be not much more than an extension of your own self-absorption, a switch of the ego-driven cry *I want* from objects or services to a person.

Does that sound harsh? I fear it does, but imagine for a moment that Janet's desire for John outlives John's desire for Janet.

Janet phones John at the office, interrupting him during meetings. She leaves bunches of flowers at his home. She sets up dinner parties and he is forced to make excuses. When he runs into her in the street John is appalled by the way she assumes a renewal of intimacy. John wants to swat her out of his life. Janet the desirable has become Janet the nuisance.

Has Janet become a different person?

Only in John's experience of her.

John's needs have changed. A few weeks ago his need was to have the ego massage and body contact Janet was delighted to offer. Now his need is to be rid of Janet so that he can get on with the rest of his life.

Unfortunately Janet still wants to be close to John and to feel that he wants to be close to her, but these needs have turned from something viewed by John as sweet, magnificent, wildly attractive (and so she perceived herself) to something irritating, ill-judged, gross (and so she now perceives herself).

Even in describing the person you desire in fact or in fantasy (warm, understanding, sensual) you are, significantly, describing what you, the desiring person, are wanting (warmth, understanding, sensuality). This does not mean that the other person has no separate existence. They certainly do. Their smile, their energy, the way they move, their responses to you, their interests, the ways in which they remind you of people you have loved in the past: these factors and many others which are less conscious all play their part. Nevertheless, to *who that person is*, and to *how that person experiences him or herself*, you bring your needs and pin them — like a tail on the donkey — with more or less accuracy.

You can be lucky when how you want that other person to be coincides well enough with how that person is in their own experience of self.

You can also be lucky when the experience of desiring itself feels reasonably comfortable for you. Then you don't need to drift into a state of obsessive self-absorption (I can't think about anyone but my beloved. *I can't think about anyone but myself wanting my beloved.*). And when desire feels comfortable for you it also saves you from needing to turn your good object (the person you desire) into a bad object (the person you no longer desire) in order to preserve intact your emotional self-image.

But what happens next, after the sighing and desiring?

Unless you have led a singularly charmed life, you will know that the effects of your desiring are always unpredictable. Your beloved may want you to desire him or her. Your desire may run its course swiftly; you may find happiness; you may have made yet another botch-up in your long career of mishaps. Who can know?

But what can be predicted is that out of the desiring always comes a message about what it is that you want and, more crucially, about *the needs which lie behind your desires*. (I need warmth. I need understanding. I need to be saved from feeling lonely.) This seems to be the case whether the desiring is specific (I want John) or abstract (I want to be loved).

It is useful to hold onto this insight, especially when your desiring has not resulted in the perfect outcome and your tendencies to self-blame (or other-blaming) are running hot. Out of every situation of desiring, *no matter what the outcome*, can emerge vital clues as to what it is you want to bring into your life.

Unravelling the needs which lie behind desiring opens you up to knowing that you are in charge of your own life, and are not waiting around for someone else to make things happen.

I want my husband to love me more is a goal difficult to achieve through sheer force of will. *I need more understanding and affection in my life* is much more broad-ranging and keeps the level of personal power higher.

I wish you would piss off may mean *I need time alone*: to recover my sense of self, to nurture my sense of self, to hang out without having to be aware of anyone else.

Your desiring — its range, its pattern, its leaps, its tentativeness — is an outward sign of internal dramas which are in their combination unique to you:

Why do I desire money more fiercely than approval?

Why do I desire comfort and reassurance more than excitement?

Why is familiar sex tolerable for me only when I pitch my mind elsewhere?

Why can I desire only from a distance?

Why is desiring so much more important to me than having?

Why is being desired less important to me than desiring?

Why does desiring seem impossible for me?

Knowing that desiring expresses your own internal dramas can take the pressure off your need to have an 'outcome' to what you desire. Part of the outcome exists: you are becoming familiar with your own needs.

Candy's experiences describe what I mean. Candy told me, 'My marriage was the usual round of activity that seems to characterise urban, middle-class marriages. I was at the centre as an organiser and facilitator but almost none of the activity was directly to do with me. I was making life flow more efficiently for Neil, my husband, and more sociably for Bella and Archie, my two children. It wasn't unpleasant, but I did feel afraid of being taken for granted and not quite knowing what to do.

'When I fell for Pablo, who was Archie's music teacher of all corny things, I was ready to leave Neil, leave our house, take the kids and move in with Pablo. What I felt was that I had been given a new lease of life.

'Neil handled it well. He asked me to give it twelve months, going on having an affair with Pablo but staying at our home. I agreed to six months and in fact at the end of that time we had worked out a *modus vivendi* which does seem to suit everyone.

'My time with Pablo is when I can relax and float and be spontaneous in a way that I couldn't manage in family life. I love Pablo, not least because it is with him that I can turn off my needs to be efficient and Mummyish.

'I think this is a phase. I somehow don't think it is going to last forever. But the relief I felt meeting Pablo, and the peace and self-esteem I've got back through having Pablo in my life, have shown me how cluttered and frenetic my life had become and how unsuited to that essentially I am.'

It is not possible to predict what the outcome of this delicate balancing act might be. It works well as long as it suits Neil, Pablo and Candy, but when one of those adults withdraws their cooperation it will shake up all three lives. What Candy is likely to be left with, however, is the knowledge that she needs more peace in her life than family caretaking allows, and that she needs to be acknowledged as a separate person: not Neil's wife, nor the children's mother, but Candy — a woman with very definite needs for solitude and the sense of renewed self which solitude can bring.

Her solitude with Pablo is not quite solitude in most people's definition, but seemed to me to fit most beautifully with Winnicott's ideal of being capable of feeling 'at one with yourself and your environment'.

Reaching into inner space

Longing for solitude as well as intimacy you put yourself imaginatively where at present you are not. Desire arises from within yourself and focuses on something outside yourself, on something or someone you do not have. You cannot desire what you have; if you have it, you do not need to desire it. You can, of course, experience a renewal of desire for someone whom you 'have' or have just 'had': long-term relationships can be testament to that.

Desiring is one of the languages of your inner space and is often directed, arrow-like, toward the inner space of another person. I want... to get inside. This translates in many people's minds into: I want to have sex.

Having sex *is* one way to reach another person's psychic as well as physical inner space. You can, with a sexual partner, set aside the masks of everyday life, and follow sex or precede it with self-revealing talk and touch and body language which describes intimately who you are. But the possibility also exists to endure sex which is profoundly disconnected.

What physical intimacy does exaggerate is a potential for vulnerability. This can be intense or even unbearable. 'Giving yourself sexually' you may lay yourself open to being attacked or misjudged or rejected more painfully than in those relationships where you keep your clothes on and perhaps your boundaries more firmly intact. Trust that *it is safe to let go* is hard to come by in sexual relationships. I became aware of that painful dilemma with almost everyone I talked to about sexual intimacy.

Rejection, too, in sexual situations is often experienced doubly. There is the loss of the actual person. More, there is loss of what most of us hope for from sexual encounters: to trust that you can be yourself, to allow someone else to be him or herself in your company, to be briefly freed from isolation.

Francesca recalls, 'The first boy I ever fell in love with was called Simon. He shared a flat with my older brother, Kit, and a couple of other guys. I thought Simon was extremely sophisticated although I'm sure now that's not how he experienced himself. He was popular with girls I think, and in those days, the late sixties, he was as cool as the culture demanded.

'I guess I pursued him and finally one afternoon he told me he wanted to have sex with me. I was incredibly nervous but determined to go through with it. I did really believe I loved this guy and I wanted desperately to be seen as his girlfriend.

'We were at a friend's house, in the sunroom and we had to pull the curtains shut. He was standing by those curtains and he told me to take my clothes off. I didn't know where to put them as I took them off and he just stood there. I put them one by one in a pile on the floor. He kept all his clothes on and just stood still by

those curtains kind of stroking his beard. Then, when I had all my
clothes off and turned around to face him, he told me to put them
on again. He had changed his mind. That's what he told me. We
were not going to have sex. I have never forgotten it.'

It is possible that Simon was a sadist who took pleasure in
Francesca's embarrassment and possible shame. Yet what is
more likely is that he experienced no desire for her beyond an
interest to see 'how far she would go', a cruel affirmation of his
masculinity at the expense of her less powerful femininity. It
may also be that in his desiring of Francesca, Simon was not lifted
beyond conflict *but experienced desire itself as a state of conflict*.

Maybe he had another girlfriend and wanted Francesca, while
also wanting to avoid offending his girlfriend and risking
losing her.

Maybe he wanted to have sex with Francesca to prove to
himself that he could have sex, and then was overcome with
doubts which paralysed him.

Maybe he wanted to have sex with Francesca's brother, Kit,
but that thought was dangerous to his sense of self.

When desire ends, or feels buried, it is sometimes because it
has run its course: each person had created someone... who
turned out to be intolerably different from their fantasies. Desire
may also end because the desiring pair have been torn apart by
conflicts. These can be internal conflicts like those Simon might
have felt, or a mix of internal and external conflicts as two people
struggle to assert their needs and have them met. *I want this but I
also want that.*

The sweep of desire which carries someone beyond conflict is
probably, in most people's lives, rarely felt. When it does come,
when it does arise from within and is met from without, it is little
wonder that people are tempted to throw caution to the winds.

Desire can feel like one of life's rare moments of liberation
from the hesitancies of the past.

The acceptable face of desire

Because sexual desiring has always had to skirt taboos, and
because it is an area of life where people frequently feel incoher-
ently defended, it is tempting to load your own and other

people's desires with moral judgements ('I should not have felt this.' 'How dare you feel that.').

Yet behind desires are always needs — probably quite legitimate needs as the individual psyche experiences them — so moral judgements are rarely helpful. Desire is not 'good' when or because it can be freely expressed. Nor is desire self-evidently 'bad' when a person cannot identify or act on their desires, or when their desires are focused on people or things or acts which are inappropriate or socially unacceptable.

Let's suppose that I am a married woman and I fall 'madly in love' with my sister-in-law. What I am doing is difficult (extremely difficult!) for a number of reasons. My husband is appalled and fearful, as well as jealous. My mother-in-law is profoundly disturbed. My sister-in-law's husband is anxious and likely to be violent in his defence of heart and home. The children from both families feel that their relationships are threatened.

All these trouble spots churn and radiate outwards, without even beginning to consider what effect my desire might have on my sister-in-law or, indeed, on my own self.

My husband/mother-in-law/best friend/marriage guidance counsellor tell me to be sensible. They might also tell me that I am not feeling what I am feeling. Or, if I am feeling it, that I should stop feeling it and get on with being a wife to my thoroughly decent husband and mother to my delightful children.

Whether I do what they urge depends on many factors. Among these may be the strength of my desire and the history of needs which lies behind it; my feelings of entitlement to determine my own life; the degree to which I feel responsible for the happiness of my husband and children; the patterns I have already established of putting myself first, middle or last.

It may, indeed, depend on whether my sense of self and inner safety come from inside or from outside myself. (Do I need you to tell me who I am? Do I need you to tell me my life is of value? Do I need you to tell me how to think or act or feel?)

How or whether I translate my desire into action may also be affected by the reaction of the person whom I am desiring: my sister-in-law. Let's suppose she too is appalled. Then, unless I am suffering from a grave state of unreality, I will probably withdraw, and for some time feel painfully isolated. After some months I may realise that the desire was 'real', but the person who awakened the desire was 'unreal' or, rather, unreal in the role in which I had cast her. She wanted to be my sister-in-law and pal, but not my bedmate. In my perception of her otherness, I had, *because of my needs*, miscast her.

If I come to that point I may seek help to eliminate my unnatural desires and make myself into the person my husband and family need me to be. Or I may make a decision that if or when it is possible, I would like to meet other women whose desires/needs are closer to my own than my sister-in-law's could ever be.

Whatever actually happens, this experience — desiring my sister-in-law — has told me something important about how my internal needs are 'represented' on the outside by someone else, whom I then want to bring into my inner world, through experiences of closeness and of sexual intimacy.

To reiterate that same crucial point: the triggers — the person who triggers my feelings of desire together with those feelings of desire themselves — show me something about who I am, what I want and whether I feel entitled to get it.

Wanting you all to myself

It is possible, through one's desiring, to make explicit a yearning to appropriate someone, almost to devour them. This has very little to do with a self-and-other relationship. It is another variation on the rampant theme of *I want*, with no accompanying questions: What are your needs? Are your needs congruent with mine?

At the age of fifty-three actor Dennis Hopper is not, to public knowledge, especially mad or bad, yet in an interview he spoke in this way about Katherine La Nasa, his twenty-two-year-old wife, a ballet dancer he met at a performance in New York.

'I don't know anything about ballet. As a matter of fact I'd never seen a ballet in my life, but I picked out the ass in the tutu that I liked and I watched it [*sic*] as much as I possibly could. There was a big party for the ballet company at Spago's, I was put at a table with the dancers and I wangled my way over to the ass I liked. I had a young woman with me who I hardly knew and she thought I was rather strange because I said to Katherine, "This is really embarrassing but you have a really great ass!" This led to other things and the next night I was back at the ballet.'

Not much later, Hopper married this 'ass' and, we can presume, the woman who went along with it.

That this man of fifty-three can talk about another human being in a piece-by-piece, split-off way is an indictment not of Hopper, who is just a more famous flawed human being than most of us, but of our society where bits and pieces of people or even their possessions are often and with conviction mistaken for the whole ('What a car!' 'Great tits.').

Obsessive interest in your own and other people's looks and material possessions, is, in general, a symptom of lack of a secure sense of self, and the genuine power-from-within that goes with that. Desiring someone else's wealth, looks or cleverness may also express envy or a belief that with the addition to your life of those assets — money, looks, brains — your life might be substantially safer or more admirable than anything you can manage on your own.

Desiring someone who has those assets — ass, tits, wallet — desiring someone *for* those assets, is an act of appropriation (I want what you have. I want to make what you have my own. I want [literally] a piece of your ass.). This is not an expression of intimacy; it is the now familiar cry of infantile narcissism. Fill me up, it pleads. Pour yourself into me, for I am empty.

Why someone would focus on ass rather than breasts, or lips or wallet adds a touch of individuality to the scenario, but basically the play remains the same. Out of my own lack of wholeness, I focus on (fetishise) a part of you.

Melanie Klein suggested that for the infant the breast and the infant's relationship to the breast represents, for a short, crucial period, Mother. Similarly, although less appropriately, a part of someone can come to represent 'lover' for an adult who is having difficulties taking on the risks of a person-with-person relationship.

Of course, any one of us will be proud of the beauty or success of our loved ones. There is nothing wrong with such pride, especially if it is laced with tolerance and good humour. Troubles arise when our desiring is conditional. If, for example, you were to fall in love with the most powerful man in your office, then found once you had married him that he was now a 'no one' out of work, your relationship may well fall apart. You loved the power rather than the man. But the power you loved came from the outside, and could never be reliable. Loving the man for *who he is* is the only kind of permanence possible. It is an illusory permanence for you will die and so will he. Nevertheless, it has an authenticity to it which is very much at the soul of intimate self-with-other relationships.

Reducing a person to an aspect of their wholeness can occur in situations of explicit hostility, as well as when admiration hides envy or hostility. The person who has betrayed you, raged against you, disgusted you, can become in your experience of that person no more whole than that act of betrayal, of rage, or disgust. ('My boss fired me, the cow.').

People who have physical handicaps, or are plain or fat or old, may also experience themselves as 'others' seen through the prism of that one characteristic. This can have dramatic effects on their experience of self, an experience continuously up-dated by self-other encounters of all kinds. Little wonder then that in the face of these reductive reactions, many people are tempted to retreat to the safety of a few close relationships, even when these may be only partially satisfactory.

Desiring, perhaps beyond any other experience of self, is not value free. People who are rich, conventionally good looking or self-promoting are not essentially more desirable. On the contrary, they may be monstrously self-absorbed. Yet they are much more likely to be desired than are people who are poor, plain or self-effacing.

Desiring is an expression of self which is affected absolutely by the morals and customs and standards as well as by the privileges and priorities of the society in which we live. This explains why we fall for the same stereotypes, or have feelings of desire which can themselves be stereotyped. Yet what is perhaps more interesting is that many people nevertheless experience desires which are actually defiant of society's stereotypes.

Falling in love with your sister-in-law may express one way in which desire potentially disrupts what is proper or 'desirable' for society at large. Depending on your point of view, you will regard such disruption as an affirmation of selfhood or as something which is selfish and destructive.

That kind of disruption seems complicated enough, but what are we to make of people who believe they desire their own young children and therefore have a right to abuse them sexually; or of people whose 'desires' come with feelings of entitlement to belittle, humiliate, subjugate or enslave the person whom they profess to desire?

In quite normal relationships one person can enslave another, not through cruelty, but ostensibly through love, making it difficult for them to spend time with others, denying them a life of their own which is not subsumed to the needs of the relationship as one person 'desires' that relationship to be.

'What we are to make of such people' depends on many factors, not least of which is our closeness to such a situation. And anyway, this immediately raises a question about whether desire — a complex of feelings which arises from within — is something which can or should be controlled. Perhaps desire itself cannot be controlled. *Probably* it cannot be controlled, at least not in the sense of ordering your emotions to turn tail and express your inner world quite differently.

But, *desiring is not acting*.

Desiring, recognising your desires, understanding something about where they have come from and where they are potentially taking you, is an experience of self that is triggered by someone or by your fantasy of Someone. It is an experience which can potentially give you a chance to know yourself — and your needs — better.

Acting upon your desires, you involve someone else. Then some negotiating must take place. This is possible for many people in a fairly unselfconscious way, at least in the short term. In the longer term, desire can get submerged beneath a weight of conflicts, both inner and outer.

For others the problems are almost immediate. These are the people whose self-absorption makes it difficult for them to acknowledge that what they want, you may not want; that what they need, you may be unwilling or unable to give. When what they want coincides with what someone else wants, they will be over the moon: when it does not, they will be howling at that same moon.

A positive use of conflict

The most comfortable relationship between desiring and acting — or not acting — is likely to exist when you are least torn between wanting two or more opposing things at the same time. Alexander Lowen certainly thinks so.

'Speaking personally, I hate having to make a decision. I feel trapped by the process. I have rarely made the right decision in my life. All the good moves I made, those that had a constructive effect on my life, were not the result of deliberate choice. I acted because my desire was so strong it allowed no choice.'

The capacity for such certainty is largely temperamental. Yet at significant moments of change in my own life I have allowed myself to be guided by dreams which have felt so different in 'weight' from everynight dreams that they have appeared to contain some essential wisdom.

Less dramatically, and in my usual round of daily life, I know that I am trying to make decisions constantly, and almost always with some degree of uncertainty, for the absence of conflict is never anything but brief. We endure conflict all of our lives.

Beyond endurance what is needed is an understanding that conflict is the grit allowing you to grow, or anyway to learn something about your own limitations and how you can resist those limitations. Conflict is part of the stuff of life. But it can also be numbing, even life-defeating.

Conflict becomes a problem when you want two or more opposing things at once. Yet even discovering what those things are is rarely easy. We tell ourselves such monstrous lies to prop up our shaky self-image! But in quiet times of self-awareness the individual nature of your conflicts can emerge.

I want to be loved; I want to be free.
I want safety; I want adventures.
I want to look up to you; I want to know your reality.
I am afraid to leave you; I want to leave you.
I want to be alone; I can't stand to be alone.
I want to be rich; I don't want to be envied.
I want to work; I want to be home with my children.
I want intimacy; I want solitude.

Those potentially mutually exclusive wants touch all our lives, sometimes making any kind of emotional expression feel dangerous. In Bronwyn Hocking's book, *Little Boy Lost*, she clarifies this dynamic: 'I felt that everything I wanted or needed to do was incompatible with something else of equal importance... The more tightly I controlled my feelings, the more I feared being trapped in the stranglehold of my repressed emotions forever... But the price of avoiding hurt in this way is a lack of any real contact with the world. Spontaneity and creativity become impossible.'

More commonly, persistent and unacknowledged conflict curdles into a state of dissatisfaction with what is happening, and a longing for what is not happening.

I can't stand to be alone; I want a lover.

My lover crowds me; I need solitude.

I can't stand my own company; I want someone to care for me.

Your needs are too great; I need a new partner.

Roberto Assagioli stressed that the problem here is *wanting two incompatible things at the same time*. This can wreck a person's peace of mind, their way of life, even their sanity, not least because it can be so difficult to recognise what is going on. Without knowing what is going on you can feel stuck, anxious, distraught, frantic or numb.

But you do not need to reach a state of enlightenment to be somewhat relieved of the worst excesses of inner confusion!

You can do this by recognising the conflicts in your own life for what they are — needs which are impossible to meet at one time — and by putting into practice what Assagioli has usefully called 'a hierarchy of needs'.

It might mean that:

- You listen to your lover complaining about her job, knowing that you can get to your desired state of solitude a little later.
- You recognise that your desire to have a child is what matters most to you and that your work life will be put on the back burner.
- You realise that as long as you are haunted by your past, making a commitment is too hard for you. You need help.
- You accept a challenging job, but attend to your fear of failure with a therapist or a friend.
- Your need for sex will have to be set aside when your partner is ill or non-existent, but that your need for companionship can be met by friends.

The person who is not aware of his or her 'hierarchy of needs', and who is feeling uncomfortable because of inner conflicts, is likely to fall into the hole of wanting 'two incompatible things at the same time' and then railing against the world, or at someone standing in for the world, because it is not possible to have them. Railing against the world is one possible outcome; withdrawal into numbness is another.

Assagioli warned of the temptation to project your conflicts onto others. 'Human nature,' he said, 'displays a strong tendency to attribute to others the attitudes, impulses, feelings and ideas present within us.'

This leads us not only into domestic strife, but, on a communal scale, into large-scale conflicts also.

It is transforming to recognise those kinds of projections as ego-defence mechanisms that actually take you away from rather than toward self-responsibility, and away from rather than toward a sense of your own power.

This dynamic of projecting your conflicts outward works two ways.

Other people's strongly-felt reactions toward you, whether these are positive or negative, can be as difficult to bear or 'contain' as the feelings you would like to disown.

Perhaps someone reacts to you with rage or hostility or contempt. You may have provoked this behaviour, consciously or unconsciously. But what is also possible is that the person is acting out conflicts erupting from *within their own psyche*. And you are the hapless person standing in the way.

Whether you become defensive and enraged, deeply hurt, or are able more or less to shrug such an assault aside, depends very much on how contained you are feeling at the time, as well as on your variable capacity to distinguish what in the attack is personal to you and what is a cry of rage against the world or an unfair, unloving past, which is for the moment represented by you.

What helps most is remembering that such a cry or attack or sly blow is a reflection of that other person's inner state; it is not an omniscient summary of you. Your *reaction* reflects your own inner state, and that can tell you which aspects of your own inner world are needy of attention.

23

Not just wanting

The words *desiring* and *wanting* seem interchangeable. Yet there are differences. Desiring involves wanting, but it is not only wanting.

I can want a fine day to get my washing dry. I can want to earn enough money to give me more writing time. These 'wants' are not trivial to me. But they are not desires. My sense of self is not threatened either by wanting those things or by getting or not getting them.

Desiring is much more dangerous to my sense of who I am, for myself and other people. It is much more dangerous because *it tells me what I do not have*. It reminds me of my own neediness, and that other people could deny me what I want. Out of my desiring I can come to know myself better; I also make myself vulnerable.

If I return to the weather and think about desire, then I am immediately back in England where I lived from 1967 to 1983. London is where most of my closest friends lived and still live, yet when I turn my mind back to the early 1980s I am desiring a warmth, a radiance of light, a sense of space and expansiveness which are particular to the South Pacific. This physical picture carries with it layers of meaning from my earliest years which I could not begin to unravel, nor would want to. Desiring finer weather than is possible in London was only part of it. The weather, the sky, the light, the foliage, the colours: those all stood for something which represented for me not-England and, more than that, a place where I might possibly feel more me, more at home.

When I think about money, and my desire to write, I remember having the safety of not being able to afford to write. Then that barrier was taken away by a friend. 'Write,' she said. 'If that is what you want to do, and if it really is only lack of money which is stopping you, I'll give you some money and you can get started.'

So then my prevarication (which kept my desire safe from the risks of acting) was taken away, and with difficulty and hesitation and only much later with a sense of inevitability, I began to write. Writing, I was able to free a part of myself which I had barely glimpsed caught up as I was in my publishing career.

The difference between wanting and desiring is very stark here. No sensible person could *want* to write. It is lonely, intensely demanding and financially ludicrous. Yet, as I have seen so often with other people whose sense of work is vocational, my *desire* to write, to understand what cannot be understood in other ways, pushes me to write even when my *wants* — for a more sociable life, or one less fraught with risk and potential failure — are also well known to my rational mind.

Desire can and sometimes does arise as a driving force; it can also be almost impossible to risk or even to identify. Sometimes even the desire to desire is lost. Fear, conformity, timidity, despair: these are the enemies of that assertion of self which tells you, *I want*.

Desiring can make someone feel intolerably vulnerable. She or he is reaching out, and risking finding no one there; worse yet, no one meeting those needs which inevitably lie behind the desiring.

This fear of finding no one stretches way back to infancy when your need to be held and accepted, not to be abandoned, was as crucial to your survival as food or sleep.

Fear, conformity, timidity, despair: few of us are entirely untarred by those painful brushes. It is certainly understandable why you might confine your desiring to predictable situations, or why you might save all your desiring for what will give you an illusion of control: money, power; more money, more power. Or why you might quench your capacity to desire until you no longer want what is not easily within reach.

You may think yourself lucky if you do not desire. Then, certainly, you cannot be wracked by grief or frustration or feelings of emptiness when what you desire does not or cannot happen, or when you get what you want, only to discover your desires are turning sour.

Not desiring may express a state of deep contentment, but it is also possible that the person who cannot desire may feel half dead, flat, empty. *And that will be how such a person experiences others*.

Gregory does not desire. 'If by that you mean wanting something so much you have to have it. I do want things to happen at work. I always work with a plan for the next six months that outlines what I expect to achieve. But that's totally realistic. Naturally I want to win when I play squash. I wanted to do well at school and university, and I did. But if you mean pining away for someone, or sending red roses in the hope that they will notice you, then no, that's not my style. I would despise it. I can't imagine wanting something that's not within my reach to get. That's a complete waste of energy, isn't it?'

Feeling emotions, feeling desire, needing: these can be problematic experiences for any one of us, but fearing to feel, fearing to desire and being unable to risk the vulnerability of acknowledging that you want something — then stretching out for it — seem to me worse. Yet it is the fate of many people for whom reaching out in infancy and early childhood was a painful, unrewarding experience.

Or is it the fate? 'Facts are not fate,' stresses Victor Frankl. 'What matters is the stand we take towards them.'

It is possible here, too, for someone to learn to take small risks. Perhaps this happens when that person comes to see that *what they fear most already lies in the past*.

Laura's awareness of this insight allows her a freedom to create a satisfying life for herself which Gregory's lack of awareness and distance from himself and others do not.

Laura speaks in a breathless, self-deprecating way. Nevertheless, she is a purposeful woman who told me, 'I was always cautious emotionally. I would say I was almost pathologically shy and when anyone approached me with any kind of intimacy in mind I could literally feel myself shrink.

'I would spend a lot of time with my brother and at work. I'm a research chemist. I was actually fine spending time alone. I admired my own self-sufficiency.

'I met Murray at work and liked him right away. He is also shy but he fell in love with me and persisted. I was appalled because I could no longer then be friendly with him. I needed to push him away once I saw him wanting to get closer to me. I actually felt very disgruntled. "How could he ruin a friendship?" I thought to myself.

'Then my brother was hospitalised with a brain tumour and because I was utterly desperate I let Murray help me, taking me to the hospital and so on. Nothing dramatic. He's not the pushy type.

'It was then that Murray realised that my brother and I don't have any other family and I told him in bare outline that we had been fostered and not very well. Months later Murray and I were walking together after work and he suddenly said to me, "They have already gone, your parents. You can't lose them all over again. I think you are so afraid of getting close to anyone because you might risk losing them. It would be awful, of course, but not as awful as losing both your parents as a baby. The most awful thing that could ever happen to you has happened already. You can't save yourself from it. It has been and gone."

'When I got home I had a terrible headache. It went on for a couple of days and I wondered if I had a brain tumour too and was going to die.

'I lay in my bed wracked with pain and had some weird dreams, and in between the dreams and the pain I had a sense of water, of the ocean, of being carried on top of water and of water rushing through me. It was an absolutely life-shattering couple of days and at the end of the time I thought, "Murray's right. Nothing could be that bad again and maybe I don't have to be the living dead. After all, it won't resurrect those who actually are dead."

'It wasn't all plain sailing then, but I had a different attitude. It was luck, of course. Murray is someone I can trust completely, although I don't ever feel that he intrudes upon me. My brother is still stuck, stuck in the past I guess. He has recovered his physical health, but is still where he was emotionally.'

Knowing Laura's family history, her emotional prognosis

would have seemed bleak. Yet she feels alive, enjoys her relationship with Murray, is able to be alone without experiencing her aloneness as a defence, and has energy left over for other people.

It is surely one of the most wonderful characteristics of human beings that we disrupt almost all attempts to categorise us. Some of us have smoothly secure childhoods and grow up to be grasping and anti-social; others appear to lack almost everything that would give stability to life, yet manage to function lovingly and generously.

I am not evoking moral superiority here; I am talking of good luck, for the capacity to be reasonably cheerful, to be loving, to trust, to welcome others into your life *does* add up to tremendous good luck — which not everyone shares fairly or equally.

24

Questions of attunement

In your desiring, as well as in the ways you act upon your desires, you will be expressing what gender means to you. You will also be vulnerable to judgements that say 'Women's desiring should be this way' and 'Men's desiring should be that way'.

It is women rather than men who seem more often to have difficulties acknowledging what they want, and asking for it in a direct way. This is because to know what it is that you want, you need to experience yourself as someone *capable of making choices*, aware of others and sensitive to their needs, yet not overly buffeted by those needs nor overly conflicted about how to balance those needs in relation to your own.

To be sensitive to what others want, and to avoid feeling overwhelmed or persecuted by those wants, you need a steady sense of self and, with that, confidence that your own needs can be met.

For many women, encouraged from birth to be attuned to others' needs but not to feel in charge of their own life, this can be difficult. Faced with the challenge of desiring, some women experience themselves passively ('I want...to be desired.'). This inevitably constructs an uneasy relationship between them and the people who have the power to desire or not to desire them.

Manipulating, acting indirectly, being petty: these behaviours are more often associated with women than with men but they are an outcome of powerlessness. Without a sense of internal power, it is extremely difficult to be direct or generous with other people.

Men, in general, have fewer problems about expressing what they need directly (I regard this as a virtue), as well as fewer problems about putting their own needs ahead of other people's (rather less of a virtue). Perhaps they have fewer problems with the internal experience that they, and not someone else, are directing their own lives.

Where men have more difficulty is in tuning in to themselves or other people: knowing what they or other people need emotionally, especially when that neediness exposes feelings of vulnerability.

Men also seem to have more difficulty with the idea that making choices is best done by engaging all parts of your being — when that is possible — rather than from one cut-off part of yourself. Making a decision with your head only, or with your sexual needs filling your mind, and discounting your own or anyone else's feelings, is potentially destructive.

Many men find it bewildering as well as frustrating that for some women an 'easy-going fuck without muddying things up with commitment' (as one man expressed it) is out of the question. For some women, feelings of affection as well as feelings of physical desire must co-exist before they can feel either aroused or satisfied.

Lisa Alther expressed it for many people when she wrote in her novel *Bedrock*: 'It was an old quandary for them. He needed sex in order to feel connected to her, and she needed to feel connected to him in order to enjoy sex.'

For such women there is a congruence between what the body wants and what their minds and hearts want. Then, even if asking or refusing is a problem, their body is, by opening up or shutting down, speaking most eloquently for them.

Regulating desire

That women can and do desire sexually is public knowledge in late twentieth-century life. But that women should be seen to act upon their desires — upon their desires to find a place in the world in their own way, as well as upon their sexual or intimacy desires — remains problematic. This is especially so when their desires do not tally with their particular man's notions of what or how women should desire.

A woman 'pursuing' a man is likely to suffer not only from his potential rejection of her for coming on too strong, but also from her own internal voices which will collude with his stereotyped judgements of her. Even when a heterosexual relationship is well established the woman is often required to keep a watch on how she expresses her sexual desires. This is largely in order to regulate her position as the desired one, the passive one, rather than as the active desirer.

Natalie is a nurse and part-time dancer in her late twenties who has been married for four years to Paddy, a builder who is eight years older. She is a lively woman who does not take easily to having her strong feelings regulated by other people.

'Paddy loves sex and so do I. Sex is very, very important in our marriage and Paddy has always been incredibly appreciative of my interest in it. I think his last wife was not really keen on sex with him at all. But there have nevertheless been some hairy moments when he has been preoccupied with work or whatever and I have made an overture to him and there has been a definite atmosphere in the air telling me that I have misjudged the situation, come on too heavy and that I should have known to hold back. But on the rare occasions when I have wanted to knock him back, with a genuine headache or period pain or whatever, he hasn't allowed me to knock him back. His needs or desires have had to be met. He'll tell me to be a good sport and suck him off, and I do it too.'

There may be more to this than emotional good manners. When a man is tired, and if intercourse is part of a couple's usual sexual routine, then he might be anxious that his 'performance' will be affected by fatigue or anxiety. Even allowing for this, women frequently complain that men's desires — often narrowly directed towards physical sex — take a priority within the relationship which their own desires do not.

Natalie again. 'There have been times when I don't want to fuck, or I don't want to fuck for the second time. There are times when I want to kiss and cuddle or talk for hours, but if Paddy is needing to fuck, we end up doing it. I know I am lucky because most of the time I really do enjoy it, but I wish that I could take my turn in deciding what's going on without that being some big issue or having to be decided in a bureaucratic kind of way. You know, like, "On Wednesdays Natalie will decide." I couldn't bear that, so we go on largely following Paddy's rhythms and needs.'

Natalie's complaints are few because in general most of her needs for intimacy and for sexual pleasure are met by Paddy, almost without Paddy having to try. What is more common, especially when a relationship has left the honeymoon phase behind, is that two people discover that they are *two* people, with two sets of desires, two sets of needs, two sets of convictions as to how sexual intimacy 'ought' to be.

This can be painful, especially if one person brings to the relationship a conviction that sex and intimacy are one and the same, while the other person sees things differently.

'How peculiar it was, she thought,' wrote Mary Gordon in her short story, 'The Other Woman', 'looking at her husband, that her body had the power to excite him, to make him lay down his book and turn to her, cupping her buttocks in his hands, wanting her like that. Her sense of the oddness of it all made her distant from him, but she began to feel his desire soothe her; it became a dwelling she could rest inside, and she thought as she met his desire with her own familiar body, How easy it is to be faithful! For it was not his body that excited her (it had never been men's bodies that had excited her), as the idea of him, of all that he was and was to her, that made her rise to meet him, desire for desire. It was the oddness of it all, and the familiarity.'

Gordon's few lines tell me that each person is, in their desiring, expressing their individuality in ways which might never be known even to their intimate partner of many years.

That there are many kinds of sexual desiring is clear, yet is sometimes hard to recognise or bear. Passionate desiring, affectionate desiring, reassuring desiring, the desire to have what someone else has, the desire to destroy: these faces of desire are rarely experienced singly. Our desiring may feel single-minded, but it is never straightforward.

The complex ways people negotiate those differences about what desiring means, what desiring brings, is very much part of an individual relationship. Perhaps it *is* the individual relationship because desiring — to be close, to be apart; to be loved, to be one's own person — extends far beyond a roll between the sheets.

Those who apparently do best in these often largely unconscious processes of negotiation will be people who have a reliable sense of individual self. They may also be least conflicted by a range of possibilities, sometimes because it suits them individually to be in roles (husband/wife) which are socially proscribed, and to 'act out' those roles unhesitatingly and even to feel 'themselves' as they do so. Yet there are also less conventional couples who seem to negotiate their desires well enough to keep both partners smiling.

And for the rest of us? There are few easy solutions, perhaps none. There are, however, those great (and by now familiar) assets which will affect for the better each and every contact you have with others:

- a sense of self
- flexibility of attitude and response
- a familiarity with your needs — and a creative spirit about how these needs can be met
- confidence that you can afford to be aware of other people's needs
- respect for other people's differences
- clarity about what you cannot tolerate
- distance from what you cannot change
- a desire to live fully in the present.

These qualities may not be of immediate help when you love your partner but no longer feel sexual desire for her, or when you tire of experiencing yourself as everyone's buddy but as no one's lover; but they will help. They will help because they are part of feeling real and of enjoying authentic relationships with other people. They are part of accepting other people's reality while not feeling dependent upon it.

An American Quaker, Elizabeth Watson, sees this as contributing to your life-long quest towards wholeness. She says, 'Let each of us work at growing into wholeness. If our lives are interesting and rewarding, sex is more likely to assume its rightful place and not be an obsession. Let us build sufficient solitude into our relationships to nurture the growth into wholeness of all parties.'

The theme of this book emerges once again: the more comfortable you are with yourself, the less you need other people and the more easily you can embrace them; not just one special person as an extension of your own self-absorption, but many people, in many different ways, experiencing their likeness to you and their differences from you as part of your intimacy with them, and as part of your knowledge of your own self.

Negotiating desire

That two people will feel and express uniting desires throughout a relationship is hard to imagine. It may not even be a good sign; then almost certainly one person has subsumed herself (*himself* is less likely) to the ideals of a 'we-self' relationship. Indeed, the degree to which *difference* of needs and outcomes can be tolerated within a close relationship is more reliable as a mark of emotional good health than sameness can ever be.

Within any sustained relationship there will be times when one person needs closeness and the other needs solitude; when one person wants to make love, the other wants to sleep or read; when one person needs to speak and the other does not want to listen; when one person pushes for change and the other opposes change.

What's to be done is often not much more demanding than explicitly acknowledging what the other person wants, while also legitimising the differences which exist between two close but separate people.

Knowing that your need has been 'heard' and understood is not the same as having that need met, yet often — with children and with adults — this acknowledgement is as much support as is necessary, especially when there are times when each person's needs are fully met ('I know you want to have sex, but tonight I'm tired.' 'I understand it's important for you to talk, but today I can't bear to listen.' 'I'm aware you want to meet more people but you will have to do it on your own. It's not what I want.').

There is in so many of us — and especially in women — an almost overwhelming need to make amends when we could be doing something which would apparently make someone else happier, but we really do not want to do it ('I'm sorry we can't have sex. I promise you that tomorrow...' 'Of course you can talk. I'll take an aspirin...' 'Meet more people? I'll go and get changed...').

There are inevitably times in a relationship when you do things you don't much want to in order to keep the wheels rolling. Concessions, deals, compromises: these are not the stuff of which romance is made, but they certainly allow many relationships to survive.

But there are also times when your integrity feels much more at stake. Consistently having sex to please someone else; listening when you are never listened to; moving when that takes you away from people who matter to you; caretaking adult children who could take care of themselves: these are all potential eroders of your sense of self. They are also expressions of fear: fear of loss, fear of not being needed.

Such fear, and with it a denial of self, can lead to a rapid eroding of that vital sense of who you are. It can also negate your possibility to desire. *I want*... becomes *I want*... *what you want*. *I want*... becomes *I want only to be wanted*. And when you no longer want me? When I have emptied myself out to be filled up with what you want — and you betray me?

Then I am likely to fill that space with hate for you.

Rage, envy, destruction

There is, wherever desire lives, the stirrings of envy and hostility, and the seeds of destruction. What others have, they may not want to share with you. What others have and you cannot have, you may want to spoil. What you have, others could take away. When you feel vulnerable you may want to destroy — especially when it is the relationship you most value or the person you love most. When you have been hurt, you may want to kill — perhaps not the person, but the relationship you have shared.

Winnicott assessed that it was a sign of maturity, and of a high degree of personal integration (being able to 'own' your feelings), when someone could accept their own feelings of destructiveness, taking responsibility for those feelings and knowing that they are 'bound up with living' and part of living fully. Yet many of us avoid this shadow. Rage, envy, hostility: that's what other people feel. When those ugly stirrings start churning, up come our ego-defence mechanisms and out go our projections.

Children do this blatantly ('I didn't want to scratch Rashid. Harry told me I had to.').

But it is not only children who act creatively in the face of their parents' looming anger. Adults too are expert at defending their sacred image of themselves as hate-free, envy-free, frustration-free, rage-free people ('I would never have got drunk if you had been on time.' 'Before I met you I was never this mean.' 'I only get angry because you drive me crazy.' 'I can't be loving when you are so cold.').

Within almost every relationship there are variations on those themes. They add up to much the same thing: each person not taking responsibility for their own feelings, their own thoughts, their own actions, their own flawed and human self.

Acknowledging to yourself that you are someone who envies, who is fearful, who is capable of hatred and of infantile rage is central to mature self-responsibility. So, too, is acknowledging that those feelings will exist in the people you love and that part of loving them is accepting the reality of those 'imperfections'.

This is certainly not easy to do when the temptation roars inside you to look around and find someone else to blame: your spouse, your boss, your child, the devil ('*They made me do it.*'). Or when the temptation arises to boot someone out because they have destroyed the hallowed picture of them you had created — and fallen for.

And it is not only your own envy of others that you may seek to avoid acknowledging. You may also fear the consequences if other people are free to envy you. If you have become successful, *will no one take care of you any more*? If you are praised for your work, *will other people try to take you down a peg or two*? If you show me around your beautiful house, *will I believe that you feel insecure*?

Other people's envy does not always manifest in feelings of hostility. On the contrary, behind adulation and excessive attention, even behind the ever-smiling facade of feminised 'niceness', can lurk envy and hostility in large doses.

Envying and being envied: neither is comfortable, both are part of a feeling life. What matters in terms of your self-and-other relationships is not that you are likely to be as capable of hostility as you are of loving, and as capable of envying as you are of generosity; but that *you do not hide from knowing this*.

'The trick,' says Nancy Friday, 'is to be able to express the hate then return to love.'

A little expressing probably goes a very long way. Most of us need a strong base of love to be able to withstand the pain and damage of hate. And that expressing of hate always, always needs to be as specific as possible ('I loathe the way you criticise me in front of other people') rather than global ('I loathe you').

'The notion that we can feel love and hate at the same time,' suggests Nancy Friday, 'is intimacy's first law. It is best learned in childhood with our first peers, our brothers and sisters. If we do not take in love's ambivalence then, it is almost impossible to come to terms with it later.'

And why not? Because we will fail to recognise our rage at the power the loved one has to hurt us. 'We do not recognise it,' Friday continues, 'as the other face of love.'

Anger, greed and ignorance, teaches Zen Buddhism, are the three enemies of reality, distorting our awareness and sabotaging 'the fullness of experience'. The more you can see through your anger, greed and ignorance, 'the more satisfying your circumstances'.

In the early days of a desiring relationship darts of jealousy and possessiveness may be seen by your lover as signs of eagerness. Scorn for past loves only confirms how lucky you are now. And while conflict can be kept at bay with mutual idealising and comfort, there is no need for anger, frustration, hostility and rage.

But those days do not last forever.

When the desired person becomes a real person, then a process of reconciliation between fantasy and reality needs to take place. Hating someone for what they are not; resenting someone for what they cannot be or do; raging against the toad who was only ever a prince in your creation of them: these are expressions of infantile rage which speak of a lack of personal integration.

Of course, enduring someone else's complex reality may not always be appropriate. You might be in a relationship which is wrong for you; it could be healthy to move on. Intimacy can fade, die and refuse mouth-to-mouth resuscitation. There is no essential failure in that.

But with those few people with whom you are on a long-haul journey, at least minimal awareness is called for of that complex self (your own self) who is hating, and why; of that self who is resenting, and why; of that self who is raging, and why; of that self who is bent on destruction, and why. For behind the raging, hating, destructive feelings are often other feelings *which may be much more dangerous to acknowledge*.

What could those feelings be? Vulnerability and fears of *not mattering*. Acknowledging them is one of the hardest tests of maturity. It is also one of the most essential.

Some people reach those feelings in themselves through their capacity 'imaginatively to put themselves into someone else's place' and to identify with the pain and vulnerability of others: perhaps their own children, perhaps a close friend or lover. Through recognising the legitimacy of someone else's anxiety or pain, they may recognise the legitimacy of their own and allow themselves the same feelings of compassion.

For others, however, emotional pain provokes no compassion, only contempt, disgust or helplessness. For those people the chance to discover their own buried pain, and to come to terms with it, can barely come about through identification. For them what needs to emerge is a desire for change. This may lead to a clearer sense that **what you can honour and tolerate in others is limited to what you can also acknowledge, honour and tolerate in your own self.**

Mourning what you cannot have

It may be that you have been focused for some time on what you want ('I want a lover.' 'I want a baby.') but cannot have. You may be having difficulty reconciling yourself to not getting what you genuinely believe you need. Perhaps what you need most is a chance to mourn.

Grief counsellors can work with people who have lost their chance to have a child with just as much skill as they work with those whose child has died. Equally, the pain of not having a lover, or of realising that you might never have that special person of your own, may also call for a period of mourning leading, if all goes well, to the relief of acceptance — which should not be confused with resignation or defeat.

A few years ago I worked in a therapy group with Ian, a gay man in his early fifties who had no interest in casual sex but in his small and rather conservative town seemed unable to meet any potential long-term partners.

Ian had explored the possibility of moving to a larger city and had not ruled this out, but he still had family responsibilities which meant that moving would be a major disruption to the people who were important in his life, as well as to himself.

A group member suggested to Ian that he write on pieces of card the qualities that the ideal lover would have brought into his life. He was to write these without censoring whether these were 'good' or 'bad' or things that he was 'entitled' to have or not.

Two weeks later, when the group met again, Ian brought the cards with him. He had written the qualities on cards which suited the mood of what he was describing. Those which carried words like 'love', 'commitment', 'understanding', were of strong, bright colours with the words written in large, beautiful letters; those which carried words like 'shared jokes', 'walks together' and 'pets' had line drawings and small decorations. When he showed us the cards which carried the words 'sexual tenderness', 'passion', 'lack of inhibition', it seemed that everyone in our small group was touched by a change of mood. These were much plainer, the words were printed neatly but without any flourishes or exuberance.

Ian's attitude to them, however, was no less positive. He intended, he told us, to use the cards practically. One or two cards each week would become his focus for a short meditation in which he would return his thoughts to the quality in question. Then he would allow what he called 'the energy of my cards' to carry him through the forthcoming week. While those chosen cards were guiding his week he would have them on his notice-board where he could glance at them frequently, reminding himself that his was a life which would include those human qualities: love, tenderness, humour, companionship, even sexual passion, although perhaps not in the way he had once imagined.

Telling us this, Ian's face reflected an aliveness which clearly he was feeling within. Life was not passing Ian by. *He was choosing*. Every aspect of his demeanour reflected this.

It is possible to see Ian's optimism as a response to a situation in which what he ultimately wants (a loving partner and a long-term relationship) might yet happen. It can be harder to be optimistic when someone feels stuck with little or no desire for the person who is already sharing their life.

In the face of the death of sexual desire, marital therapists usually suggest that the marriage or partnership will come to an end unless the non-desiring partner has no choice but to stay. The no-choice might be economic; it might be because there are children neither parent wishes to leave. The no-choice might be religious or moral. The no-choice might also come if the couple experience each other (unconsciously perhaps) as much-needed parents. Then, too, it may be impossible to leave home.

There is certainly no moral highground in this kind of dilemma, especially when sex between people has such individual meaning. For some people to be denied sexual contact by their partner would be devastating. Perhaps for them sexual contact is a crucial means to express love, or to feel safe, or to maintain self-acceptance. Without it they may feel intolerably crushed, or even adrift. Other people may experience sexual contact quite differently: nice if you have it, not a big problem if you don't.

What sex means to each person will become very apparent when sexual desire subsides or dies. Then is the time to find out what needs underpin each individual's experience of sexual desire and how variously and creatively those needs can be met. In the having of a sexual relationship, or even in circumventing it, lateral thinking is often the best 'aid' a couple can have.

A couple might decide, for example, that the partner who 'needs sex' will be free to have other sexual relationships. Another couple may decide to put a time limit on their non-sexual togetherness in order to avoid feeling trapped. Caressing, massaging or playing sports together may stand in for sexual contact for some people, while for others an almost total physical distancing may be easiest to cope with.

Talking to people about sexual desire, thinking about sexual desire, I frequently came up against the conundrum: why does sexual desire die? ('A year ago I couldn't wait to get you into bed. Now I am staying late at work and searching for new excuses.')

Once again we face the exquisite subjectivity of individuals. Daily familiarity increases desire for some people: the desire to affirm a relationship in which each person feels trusting, wanted, and 'themselves', in which they can 'let go' *because* they are trusting, wanted and 'themselves'.

Others might not recognise such cosy, affirming impulses as desire at all. They may experience themselves as needing a much greater level of excitement and physical sensation (much hotter sex) than daily familiarity can generally allow. From those two sets of attitudes alone would come very different conclusions about when desire has come to an end.

Desiring sexually, while also suppressing feelings of anger, hostility, rage or resentment, is usually pretty tricky, although some couples who are compulsively expressive of their rage and hostility may also have tempestuous sex, desiring... what? Sensation, a feeling of connection, a sense of relief that despite their ghastly name-calling or even physical assaults, they have not been totally rejected?

Some people connect with emotions *and* with bodies; other people are capable of experiencing physical relief with partners from whom they feel emotionally disconnected. The idea of sex as a physical release can turn them on, even if they have long ago turned off to the relationship itself and to the emotional needs of their partner.

There are no rules. What there is, with luck, is the capacity to change if your way of desiring feels uncomfortable for you.

Scarcity value often revives sexual desire. People whose partners have left them or who are contemplating leaving them may suddenly feel fresh rushes of sexual passion. Fear, anxiety, envy, even hostility: these can all be powerful aphrodisiacs if you are facing the loss of someone who represents part of your safety.

This is because we pile onto what we call sexual desire many emotions and needs, not least of which is our need to be desired. *Tell me that I matter.* In some people this is so overwhelming it literally drives their lives — pushing them from one bed to the next — at least until they come to trust that they matter to themselves.

In others to be desired sexually is virtually an irrelevance. What they might seek is esteem and appreciation from others, or moments of shared goodwill and understanding, or a barrel of laughs and a day at the races.

25

Bringing intimacy to solitude

You can in solitude experience intense moments of sexual intimacy with your own self, or with fantasised or idealised others whom you can create entirely to your own satisfaction.

Exploring your fantasies while also familiarising yourself with your own body can liberate aspects of your desiring self and bring to your conscious mind new information about what you want and need. How comforting such an experience might be for you depends very much on whether this fits with the way you want to see yourself, and on the attitudes you have been taught to hold as to whether the having and expressing of sexual feelings is valid for yourself alone, or 'proper' only when shared with a partner.

When describing her desiring self, Alice seemed hesitant to see her sexual desires enacted in real life encounters. Yet her inner life, of which her feelings of desire are directly expressive, is rich and unexpected. Questioning herself as a sexually desiring woman, Alice said that she experiences a mismatch between desires for real persons and desires for real flesh.

'If the people one desires are not available you have to deal with that in some way: having them is not one of the ways which is available. If you desire someone outside intimacy, just because you fancy them, because they fit a particular set of appearances or body types or whatever, there's not really much point in bothering because the *person* isn't going to be there. It wasn't a person-to-person response which triggered your response of desire in the first place.'

That mismatch between the person and the triggers for desiring, a mismatch Alice captures exquisitely, is at the heart of the breakdown of many relationships, especially when they are short term.

But does the absence of lovers mean for Alice that her body receives too little attention? Not so, she says.

'My body doesn't get much attention from anybody else. It gets lots of attention from me. It also gets quite a lot of attention from whoever is inhabiting it at the time. I get hit by sexual desire all the time but I can manage better desire by keeping it in the realm of daydream and following it through in a masturbatory fantasy.

'I spend literally hours day-dreaming. The day-dreams are peopled, filmic, novelistic, unfolding with differentiated sets of characters who are entirely fictional.

'One rolling soap is me in other guises, being more than one character. A pair of lesbian lovers with various problems, and I am both those people, both the cause of the anguish and the sufferer of the anguish. That day-dream is almost entirely about working out feelings of rejection or self-doubt or love being lost.

'At times in my non-day-dreaming life, I get confronted with feelings like loss of self-esteem or rejection or fear of failure of an intimate sexual relationship and in my real life, at some point in the same day, I will go into such a day-dream. There are times when I am resentful of having to make ordinary flesh-and-blood contact with people because it gets in the way of that.'

Remembering her childhood, Alice said: 'I have always done this, even when I was a tiny child. Then I was the daughter of a god, much misunderstood by all the other daughters...'

Alice's rich inner sexual life is in part a blessing. It allows her to work through many emotions in a fairly conscious yet not overly controlled way, as well as giving her a varied and largely satisfying sexual life. On the other hand, precisely because she is so densely peopled from within, she can 'afford' to be cautious, maybe overly cautious about risking sexual contact with people other than herself, cautious about risking needing, wanting, reaching out — and being rejected.

I asked, somewhat tentatively, whether Alice expected a real live person eventually to occupy some of the inner space given over to her fantasy people. Was she, I wondered, clinging tenaciously to a state of unreadiness?

'That would shift the emphasis from where I would want to place it. My own emphasis is that I haven't found anyone good enough, I mean, good enough for Alice. However, I do want to discover the secret of losing or casting off passivity. If you are almost entirely passive you are eternally dependent on other people's perceptions of who or what you are in order for them to think, "She's a person who could..." which means that if some element of self-esteem comes from being in the world, you are giving to other people the right to determine whether you should be given that degree of self-esteem.'

Perhaps having sexual contact with real live people is psychologically dangerous for Alice, or perhaps combining love and sex is what unconsciously threatens her, for she is a woman who has intense, loving, non-sexual friendships. It does seem to be the combination of real people with sexual feelings which strikes warning bells too loud for her unconscious to ignore.

Having sex with real, live partners involves, for some people, little risk. (I am not referring to the risk of AIDS here, or of catching herpes or crabs. I am referring to emotional risks, like feeling lost in the relationship, or overwhelmed, or bored, or distanced, or used or coerced.) Sexual contact can for such people be compartmentalised, separated from emotions and treated as a function. Sexual contact can even act as a barrier against potential intimacy. Listen to Louis describe that defence exactly.

'I never have sex with the same woman or man for more than a month or two. By then I'm always bored. I'm just like that. I like novelty. For me there's no better time than the first time, or maybe the first few times. I get off on seeing how crazy they are to get into bed with me. That turns me on and then the girl or guy goes wild too. That's what I like, not Mummy-and-Daddy sex under the blankets with the lights out. That's for old age or for those who can't get what I can.

'It's not different with men or women, but men handle it better. I mean, when I have to say, "It's been great but..." I know I'm hardly ever going to get into a heavy scene with a guy. What I often get is a great farewell fuck. But the girls cry and carry on.

'The only person I can liken myself to is that character Richard Gere played in *American Gigolo*. I even bought the video I liked it that much. You know how the Gere character could fuck like an angel and the women who paid him were really into the fucking and it was all because he was kind of above it? Lovely to them, but somehow not there. That's me. And it drives them crazy. It's irresistible, I tell you.'

Perhaps as you read Louis' words you are feeling distaste, or maybe envy? Close to, Louis is hard to listen to but also hard to dislike. He is a sweet-looking man in his thirties, a teacher who is self-absorbed but very funny when he isn't talking about sex, and quite funny then sometimes too — if you are not one of his current, former or future partners.

Intimacy is not something Louis can, in his terms, 'handle', at least not intimacy in the way it has been unfolding in this book: *one person willing to engage with the reality of someone else — and to risk being changed by that experience.*

For Louis, intimacy which involves feelings as well as bodies would mean risking more of himself than he brings to his role as gigolo. It would also mean risking the other person bringing to the relationship more than the demands of a playmate. When that point comes in a relationship, Louis literally shuts the door.

Louis needs admiration, lots of it. Alas for Louis and his lovers, he can't give admiration — at least not beyond admiring those aspects of the person which fit in with his temporary need of them.

And why can't he give admiration? Maybe he is not safe enough internally to 'leave himself behind'.

When I spoke to Louis about getting to know someone in their wholeness, he shook his head. He also grinned; charm is his closest ally.

'That's not for me. The fucking is enough. Sometimes with some people, men mostly, there's a moment in the sex when I think, "God I want to climb inside this guy and stay there", but usually when I have done as much of that climbing inside as is humanly possible the feeling goes. Thank God!'

Louis needs the intensity of new sex. Experiencing that intensity, he feels alive. But it is a life limited to a narrow range of emotions and limited by a compulsive need for repetition. As one lover goes out the door, another enters, but there is very little individuality about these lovers in Louis' experience of them.

Through the anonymity of sex Louis feels alive, admired, sexually satisfied; he is having fun. But he is not having self-and-other relationships. For Louis trusting — self-trusting, as well as trusting others — is too dangerous, so in sex too he must keep his barriers firmly in place. His love-making with others, sexually uninhibited as it might be, seems to have all the characteristics of two strangers meeting, with little human relatedness taking place and little sense of meaning.

So, what is Louis desiring? Not contact, not closeness, not a shift in two lives brought together by the alchemy of sex. No, not that, but an attractive body *which can arouse him* to experience a hit of bodily sensation which will, in turn, and like any other narcotic, defeat the grumblings of fear; not least the fear of isolation, meaninglessness and death.

But when a body no longer arouses him it must be shuffled off, and the person with it.

Straight? Gay? Should it matter?

When people are, in their sexual practices, exclusively heterosexual or gay, it is almost inevitable that they will carry misunderstandings and prejudices about the desires and sexual practices of the 'other' group. This is often couched in terms of hostility which is especially marked in the attitudes of heterosexual people toward gay people. (Most gay people have far more knowledge about heterosexual people than heterosexual people have about gay people. This is not surprising. Gay people were raised in heterosexual families and live in a world where heterosexuality is the norm.)

Despite having the dominant culture so firmly on 'their side', heterosexuals still shore up their prejudices with certainty and self-righteousness. Homophobia runs deep in our communities; it attacks even our capacity to desire freely.

Identifying with certain modes of desiring, certain objects of desire, specific acts: none of this happens by chance. However you express it, this is, again, part of the language of your own inner world.

You may find solace and security from identifying with a way of life that is upheld by the dominant culture (heterosexual, married). You might, on the other hand, find solace and stimulation, a welcome feeling of being 'different but at home' as one gay man said to me, as part of a minority community. But whether you are in a heterosexual relationship, a gay relationship, a multiple relationship or in no relationship at all, you *are still your own self*. The other person, or even a lifestyle that feels 'right', can help in your quest to know and express *who I am*, but it does not save you from the essential task of finding your own solid ground within.

More specifically, it does not save you from the temptation to overload your sexually intimate relationship with needs from your past, as well as all your current desires for security and protection.

Of course, within each relationship you are responded to somewhat differently, and so your sense of self shifts. You can, in your experience of self, feel enhanced by one person, diminished by another, or enhanced by one lifestyle and diminished by another.

But the quality of your relationships is much less affected by whether your sexually intimate relationships are gay or straight, married or multiple, than by whether you feel in touch with and true to your own inner world. *Only from that freedom comes the capacity to be self-affirming, and to have authentic, mutually affirming relationships with others.*

When I talked to heterosexual men about their perceptions of sexual intimacy between homosexual men I was often assured that homosexual men are not sexually intimate — 'they just fuck'.

I would interpret this point of view as a projection, perhaps one laced with envy. There are undoubtedly gay men who 'just fuck', and there are undoubtedly heterosexual men who would like to 'just fuck' if only women would let them.

Theo strongly rebuts the 'just fucking' theory. Of male homosexual sex he says, 'Even in sex as recreation there is intimacy. That fleeting sexual encounter can be just so intimate that it can leave you with a great hole when it is not there. The sexual attraction thing is so potent for a male, especially at a young age, and I never separated them out, sex and love, so in terms of getting my intimacy needs met, they're all part of the same thing.'

Theo adds some interesting generalisations about heterosexual men and their attitudes towards actual or potential partners.

'One of the differences between gay men and heterosexual men is that for heterosexual men, sex is power. For homosexual men, sex is ecstasy and love. Heterosexual men never talk about how fantastic it was for them, and what she did to them. When gay men talk it is in terms of pleasure and sensuality. Even the most anonymous sexual contact that I've had there was always a moment of extraordinary giving and of *holding*. It means, I think, that heterosexual men are not game to *give themselves up to that*. For gay men there is nothing of that sort of sexual hang-up.'

Few heterosexual men will admit to envying homosexual men anything at all, although heterosexuals' insistence on decrying gay promiscuity speaks of a deep, unacknowledged envy ('I don't want to be like him, but I want what he has.'). Would acknowledging their envy threaten heterosexual men's hard-won masculinity? I can't know. What I do know is that every gay man I spoke to told me how widespread is heterosexual men's 'dabbling' in gay sex and how many straight men visit gay bars or have fleeting sexual encounters in public places. How does this fit in with each man's sense of himself as a desiring person, as a man who must compartmentalise part of his desiring life and shroud it in secrecy, even from himself?

Each story would be different. What may be common to them, however, is a capacity to compartmentalise, to split off, to be Box by day and Cox by evening. This compartmentalising is not always done easily and it is rarely achieved without cost. But it is a dynamic that women, in general, find hard to emulate.

Heterosexual women's fantasies about lesbians were, as I listened to them, more overtly envious than heterosexual men allowed themselves to be. Yet it was less often the sex that was envied — or even especially well understood — but rather a perception that lesbian couples might understand and meet each other's emotional needs.

Heather's views were typical. 'I have often felt enraged that even though I try to be honest and talk about what I want, I rarely have the feeling that my husband has a clue what I'm saying. I've often said to myself, "If only I was a man trying to love a woman

I'd do it so differently" and I guess that's what two women together can do: know what each other wants, and know how to meet those wants.'

But in relationships where people bring their deepest fears from the past, as well as their greatest hopes for redemption, all intimacy problems are not solved through 'being understood'. You may never be better understood than by your therapist, but the needs people bring to intimate sexual relationships go beyond the need for understanding.

Feeling understood

Roger was adamant that he wants 'to be understood, yes, but I want to be enigmatic and mysterious as well. It's partly controlling, and partly an affirmation of my own space. The concept of fully knowing is meaningless to me.'

And speaking of a former relationship, where sharing intimate thoughts and feelings had been highly prized, Catherine said, 'Jonathan certainly understood me, but this did not mean that I felt *met*. Nor that my soul was being fed. For all that understanding I could not allow any soul warmth. It would have been too invasive. Understanding can be wonderful, but it can also be a power trip.'

Understanding someone else; attempting to please someone else; feeling empathic: these all seem highly desirable aspects of sexual intimacy. And they can be. But only when each person's psychological boundaries are intact. Without these you can quickly feel invaded, emptied, confused, numbed or violent. 'The more I tried to please Jonathan,' said Catherine, 'the less I had of myself. *And the more I needed him to shore me up.*'

I am not arguing against the cultivation of understanding within a relationship. What I am saying is that when the separate boundaries between two people blur, and they become vague about where self-responsibility begins and ends, it can set up a dynamic which hinders or even defeats intimacy.

Elizabeth and Kim's saga of desiring and disappointment shows this. They are talented, their work areas are compatible, people adore seeing them together. But Kim can't settle down.

She is constantly postponing their plans to buy a house together and often seems irritable when they are the no-audience couple at home rather than the ideal couple out in the world.

Kim is convinced that she wants the relationship to work. If a relationship could work for her, it would be with Elizabeth, or so she thinks. Sometimes she feels something different. Maybe she mistrusts Elizabeth? Or maybe, despite everything, Elizabeth is not quite the right woman for her? Elizabeth is clever and funny, charming and kind, but ... there is something stirring in Kim, a feeling of unease she cannot locate but which shows itself in her irritability and her unwillingness to surrender herself temporarily in love-making.

Elizabeth is tormenting herself, wondering what she is doing wrong. If Kim is not happy, then surely that is her fault. Shouldn't she be able to make Kim happy? She has never loved anyone as much as she loves Kim. Why is she failing?

The harder Elizabeth tries to see herself reflected back as someone who can 'make Kim happy' the more 'unattainable' Kim or Kim's happiness feels to Elizabeth. Oddly enough, this goes for Kim too. She feels about as unattainable to herself as she apparently does to Elizabeth. Neither of them likes this; neither of them is happy. The 'ideal couple' is unravelling.

Kim does not remember and no one has ever told her that when she was a baby her mother was depressed. She coped with her three children's physical needs well enough but Kim was demanding. She didn't want to hit Kim. Instead she would shut Kim into her room and bring her out only when Kim's father was due home. No family member could emotionally afford to acknowledge Kim's mother's distress, and certainly no family member wanted to rehash unhappy memories when the woman eventually perked up.

Yet feeling trusting enough to make a commitment to Elizabeth, and to abandon herself however briefly to love-making with someone she loves and who has the power to reject her: *these are 're-appearances' which the infant Kim, the forgotten Kim, is making in the life of adult Kim.*

It is possible to predict that the more strenuously Elizabeth tries to 'help' Kim or even to 'reach' her, the more likely it is she will drive Kim away. Her anxiety will attach itself to Kim's guilt-in-the-present and discomfort-from-the-past. That combination will be too much for Kim to bear. Kim will then escape to a relationship with someone less 'real' than Elizabeth is, someone with whom she can be close rather than intimate, 'sexy' rather than nurturing, 'funny' rather than exposed. And Elizabeth will be left with feelings of loss, regret and failure.

Elizabeth could help Kim, *but only by helping herself.*

She could (if she is lucky, if she is supported) come to see that everything that happens in Kim's life in the present *does not come about because of their relationship.*

She could accept that in some of the internal dramas in Kim's life she, Elizabeth, is barely present, except as a catalyst.

When Elizabeth perceives something is troubling Kim, she could choose not to centralise herself in that drama ('What have I done wrong? What should I do now?'). Instead, she could leave Kim alone.

This may give Kim the chance to come *toward* Elizabeth, rather than feeling she must push her away if she is not to die from internal suffocation. It may even give Kim the chance to discover that loving someone does not necessarily mean that she will be put in a metaphorical closed room.

And what would be in it for Elizabeth? The survival of a relationship that means a great deal to her would be one benefit. And freedom from the mixture of humility and grandiosity which tells her that when things are not going right, *it must be her fault* and even if she is not at fault, *that she ought to be able to help.*

Closeness and space

Intimacy has been beautifully defined by Lucy Goodison as 'a very strong energy exchange with another person', but for intimacy to be sustaining, rather than overwhelming, you need the other side of the coin also — solitude — which Lucy has called 'A very intense connection with the energy of your own body.' That may not be exactly how you experience it, but the need for connection with others, *while also remaining connected to yourself*, is something you will recognise.

To make any relationship 'work' with another human being, you probably need closeness and acceptance and also separateness, self-sufficiency and space. You need to be reasonably aware of your own feelings; aware of how those feelings have been affected by your past; and how your feelings are affecting others in your current relationships.

This fine balance between intimacy and solitude is not easily achieved or sustained. When you are attempting to create this balance in your life, while also living in partnership with someone else, their respect for your separateness, as well as their joy in your connectedness, will enhance your efforts immeasurably. Whether this person is of the same gender as yourself, or is, more conventionally, of the other gender, seems of negligible importance. It will affect you, of course: how you see yourself and, most certainly, how you are perceived by others. But the twin desires for intimacy and for solitude rise above questions of social conformity; they go straight to the heart of our deepest human strivings.

26

Cupid's arrows

Like most boys of six, my son Gabriel came to detest public kissing. To take revenge I told him the story of Cupid, the fat little angel with its quiver full of arrows. One of these arrows, I assured Gabriel, can pierce your heart slyly; you won't even know that it's there. But the next person you see you will fall in love with, and you will kiss that person often, even in public.

Gabriel's reaction was of such horror that I had to relent and tell him I was joking. Or half joking. For sometimes lust — or love — does strike so swiftly and apparently arbitrarily that it would seem Cupid may be at work. Yet, in retrospect, many people would acknowledge a certain kind of readiness — whether or not this is conscious — for that moment when Cupid's arrow changes the course of a life.

Francesca, now in her forties, believes that she can see clearly that she has 'been pushed forward in the ways I needed to be' by the major love affairs in her life.

'The first man I was seriously in love with was a real liberator for me. He was an intellectual and I was very afraid of my own genuine interest in intellectual matters. He gave me the feeling that I had a right to take up those issues. I was often intimidated by him but he pushed me on and took me seriously which was pretty amazing as I was in no condition to take myself seriously.

'What did I need from him? Well, in addition to that validation of who I was and am, I needed love. He was able to show that. And I was able to accept it, and largely to believe I was worthy of it, like any real person. Irresistible! But he was also something of a Svengali. He wanted to interpret me to the world and even to myself. That made it hard for me literally to breathe within the relationship. At first I withdrew from him physically. I became more and more distanced from him sexually. I would have sex with him but would be switched off or very unhappy. But that sexual withdrawal made him so unhappy it felt like I had no choice but to get out, even though there was a lot of love still. It was terribly hard to make the break. I went on needing his approval and his love for years. And I also went on dallying with the temptation to believe that he knew more about me than I ever could. His certainty about things was something I could never compete with, yet oddly enough he is tremendously uncertain about himself and that has in some ways diminished his working life, while I have gone on and done at least as well as he ever told me I could do.

'My second major affair was with a woman. I had had several affairs with women and felt very eager to be sexually in touch with women, but with Caro I fell deeply in love and I can still recall how incredible it was, to be in love with this fantastic woman, to have access to her body and her mind, and to be loved by her in return. For months it felt like heaven. I had been having therapy and I abandoned that, believing that I was on top of the world and would stay there forever. The sexual relationship with her ended in an oblique and painful way, but for a couple of years it was wonderful. I used to feel sorry for heterosexual women who would never know what it was like to have the intense friendship women are used to having with each other, plus an incredible eroticism and sexual satisfaction as well. But when things began to get a bit shaky between us I found myself once again withdrawing sexually, not feeling so eager, trying to find excuses. It was as though I had to get away because I could not put into words what was going on. But I think retreating totally is not the answer and may never be the answer. Whatever you are retreating from follows you around like a faithful puppy.

'Why Caro? She was loveable. Admirable, funny. Of course, difficult and prickly too — and demanding. More than she realised. Who isn't? I suppose in retrospect I'm aware that I wasn't sure I could love that deeply and to discover I could — and a woman — it blew my mind apart.

'That relationship ostensibly broke up because I fell for a much younger woman and Caro couldn't handle it. I don't blame her. I behaved badly, or anyway single-mindedly. I was in my early thirties then and Janie was only twenty. She was gorgeous and I was besotted, I guess befuddled with lust, but it was also that she was so young and I was moving towards more and more of a need to have a child. It sounds bizarre because my feelings for her were so sex-driven, but sometimes I would look at her face asleep on the pillow, she would look about twelve when she was asleep, and I would feel no lust at all but just incredible tenderness and the need — which I then thought could not be realised — to have a child of my own.

'The relationship with Janie also ended. I felt overloaded with her demands. I could not put up with them. Also I was not really separated from Caro or even from Luca. Perhaps that made Janie more frantic than she would otherwise have been, but I was too needy myself to want to be her mummy as well as her lover.

'After that I had a period of semi-solitude, feeling pretty raw and ill-equipped for big relationships. Then, slowly, I began a more conventional relationship, with Dave, the man who is the father of my three children. I needed the children and possibly a less overwhelming kind of relationship than I had had in the past. More conventional, more space maybe? He admired and needed me, and later it turned out he needed the children too, although now he needs me much less. Or perhaps I have made myself much less needable. We are still together, and we are both very keen on the boys, but our own relationship is not ideal. Still, if you believe as I do that you grow by changing, then 'ideal' is a word you can only use for a limited time.

'My sexual desires have been like catapults, lurching me towards the right person at the right time who has made dramatic shifts in how I could see myself and how I could act, although, alas for them, often the insights come much later on! But each time there has been a great deal of love, and of good will, and of interest and tenderness and exciting ideas, all of which I feel have made me the person I now am. Whereas the instant lust affairs, the one-night or one-month stands, have dissolved into the past with hardly a trace.'

Francesca's sense that sexual desire has been a catalyst for emotional and spiritual change in her life is echoed by many people I have spoken to. I recognise this pattern in my life also.

Close to someone else, you take with more or less consciousness and gratitude what they have to give, sometimes scarcely noticing that this may be new knowledge of your self, knowledge which might ease the limitations of your past, and open up for you a possibility of greater wholeness in the future.

Open to your self and other people, you can gain or regain the confidence to trust, to let go and then to change in the ways necessary for you to find out not only *who you are*, but how best to express that in times of solitude and intimacy.

There are many ways in which change can begin. And no way of knowing when change is ending, except death. But it is desire, the desire for something or for someone, or the desire to be at the centre of your own life conscious of what you want, that can be the most dynamic of pointers, setting your life off along a fresh track in which you do not simply discover someone or something new, but also what is new or undiscovered in your own self.

Dante spoke warmly of 'an intellectual life filled with love'. That beautiful phrase describes to me a life in which thinking (about people, about how we live, about life's meaning for ourselves and for other people) is honoured, but also suffused with love which leads to connection, to spontaneity of feeling, and from there to action if that should be appropriate.

It is a phrase to describe a life which takes into account the needs and desires of others, and balances them with your own.

Like the setting of the sun and the rising of the moon; like the falling of the leaves and the arrival of buds; like the daily ebb and flow of the ocean's tides; like the recognition of your self in other people and the discovery of your own uniqueness, an image of a cycle arises once more.

Trusting ourselves, we feel alive; feeling alive, we can reach out and trust others. Trusting others, we can cherish what they have to give. Taking what they have to give, we feel more alive.

Part 1

p. 7 'I have a body...distinct from all of them.' Ferrucci, 1982, p. 67.

p. 8 'The ego is... the horse.' Freud, 1923.

p. 8 'The experience of Self...cannot touch.' von Franz, 1975, p. 73.

p. 20 'The more possible... he has become.' Guntrip, 1971, p. 181.

p. 22 'The life of... own life.' Winnicott, 1986, p. 27.

p. 22 David Jansen, class notes. Relationship Development Centre, Sydney, 1988.

p. 23 'The phenomenological basis of the word self.' Deikman, 1982, p. 92.

p. 23 Krishnamurti's phrase, 'little man within', and also 'What you now feel...' Wilber, 1981, p. 70.

p. 27 Winnicott's work on the capacity to be alone is crucial to this book. *See* 'On the Capacity to Be Alone' in Winnicott, 1965; *see also* Davis & Wallbridge, 1981.

p. 34 'Over the years... self.' Miller, 1983, p. 47.

p. 36 'Shortly before... to myself.' Wolff, 1969, p. 67.

p. 37 *See* Segal (2nd edn), 1975; *see also* Friday, 1986.

p. 38 'Independent... happens in a relationship.' Rubin, 1983, p. 53.

p. 41 'There is no confusion... other exist.' Stern, 1985, p. 10.

p. 44 'Catherine Hillery... do them.' Colegate, 1988, p. 123.

p. 46 'Irrational rage... sentimentality.' Lowen, 1983, p. 62.

p. 46 'Of feeling... worthwhile outside.' Sennett, 1977, p. 72.

p. 47 'The manifest... begins to care.' ibid., p. 71.

p. 50 'becomes an important... person.' Fraiberg, 1968, p. 191.

p. 50 'Interpersonal... other humans.' Stern, 1985, p. 151.

p. 51 'The best hope... one's whims.' Lasch, 1984, p. 178.

p. 58 'For many... for him, either.' Makeba, 1988, pp. 19–20.

p. 58 'Accepting myself... familiar.' Reboin, 1986, p. 182.

p. 60 'The seminar... transcended them.' Gerhard Adler, 1979, p. 89.

Part 2

p. 66 'The tight pants...' Kaufman, 1987, p. 3.

p. 74 'The gay child... survive.' Morse & Larkin, 1988, p. xxv.

p. 76 Joanna Ryan, private discussion, London, 1988.

p. 77 Harrison, 1987, p. 142.

p. 78 ibid., pp. 142–3.

p. 79 Wiebke Wüstenberg, private discussion, Sydney and Frankfurt, 1987–1988.

p. 82 Fraiberg, 1968, p. 189.

p. 83 '... made a problem of...', 'Heterosexual men...', '... is written... men's sun.' Rutherford, 1988, p. 43.

p. 84 'All I can... Biggles.' Baker, 1988, pp. 247, 255.

p. 84 'Few marriages... reversed.' Dicks, 1967, p. 33.

p. 85 'If human infants... crisis.' Guntrip, 1971, p. 114.

p. 85 'In the unconscious... excluded.', 'The fear... not inevitable.' Seidenberg, 1973, p. 326.

p. 86 'Like most boys... you get hurt.' Wilson-Fuller, the *Australian Magazine*, 5–6 November, 1988, p. 13.

p. 89 'The boy-child... with her.', 'A serious lack... identity.', 'If father... the transition.', '... need to have... without passivity.' Cathie, 1987, p. 9.

p. 97 '... claims... world)', 'He embraces... the world.' Kaufman, 1987, p. 11.

p. 99 'Whenever Preston... saying.' Bryers, 1987, p. 210.

p.101 'By the time... thrashings.' Ireland, 1988, pp. 90–1.

p.104 'Over coffee... like a brother's.' Michael Lassell, 'How to Watch Your Brother Die', in Morse & Larkin, 1988, pp. 224–5.

p.108 'Faced with... into himself.' Sanger & Kelly, 1988, p. 23.

p.122 'In that moment... outside world.' Garner, 1980, p. 141.

p.122 'Feminism has... and feelings.', 'Often we arrive... or child.' Seidler, 1988, pp. 280, 290.

p.126   'Children are... lives began.' Slater, 1976, p. 122.
p.130   'As families... each day.' Bowen, 1978, p. 520.

Part 3

p.133   'The greater part... existence.' Wolff, p. 161.
p.136   'I may... what I see.' Sutherland, 1977, p. 75.
p.136   '... calm, restful... is around.' Winnicott, 'On the Capacity to Be Alone', 1965, p. 54.
p.137   'being alone... someone else is present.' ibid.
p.137   'The baby gains proof... the world.' Guntrip, 1971, p. 117.
p.166   'Man wants... a piece.', 'Either he... to fail.', 'The other... cohesive whole.' Symington, 1986, pp. 46–7.
p.170   'It is just... missing.' Anthony Storr, reviewing Miller, 1981, in the *New Republic*, 1981.
p.175   'creative and... the environment.' Guntrip, 1971, p. 50.
p.178   'Only she... in the end.' Rich, 1978, p. 33.

Part 4

p.179   Malone & Malone, 1987, p. 51.
p.186   'Self-esteem... capacity to love.' Symington, 1986, p. 170.
p.208   'The person... away from.' Fairbairn, in Guntrip, 1971, p. 116.
p.210   'It is a banality... others.' Wolff, 1969, p. 168.
p.215   'Who is there?... God replies.' Deikman, 1982, p. 88.
p.219   'Feminists were... all right.' Dennis Altman. 'The Myth of Endless Love', *National Times*, 3–9 February 1984, pp. 8–9.
p.220   Lucy Goodison, private discussion, London, 1988; *see also* Goodison, 1990.
p.229   'Hand in hand... uncoupled.' Stein, 1985, p. 175.
p.231   'We need... learn it.' Rilke, 1987, p. 85.
p.242   'The family's capacity... your own.' Napier & Whitaker, 1978, pp. 93.
p.243   'It is very difficult... same time.' ibid., p. 116.
p.243   'to ask... themselves.' ibid., p. 119.

Part 5

p.247   'Our love ... must happen.' Parker-Rhodes, 1985, p. 45.

p.249   'The experience ... of trust.' Pincus, 1978, p. 144.

p.257   'It is precisely ... true selves.' Lucy Goodison, private discussion, London, 1988; *see also* Goodison, 1990.

p.257   'Lesbianism ... my being.' Audre Lord in Linden et al, 1982.

p.258   'That the ability ... of life.' Schneiderman, 1983, p. 73.

p.267   'I don't know ... the ballet.' Dennis Hopper quoted by Susan Wyndham in 'Mr Hopper Rides Again', the *Australian Magazine*, 7–8 April 1990, pp. 31–8.

p.271   'Speaking personally ... choice.' Lowen, 1980, p. 259.

p.272   Hocking, 1990, pp. 118–20.

p.272   Roberto Assagioli, 'The Resolution of Conflicts'; *see also* Sam Keen, 'The Golden Mean of Roberto Assagioli, *Psychology Today*, December 1974.

p.280   'It was an old ... enjoy sex.' Alther, 1990, p. 263.

p.282   'How peculiar ... familiarity.' Gordon, 1987, p. 149.

p.287   'The trick ... to love.', 'The notion ... later.' Friday, 1986, pp. 539, 527.

p.302   'a very strong ... person.', 'A very intense ... body.' Lucy Goodison, private discussion, London, 1988.

Adler, Alfred, *The Pattern of Life*, Kegan Paul, Trench, Trebner, London, 1931.

Adler, Gerhard, *Dynamics of the Self*, Coventure, London, 1979.

Alther, Lisa, *Bedrock*, Alfred A. Knopf, New York, 1990.

Assagioli, Roberto, *The Act of Will*, Viking, New York, 1973.

——— , *Psychosynthesis, a Manual of Principles and Techniques*, Hobbs Doorman, New York, 1965.

Baker, Garth, 'World according to Garth', in King, M. 1988.

Balint, Michael, *The Basic Fault*, Tavistock, London, 1968.

Becker, Ernest, *The Denial of Death*, The Free Press, New York, 1973.

Bowen, Murray, *Family Therapy in Clinical Practice*, Jason Aronson, New York, 1978.

Bowlby, John, *Attachment and Loss*, 3 vols, The Hogarth Press, London, 1963, 1973, 1980.

Bryers, Paul, *Coming First*, Bloomsbury, London, 1987.

Cardinal, Marie, *The Words to Say It*, Picador, London, 1984.

Cartledge, Sue & Ryan, Joanna (eds), *Sex and Love*, The Women's Press, London, 1983.

Casement, Patrick, 'Interpretation: fresh insight or cliché?', *Free Associations* No. 5, London, 1986.

Cathie, Sean, 'What does it mean to be a man?', *Free Associations* No. 8, London, 1987.

Chapman, Rowena & Rutherford, Jonathan, *Male Order: Unwrapping Masculinity*, Lawrence & Wishart, London, 1988.

Chodorow, Nancy, *The Reproduction of Mothering: Psychoanalysis and the Sociology of Gender*, University of California Press, Berkeley & Los Angeles, 1978.

Clark, Ronald, W., *Freud: The Man and the Cause*, Granada, London, 1982.

Colegate, Isabel, *Deceits of Time*, Viking, London, 1988.

Davis, Madeline & Wallbridge, David, *Boundary and Space: An Introduction to the Work of D.W. Winnicott*, Karnac Press, London, 1981.

Deikman, Arthur J., *The Observing Self: Mysticism and Psychotherapy*, Beacon Press, Boston, 1982.

Demetrakopoulos, Stephanie, *Listening to Our Bodies*, Beacon Press, Boston, 1983.

Dicks, Henry V., *Marital Tensions: Clinical Studies towards a Psychological Theory of Interaction*, Routledge & Kegan Paul, London, 1967.

Dinnerstein, Dorothy, *The Mermaid and the Minotaur: Sexual Arrangements and Human Malaise*, Harper Colophon, New York, 1976.

Eichenbaum, Luise & Orbach, Susie, *Outside In, Inside Out*, Penguin, Harmondsworth, 1982.

——— , *What do Women Want?*, Michael Joseph, London, 1983.

Ernst, Sheila & Goodison, Lucy, *In Our Own Hands: A Book of Self-Help Therapy*, The Women's Press, London, 1981.

Ernst, Sheila & Maguire, Marie (eds), *Living with the Sphinx: Papers from the Women's Therapy Centre*, The Women's Press, London, 1987.

Fairbairn, W.R.D., *An Object Relations Theory of Personality*, Basic Books, New York, 1954.

Ferrucci, Piero, *What We May Be: The Visions and Techniques of Psychosynthesis*, Turnstone Press, 1982.

Fraiberg, Selma H., *The Magic Years: Understanding and Handling the Problems of Early Childhood*, Methuen, London, 1968.

——— (ed.), *Clinical Studies in Infant Mental Health: The First Year of Life*, Tavistock Publications, London & New York, 1980.

Frankl, Viktor E., *Man's Search for Meaning*, Beacon Press, Boston, 1939.

——— , *The Will to Meaning*, Souvenir Press, London, 1971.

Franz, Marie-Louise von, *Carl Gustav Jung: His Myth in Our Time*, G.P. Putnam's Sons, New York, 1975.

Freud, Sigmund, *The Ego and the Id* (1923 *Standard Edition*, vol.19, Hogarth Press, London, 1961).

────, *The Standard Edition of the Complete Psychological Works of Sigmund Freud*, ed. James Strachey, 24 vols, Hogarth Press, London 1953–1964.

Friday, Nancy, *Jealousy*, Collins, London, 1986.

Garner, Helen, *Honour and Other People's Children*, McPhee Gribble, Melbourne, 1980.

Garner, Shirley N., Kahane, Claire & Sprengnether, Madelon, (eds), *The (M)other Tongue: Essays in Feminist Psychoanalytic Interpretation*, Cornell University Press, Ithaca and London, 1985.

Gilligan, Carol, *In a Different Voice: Psychological Theory and Women's Development*, Harvard University Press, Cambridge, Mass., 1982.

Goodison, Lucy, *Moving Heaven and Earth: Sexuality, Spirituality and Social Change*, The Women's Press, London, 1990.

Gordon, Mary, *Temporary Shelter*, Bloomsbury, London, 1987.

Gosskurth, Phyllis, *Melanie Klein: Her World and Her Work*, Hodder & Stoughton, London, 1986.

Guntrip, Harry, *Psychoanalytic Theory, Therapy and the Self: A Basic Guide to the Human Personality in Freud, Erikson, Klein, Sullivan, Fairbairn, Hartmann, Jacobson & Winnicott*, Basic Books, New York, 1971.

Harrison, Fraser, *A Father's Diary*, Collins, London, 1985.

────, *A Winter's Tale*, Collins, London, 1987.

Hocking, Bronwyn, *Little Boy Lost*, Bloomsbury, London, 1990.

Horney, Karen, *New Ways in Psychoanalysis*, Norton, New York, 1939 and 1966.

Ireland, Kevin, 'One of the Bohemians', in King, M. 1988.

Joseph, Gloria I. & Lewis, Jill, *Common Differences: Conflicts in Black and White Feminist Perspectives*, South End Press, Boston, 1981.

Jung, Carl G., *Symbols of Transformation*, Princeton University Press, Princeton, N.J., (2nd edn), 1967.

────, *Memories, Dreams and Reflections* Routledge & Kegan Paul, London, 1963.

Kagan, Jerome, *The Nature of the Child*, Basic Books, New York, 1985.

Kaufman, Michael (ed.), *Beyond Patriarchy*, Oxford University Press, Toronto, 1987.

King, Michael (ed.), *One of the Boys? Changing Views of Masculinity in New Zealand*, Heinemann, Auckland, 1988.

Klein, Melanie, *Envy and Gratitude*, Dell, New York, 1975.

——— , *The Psychoanalysis of Children*, Dell, New York, 1932, 1975.

Kohut, Heinz, *The Analysis of the Self*, International Universities Press, New York, 1971.

——— , *The Restoration of the Self*, International Universities Press, New York, 1977.

Lacan, Jacques, *The Four Fundamental Concepts of Psychoanalysis*, Penguin, Harmondsworth, 1977.

Laing, R.D., *The Divided Self: A Study of Sanity and Madness*, Tavistock, London, 1960.

——— , *Self and Others*, Tavistock, London, 1962.

Lasch, Christopher, *The Culture of Narcissism: American Life in an Age of Diminishing Expectations*, Norton, New York, 1979.

——— , *The Minimal Self: Psychic Survival in Troubled Times*, Norton, New York, 1984.

Linden, R.R., Russell, D.E.H. & Star, S.L., *Against Sado-Masochism*, Frog in the Well Press, 1982.

Little, Margaret, 'On the value of regression to dependence', *Free Associations* No. 10, London, 1987.

Lowen, Alexander, *Fear of Life*, Macmillan, New York, 1980.

——— , *Narcissism: Denial of the True Self*, Macmillan, New York, 1983.

McDougall, Joyce, *Theatres of the Mind: Illusion and Truth on the Psychoanalytic Stage*, Free Association Books, London, 1986.

Makeba, Miriam & Hall, James, *Makeba: My Story*, Bloomsbury, London, 1988.

Mahler, Margaret S., Pines, Fred & Bergman, Anni, *The Psychological Birth of the Human Infant: Symbiosis and Individuation*, Hutchinson, London, 1975.

Malone, Thomas P. & Malone, Patrick T., *The Art of Intimacy*, Simon & Schuster, New York, 1987.

Maslow, Abraham, *The Farther Reaches of Human Nature*, Viking, New York, 1971.

Metcalf, Andy & Humphries, Martin, *The Sexuality of Men*, Pluto Press, London, 1985.

Miller, Alice, *The Drama of the Gifted Child and the Search for the True Self*, Faber & Faber, London, 1983 (published in the USA as *Prisoners of Childhood*, Basic Books, New York, 1981).

———, *For Your Own Good: Hidden Cruelty in Childrearing the Roots of Violence*, Faber & Faber, London, 1983.

———, *Thou Shalt Not Be Aware*, Pluto Press, London, 1987.

Modjeska, Drusilla, *Poppy*, McPhee Gribble, Melbourne, 1990.

Morgan, Robin, *The Demon Lover: On the Sexuality of Terrorism*, Methuen, London, 1989.

Morse, Carl & Larkin, Joan (eds), *Gay and Lesbian Poetry in Our Time*, St Martin's Press, New York, 1988.

Napier, Augustus Y. & Whitaker, Carl A., *The Family Crucible*, Harper & Row, New York, 1978.

New, Caroline & David, Miriam, *For the Children's Sake*, Penguin, Harmondsworth, 1985.

Nin, Anais, *Journals*, 7 vols, Quartet Books, London, 1973–1980.

Norwood, Robin, *Women Who Love Too Much*, Arrow, London, 1986.

O'Connor, Peter, *Dreams and the Search for Meaning*, Methuen Haynes, Sydney, 1986.

———, *Understanding Jung Understanding Yourself*, Methuen Haynes, Sydney, 1985.

Orbach, Susie, *Hunger Strike: the Anorectic's Struggle as a Metaphor for Our Age*, Faber & Faber, London, 1986.

Parker-Rhodes, Damaris, *The Way Out Is the Way In*, Quaker Home Service, London, 1985.

Pedder, Jonathan, R., 'Some biographical contributions to psychoanalytic theories', *Free Associations*, No.10, London, 1987.

Piercy, Marge, *Stone, Paper, Knife*, Pandora, London, 1983.

Pincus, Lily & Dare, Christopher, *Secrets in the Family*, Faber & Faber, London, 1978.

Post van der, Laurens, *Jung and the Story of Our Time*, The Hogarth Press, London, 1976.

Reboin, Faith, 'Lesbian Grandmother', in Adelman, Marcy (ed.), *Long Time Passing: Lives of Older Lesbians*, Alyson Publications, Boston, 1986.

Rich, Adrienne, *The Dream of a Common Language*, Norton, New York, 1978.

Rilke, Rainer Maria, *The Selected Poetry of Rainer Maria Rilke*, Picador, London, 1987.

Rowan, John, *The Horned God: Feminism and Men as Wounding and Healing*, Routledge & Kegan Paul, London, 1987.

Rubin, Lillian, *Intimate Strangers*, Harper & Row, New York, 1983.

Rutherford, Jonathan, 'Who's that Man?', in Chapman, R. & Rutherford, J., 1988.

Ryan, Joanna, 'Lesbian Therapists: Some Practical, Political and Theoretical Issues', Feminism and Psychotherapy Conference, Leeds, 1987.

Rycroft, Charles, *Anxiety and Neurosis*, Allen Lane, London, 1968.

——, *A Critical Dictionary of Psychoanalysis*, Penguin, Harmondsworth, 1979.

Samuels, Andrew, Shorter, Bani & Plaut, Fred, *A Critical Dictionary of Jungian Analysis*, Routledge & Kegan Paul, London, 1986.

—— (ed.), *The Father: Contemporary Jungian Perspectives*, Free Association Books, London, 1985.

Sanford, John A., *The Invisible Partners*, Paulist Press, New York, 1980.

Sanger, Sirgay & Kelly, John, *The Woman Who Works, the Parent Who Cares*, Bantam, New York, 1988.

Scarf, Maggie, *Intimate Partners: Patterns in Love and Marriage*, Century Hutchinson, London, 1987.

Schneiderman, Stuart, *Jacques Lacan: The Death of an Intellectual Hero*, Harvard University Press, Cambridge, Mass., 1983.

Segal, Hanna, *Introduction to the Work of Melanie Klein*, The Hogarth Press, London, 2nd edn, 1975.

Seidenberg, Robert, 'Is Anatomy Destiny?', in Miller, Jean Baker (ed.), *Psychoanalysis and Women*, Penguin, Harmondsworth, 1973.

Seidler, Victor J., 'Fathering, Authority and Masculinity', in Chapman, Rowena & Rutherford, Jonathan (eds.), 1988.

——, 'Reason, Desire, and Male Sexuality', in Caplan, Pat (ed.), *The Cultural Construction of Sexuality*, Tavistock, London & New York, 1987.

Sennett, Richard, 'Narcissism and Modern Culture', in *October*, vol.4, Fall 1977.

Sheehy, Gail, *Passages*, Dutton, New York, 1976.

Skynner, Robin, *Explorations with Families: Group Analysis and Family Therapy*, Methuen, London, 1987.

Slater, Philip, *The Pursuit of Loneliness*, Beacon Press, Boston, 1970, 1976.

Smith, Gavin, 'The crisis of fatherhood', *Free Associations* No. 9, London, 1987.

Sohl, Robert & Carr, Audrey (eds), *The Gospel According to Zen*, Mentor, New York, 1970.

Stein, Robert, 'Coupling/Uncoupling', in Welwood, J., 1985.

Stern, Daniel N., *The Interpersonal World of the Infant: A View from Psychoanalysis and Developmental Psychology*, Basic Books, New York, 1985.

Stoller, Robert J., *Presentations of Gender*, Yale University Press, New Haven & London, 1985.

—— , *Sex and Gender*, Science House, New York, 1968.

Strouse, Jean (ed.), *Women & Analysis*, Dell, New York, 1974.

Sutherland, Stuart, *Breakdown*, Paladin, London, 1977.

Symington, Neville, *The Analytic Experience*, Free Association Books, London, 1986.

Viorst, Judith, *Necessary Losses*, Simon & Schuster, New York, 1986.

Waddell, Margot, 'The Marilyn Monroe Children's Fund', in *Free Associations*, No. 9, 1987.

Watson, Elizabeth, *Sexuality: A Part of Wholeness*, Family Relations Commitee, Philadelphia, 1982–1983.

Welwood, John (ed.), *Challenge of the Heart*, Shambhala, Boston, 1985.

Whitaker, Carl, A., 'The Growing Edge in Techniques of Family Therapy', in Haley, J. & Hoffman, L. (eds), *Techniques of Family Therapy*, Basic Books, New York, 1967.

Wickes, Frances G., *The Inner World of Choice*, Coventure, London, 1977.

Wilber, Ken, *No Boundary: Eastern & Western Approaches to Personal Growth*, New Science Library, Boston & London, 1981.

Winnicott, D.W., *The Family and Individual Development*, Tavistock, London, 1968.

—— , *Holding and Interpretation: Fragment of an Analysis*, Pelican, Harmondsworth, 1986.

—— , *Home is Where the Heart Is: Essays by a Psychoanalyst*, The Hogarth Press, London, 1972 and 1986.

—— , *The Maturational Processes and the Facilitating Environment*, The Hogarth Press, London, 1965.

—— , *Playing and Reality*, Penguin, Harmondsworth, 1980.

—— , *Therapeutic Consultations in Child Psychiatry*, The Hogarth Press, London, 1971.

—— , *Through Paediatrics to Psychoanalysis*, The Hogarth Press, London, 1978.

Wolff, Charlotte, *On the Way to Myself*, Methuen, London, 1969.

Yalom, Irvin D., *Existential Psychotherapy*, Basic Books, New York, 1980.

—— , *The Theory and Practice of Group Psychotherapy*, Basic Books, New York, 1975.